The Threat From Within

The Threat From Within

Recognizing Al Qaeda–Inspired Radicalization and Terrorism in the West

Phil Gurski

ROWMAN & LITTLEFIELD
Lanham • Boulder • New York • London

Associate Editor: Marie-Claire Antoine
Marketing Manager: Deborah Hudson
Production Editor: Laura Reiter
Interior Designer: Deanta Publishing Services
Cover Designer: Matt Pirro
Cover Art: ©Zou Zheng/Xinhua/Alamy Live News

Published by Rowman & Littlefield
A wholly owned subsidiary of The Rowman & Littlefield Publishing Group, Inc.
4501 Forbes Boulevard, Suite 200, Lanham, Maryland 20706
www.rowman.com

Unit A, Whitacre Mews, 26-34 Stannary Street, London SE11 4AB

British Library Cataloguing in Publication Information Available

Library of Congress Cataloging-in-Publication Data
Gurski, Phil.
The threat from within : recognizing Al Qaeda-inspired radicalization
and terrorism in the West / Phil Gurski.
    pages cm
Includes bibliographical references and index.
ISBN 978-1-4422-5560-9 (cloth : alk. paper) — ISBN 978-1-4422-5561-6
(pbk. : alk. paper) — ISBN 978-1-4422-5562-3 (electronic) 1. Terrorism—Prevention.
2. Qaida (Organization) 3. Islamic fundamentalism. I. Title.
HV6431.G88 2016
363.32509182′1—dc23   2015021305

∞™ The paper used in this publication meets the minimum requirements of American
National Standard for Information Sciences—Permanence of Paper for Printed Library
Materials, ANSI/NISO Z39.48-1992.

Printed in the United States of America

To the men and women on the front lines at CSIS with whom I have had the honor of working and whose largely unrecognized dedication and professionalism helps to keep Canada and Canadians safe

To law enforcement across Canada and around the world who put their lives on the line every day on our behalf

And to my family, whose love and support for me is manifest each and every day

Contents

Author's Note

The views and analyses presented here are not representative of CSIS or of any other government of Canada agency. Any error of fact or analysis is the author's alone.

Preface

Canadians and the world were shocked by the horrible events of October 22, 2014, when Muslim convert Michael Zehaf-Bibeau killed Nathan Cirillo, a young reservist from Hamilton, Ontario, serving as honor guard at the National War Memorial in Ottawa, and Zehaf-Bibeau subsequently attempted to storm the Canadian Parliament. We cannot forget as well the death of Warrant Officer Patrice Vincent in Saint-Jean-sur-Richelieu, Quebec, struck by a car and killed two days earlier by another convert. Other events in Sydney and Paris were equally horrific.

In each instance, once the attackers were killed, the questions came fast and furiously: Who were they? Why had they done this? Were they acting alone? Were these acts of terrorism? What does this all mean?

This book is an attempt to answer some of these questions. There has been a lot of interest in terrorism in Canada and the West in recent years and a need for more information. More and more researchers in Canada are (finally) turning their attention to the matter, and a host of experts is sharing their views on such programs as CBC's flagship newscast, *The National*.

Each of these attacks was a fulfillment of what Canadian security officials have been saying for a long time: a terrorist attack will be a matter of *when*, not if. While it may once have been possible for Canadians to disbelieve the inevitability of a terrorist attack here—all the so-called plots had been successfully thwarted before October 2014—it is unlikely they will do so now. Opinion polls in early 2015 show that the fear of terrorism does resonate with ordinary Canadians.

In these pages, we will explore the many aspects of a particular brand of violent extremism: that inspired by Al Qaeda. We will try to understand what is driving it, what it looks like, and what can be done about it. In the end, we will look at what is currently being done and what other avenues need to be considered to obviate the threat.

The slaughter of reservist Nathan Cirillo, and the murder two days earlier of Warrant Officer Patrick Vincent, demonstrate without question that we cannot ignore the threat of violent extremism in Canada. These attacks will most likely not be the only ones. We need to have a better picture of what this all about. But we need to keep this threat in perspective. Let us discuss and debate the phenomenon.

Introduction

MADE IN ORLEANS

Orleans is a suburb east of Ottawa, popular with civil servants. Increasingly beset with the big box–store plague all too common in large Canadian cities, it is comfortably middle class with a healthy split between francophones and anglophones. It was here that Momin Khawaja was born to Pakistani immigrants in 1979.

Khawaja and his siblings led, by all appearances, a comfortable life in the nation's capital. In 2000 his father, Mahboob Khawaja, had earned a PhD in social sciences from Syracuse University and later went on to write several books on Muslims and their place in Western culture. In 2000 the University Press of America published a version of Mahboob's PhD thesis as *Muslims and the West: Quest for Change and Conflict Resolution*. His son, Momin, was perfectly integrated into Canadian society, and Momin himself told a reporter that his childhood had been normal. He'd excelled at high school and had once even scored the second highest mark on an Ontario-wide math exam. His family's house had a basketball net in the driveway, and his high school years were marked by a souped-up car and hip-hop music.

The family had moved to Saudi Arabia for a few years when their father had accepted work in the kingdom but had returned to Canada where Momin completed high school and finished a program in computer science at Algonquin Community College in Ottawa.

But during his second year at Algonquin, Khawaja underwent major personal changes. Although he'd always been a practicing Muslim, he now grew a beard, started praying five times a day, stopped dating and drinking, and began to look for a Muslim partner. None of these is of concern from a security perspective, of course. But in the aftermath of the terrorist attacks

1

of 9/11, Khawaja had become obsessed with the plight of Muslims around the world and believed that the United States was sponsoring terrorism and oppressing Muslims.

Today Momin Khawaja is serving a life sentence at the Special Handling Unit of the prison complex in Sainte-Anne-des-Plaines Prison in Quebec for his role in a 2004 plot to detonate a six-hundred-kilo bomb in London, England. At the time of his arrest he was contracted as a computer-software developer for the Canadian Department of Foreign Affairs.[1]

CHAPTER ABSTRACT

And so we set the stage for our discussion. In the following, we discuss the book's intent, provide a basis for understanding the terminology to be used (*terrorism, radicalization, Al Qaeda–inspired, narrative, lone wolves*, etc.), and seek to determine how big the problem is in Canada—all this, perhaps most importantly, from the perspective of a former Canadian intelligence analyst.

WHAT THIS BOOK IS ABOUT

In the following, we examine what drives Al Qaeda–inspired radicalization to violence in Canada and the West, how to detect it, and how to confront it. We discuss behaviors and ideologies observable and tangible in radicalized individuals or in those on the path to violent radicalization. I have drawn from cases of individuals in Canada who have radicalized and moved on to a variety of extremist activities—plotting acts of terrorism in Canada or abroad, traveling to join terrorist groups, or participating in violent jihadi conflicts outside of this country. I hope our discussion here will serve those in Canada—intelligence and law enforcement, community and religious leaders, teachers, parents, and others—who may be in a position to detect individuals who appear to be on the path of radicalization and intervene before they can do violence. And our examinations will hopefully be a valuable primer on terrorism in Canada for university-level students of international security.

My purpose in writing this book is not to contribute to the growing literature on theories of radicalization or terrorism—much of which, as acknowledged by some in the terrorism-studies field, has not been based on primary data nor extrapolated from small data sets.[2] Rather, the focus here is on practice and detection, not a discussion of the merits of one theoretical approach over another. That said, many good books on terrorism are available and well worth reading, and appendix 1 of this book lists what I consider to be among the best of those works.

My comments and analyses throughout are based on many years of observation as an intelligence "insider," if you will, and on the considerable thought I've given to the meaning of the data to which I was privy. I have made no effort to impose a particular theoretical framework on the available data to confirm a predetermined hypothesis. I leave such literature review to other more academically-oriented publications, as I am not an academic with a particular methodological approach to promote.

What this book does offer is a realistic overview of the threat from Al Qaeda–inspired extremism in Canada. There has been little discussion in the academic literature on this threat from a Canadian angle—although a recent spate of terrorism cases has meant increased coverage by Canadian Press—and none from a former intelligence practitioner's perspective. To the best of my knowledge, the publication of this Canadian-insider perspective and analysis is the first of its kind. It will hopefully dovetail with the new information emerging in recent years from a number of research initiatives in Canada[3] and provide a useful addition to an impoverished field.

A FEW DEFINITIONS

Any book dealing with terrorism and national security threats must establish from the outset the parameters of the issue at hand. This means defining terms that mean different things to different people. A great deal has been written, especially over the past decade, on terrorism, particularly the Al Qaeda brand, and debates over terminology abound. In order to clarify our discussion, I use the following terms and concepts—and though there may be better definitions or terms, I will consistently use these ones.

Terrorism and Extremism

Probably as many interpretations of *terrorism* and *terrorist activity* exist as there are national jurisdictions. In Canada offenses classified as *terrorism* are delineated in section 83 of the Canadian Criminal Code, which states that a terrorist act is one committed

(A) in whole or in part for a political, religious, or ideological purpose, objective, or cause and

(B) in whole or in part with the intention of intimidating the public, or a segment of the public, with regard to its security, including its economic security, or compelling a person, a government, or a domestic or an

international organization to do or to refrain from doing any act, whether
the public or the person, government, or organization is inside or outside
Canada, and

(ii) that intentionally

(a) causes death or serious bodily harm to a person by the use of
violence,

(b) endangers a person's life,

(c) causes a serious risk to the health or safety of the public or
any segment of the public,

(d) causes substantial property damage, whether to public or
private property, if causing such damage is likely to result in
the conduct or harm referred to in any of clauses (A) to (C)
or

(e) causes serious interference with or serious disruption of
an essential service, facility, or system, whether public or
private, other than as a result of advocacy, protest, dissent, or
stoppage of work that is not intended to result in the conduct
or harm referred to in any of clauses (A) to (C), and includes
a conspiracy, attempt, or threat to commit any such act or
omission, or being an accessory after the fact or counselling
in relation to any such act or omission, but, for greater
certainty, does not include an act or omission that is committed during an armed conflict and that, at the time and in
the place of its commission, is in accordance with customary
international law or conventional international law applicable to the conflict, or the activities undertaken by military
forces of a state in the exercise of their official duties, to the
extent that those activities are governed by other rules of
international law.

This rather long-winded definition states, essentially, that terrorism is ideologically-motivated violence seeking to force change at the social or political
level.

The Australian Security Intelligence Organisation Act 1979—a close coun-
terpart to the Canadian Security Intelligence Service—states that terrorism is
"acts or threats of violence or unlawful harm that are intended or likely to
achieve a political objective, whether in Australia or elsewhere, including
acts or threats carried on for the purpose of influencing the policy or acts of
a government, whether in Australia or elsewhere." I find this to be a concise,
clear definition of what terrorists are trying to achieve.

We could debate forever on what constitutes a *terrorist*. For the purposes
of our discussion, I limit my analysis to those individuals and groups that

carry out significant acts of violence in accordance with the broadly termed "Al Qaeda narrative" (to be discussed in much detail below).

Bringing the conversation back to this country, however, terrorism investigations in Canada are usually carried out by the Royal Canadian Mounted Police in its role as both the federal and national security police force (the RCMP is also the provincial force of jurisdiction in eight of Canada's ten provinces and all three territories). But it is not the only organization involved. For its part, the Canadian Security Intelligence Service undertakes terrorism investigations and collects information under sections 2 and 12 of the CSIS Act. These clauses are worth repeating here.

Section 12 of the CSIS Act states that "the Service shall collect, by investigation or otherwise, to the extent that it is strictly necessary, and analyse and retain information and intelligence respecting activities that may on reasonable grounds be suspected of constituting threats to the security of Canada and, in relation thereto, shall report to and advise the Government of Canada."

Section 2 of the act defines what is meant in section 12 by *threats to the security of Canada*: section 2 (c) relates specifically to terrorism as "activities within or relating to Canada directed toward or in support of the threat or use of acts of serious violence against persons or property for the purpose of achieving a political, religious, or ideological objective within Canada or a foreign state." Note the importance of the "motivation" clause—*political, religious, or ideological objective*. Violence perpetrated without any one (or several) of these motivators is not terrorism; it is simply violence. The constitutional and charter validity of the motivation clause in the section on terrorism in the Canadian Criminal Code was challenged during the 2008 trial of Momin Khawaja, a Canadian citizen, but was ultimately upheld by the courts.[4]

Any definition of *terrorism* will likely include some version of the motivation clause. In general, the terms *terrorism* and *violent extremism* tend to get used interchangeably in the mass media and will be used in a similar fashion here.

From a layperson's perspective, terrorism involves

- a serious act of violence
- people who may or may not be associated with or directed by a recognized state
- violence targeted at noncombatants
- a desire to effect change through the use of violence
- and motivation that is somehow political, religious, or ideological in nature.

I recognize that a subset of terrorism has been termed *state-sponsored*. As it does not apply to the particular brand of terrorism discussed in this book, I leave it aside. I also know that attacks on military troops are sometimes called acts of terrorism. There are probably finer distinctions to be made here (if the member of an armed forces is off duty, is it terrorism?), but I, too, set those distinctions aside.

It has been interesting to watch the debate in the media and in politics over what to call the attacks in Saint-Jean-sur-Richelieu and Ottawa in October 2014. Prime Minister Stephen Harper called the attacks *terrorism*, while Opposition Leader Thomas Mulcair labeled them *criminal acts*. While there are still many more questions yet to be answered (and some never will be, in light of the deaths of both assailants), it seems clear that both men, Martin Couture-Rouleau and Michael Zehaf-Bibeau, were radicalized within the Al Qaeda framework (ideology), sought to punish Canada for its policy in Iraq (seek to change minds and influence opinion), carried out a serious act of violence (resulting in two deaths plus their own demise), and attacked the Canadian military and government—Parliament (symbolic targets).

Al Qaeda–Inspired Extremism

Since the attacks of September 11, 2001 (hereafter 9/11), a debate has raged over what to call this particular brand of terrorism. Among the words used by various sources at one time or another are *Islamic terrorism*, *Muslim terrorism*, *Islamo-fascism*, *global jihadism*, *Salafi jihadism*, *nihilist violence*, and others. The terms that include the words *Islam* or *Muslim* have been the most divisive, as they problematically suggest that this form of terrorism has a link to the faith of over a billion Muslims. Some fear that the use of such terms is not only inaccurate but also puts barriers between governments and security and law-enforcement agencies and the communities with which they work to prevent terrorism. There is no question that some, particularly on the political right, have made unhelpful comments and charges that Islam is inextricably linked to terrorism or that Islam is a "terrorist faith." Such statements have undoubtedly contributed to what has been called the "securitization" of the Muslim community in Canada and other Western countries, in which Muslims are seen primarily through a security lens and questions are asked whether they pose a threat to greater society.[5] It has been my experience that an unfortunate "slip of the tongue" by a cabinet minister or member of Parliament (intentional or otherwise) makes it more difficult to engage communities in Canada on this topic.

A term widespread in academic literature is *Islamist extremism*. Note the subtle but important difference between *Islamic* and *Islamist*: The former is the adjectival form of the noun *Islam*, referring to the activities and beliefs of the world's Muslims. The second implies support for or belief in the application of a particular fundamentalist brand of Islam; the "extremism" part implies that this application is to be achieved by extreme (read, *violent*) means. Despite its solid basis in the literature, the term nevertheless still uses a word from the "Islam" list and is hence seen as offensive by some. Here, therefore, the term *Al Qaeda–inspired* will be used.

The question of terminology is a contentious one. There are some who see any effort at finding terms that do not include the "I-word" to be nothing more than political correctness run amok.[6] Those on the right will go so far as to state that Islam is inherently violent (even notoriously leftwing comedian Bill Maher described Islam as the "mother lode of bad ideas"[7]). An effort by the Muslim community in Manitoba to produce a guidebook on radicalization and suggest terminology that did not refer to Islam was roundly criticized in Canadian media.[8] The handbook did indeed contain material that the RCMP, one of the contributors to the manual, considered to be "adversarial."[9]

Although this book will not use the term *Islamist extremism*, it will speak of jihad, hijra, and other terms used by violent extremists. To do otherwise would undermine a better understanding of this phenomenon. These terms, and others, will be explained when they appear. It should be remembered that we are trying to comprehend how extremists use these terms, not how they are defined in the mainstream.

So, while less controversial from a faith or linguistic perspective, the term *Al Qaeda–inspired* nevertheless requires some further explanation. An individual "inspired" by Al Qaeda may have nothing to do with the terrorist group known as Al Qaeda or its affiliates. An extremist need not be a card-carrying member of any organization to be inspired by it. Furthermore, Al Qaeda did not invent terrorism. The particular narrative that supports this form of terrorism predates Al Qaeda and will survive its eventual demise. Still, Al Qaeda today remains the best-known source of this narrative (see below), and, hence, the term *Al Qaeda–inspired* will be used throughout this book.

What do we do about groups like the Islamic State? Al Qaeda has rejected IS's brutal violence, and the latter has ignored the former's calls to join the greater cause.[10] Nevertheless, the narrative promoted by IS is virtually identical to the Al Qaeda narrative, and IS did originate from within the Al Qaeda orbit. So, despite the recent rise in influence of IS and reports that attacks in the West have been inspired by the group, *Al Qaeda–inspired* is still a valid term. Whether we call it *Al Qaeda–inspired* or *IS–inspired*, the fundamentals of the underlying ideology are the same.

Note that, in the security intelligence field, terrorism subsumed under the Al Qaeda catchall is actually executed by three types of organizations:

1. *Al Qaeda core* is the original group created in large part by the late Osama Bin Laden and now headed by his lieutenant Ayman al-Zawahiri.

2. *Al Qaeda affiliates* are groups that either carry the Al Qaeda brand name (Al Qaeda in the Arabian Peninsula, Al Qaeda in Iraq, Al Qaeda in the Islamic Maghreb, etc.) or enjoy a relationship (financial, ideological, personnel, etc.) with the original Al Qaeda core (Al-Shabaab in Somalia, Jemaah Islamiya in Southeast Asia, Jabhat Al Nusrah in Syria, and Boko Haram in Nigeria are four good examples).
3. *Al Qaeda–inspired* individuals and groups subscribe to the ideology propagated by Al Qaeda but have no links to the group or its affiliates.

It is important to note that individuals and groups at all three levels have the same essential beliefs, even if their goals are different; that is, the nature of their activities may be focused on local, regional, or global levels—although it is not uncommon for individuals and groups to move among these levels as circumstances and opportunities shift. Most of the analysis in this book is drawn from cases of individuals and groups in Canada belonging to the Al Qaeda–inspired category denoted above, although it is possible that individuals may also have had links to either or both of the other two levels of Al Qaeda at some time.

The Al Qaeda Narrative

As noted, if violence is to be construed as terrorism, it must be carried out along ideological, political, or religious lines. Al Qaeda–inspired violence is no different. Al Qaeda justifies—and mandates—the use of violence, taking ideas from all three motivational spheres.

The Al Qaeda narrative (also widely known as the *Al Qaeda common narrative* or the *single narrative*) is a worldview, elegant in its simplicity and appealing to a large audience. (It should be noted that, even if the vast majority of those exposed to the narrative do not act or condone terrorism, they may be sympathetic to parts of it.) The narrative constructs a series of stories that seeks to explain why the world is the way it is and to offer a solution to right wrongs. While Al Qaeda is not the owner of this mode of terrorism, it is, however, the best-known representative, and practitioners have taken to using it as the primary example of a particular terrorist phenomenon.

Stories are powerful tools. They teach us when we are young, and we continue to use them to understand what we see and experience. And the Al Qaeda narrative has—arguably—successfully interpreted fourteen hundred years of history and conflict, distilled into a potent formula. In its essentials, the narrative can be summarized as follows:

1. The West hates Islam and Muslims.
2. The West is in a state of perpetual war with Islam and Muslims.
3. True Muslims have a divine mandate to fight in violent jihad.[11]

This book will closely detail all three aspects of the narrative, how people come to believe in it, and how those seeking to stop terrorism can recognize how it is being used to justify violence. A few preliminary comments should be made, however.

1. "The West" is a big tent. It includes not only the "traditional" West (the United States, UK, Canada, and Western Europe) but also Israel, Russia, China, India, and anyone else seen as an enemy of Islam. Muslim countries closely allied to the West—Saudi Arabia, Jordan, and so on—are usually folded into this group.
2. The West is accused of having rejected Islam since the faith's founding and has been seeking to destroy it through warfare and other means ever since.
3. The religious nature of Al Qaeda–inspired terrorism is often ignored or underemphasized, sometimes because of the sensitive nature of tying a particular faith (Islam) to terrorism. It is my view that this oversight is a mistake, and much of this book will examine how groups like Al Qaeda use Islam to justify violence.

Radicalization

This term is perhaps the most controversial of all. At its most basic level, *radicalization* is the process through which someone becomes a radical. For many, thankfully, there is absolutely nothing wrong with being a radical. It is certainly not illegal—at least, not in Canada. Arguably some of the most important changes in Canada now positively viewed by the majority of Canadians were, at one point, the fantasies of "radicals." Among these developments are women's suffrage, universal healthcare, and gay marriage. In their time, each was seen as radical and undesirable—if not outright illegal—and they are largely part of the normal Canadian social fabric (would anyone seriously suggest in the twenty-first century that women in Canada should not have the vote?).

So, if radical ways of thinking and acting are not problematic in and of themselves, why should we concern ourselves with them? From a security and law-enforcement perspective, radical activities pose a threat to Canadian *national* security when they advocate the use of violence to further a cause. And yet most Canadians would distinguish between thinking about or advocating violence and actually *using* violence. The latter is clearly more of concern than the former. As a senior Royal Canadian Mounted Police official noted in October 2014, the Canadian government could not arrest and charge Martin Couture-Rouleau because of what he was thinking ("We could not arrest someone for having radical thoughts. It's not a crime in Canada"[12]). Furthermore, do we want the Canadian government or its security intelligence and law-enforcement agencies—or the public, for that matter—to monitor or police radical thoughts that *may* result in actual violence?

This, I think, is the challenge facing both CSIS and the RCMP—and, to a larger extent, all of us. Terrorists and radicalized violent extremists are not born; they are made. They pass through some sort of process that convinces them—or during which they convince themselves—that violence is possible, desirable, preferred, justified, or even divinely inspired, sanctioned, and mandatory. It would seem unlikely that people move directly from zero to violence in one giant leap. It is more typical for an individual or a group to travel along an idiosyncratic pathway, during which the necessity for violence is (perhaps slowly) introduced and imposed.

So, at what point do these individuals and groups pose an actual threat to Canada? If our security and law-enforcement agencies wait until the eve of an attack to begin an investigation, it is more likely that the perpetrators of such an attack will be successful. Act too early, however, and the intelligence and evidence may not be strong enough to act upon or the investigation may be seen as an infringement of constitutionally-protected activity.

In order to gain a general or universal understanding of why individuals embrace violence as a legitimate tool for change we must gather as much information as possible on each violent radical's background, influences, and environment. This information may become available at a time when violence is seen as a *potential* solution or justifiable act. It is acknowledged that some Canadians will consider it problematic—and undesirable—to look at this stage. Nevertheless, waiting too long to look into radicalization means our understanding is poorer and the chances of successful attacks are greater.

Is there a way to focus on only the forms of radicalization that should be of interest to Canadians? Can we agree on a definition that captures the problematic cases? As it turns out, the RCMP has a useful definition of radicalization, taken from their publication *Radicalization: A Guide for the Perplexed*. "Radicalization," the RCMP says, is "the process by which individuals are introduced to an overtly ideological message and belief system that encourages movement from moderate, mainstream beliefs towards extreme views." It goes on to state, "While radical thinking is by no means problematic in itself, it becomes a threat to national security when Canadian citizens or residents espouse or engage in violence or direct action as a means of promoting political, ideological, or religious extremism."[13] These two sentences highlight the essence of the problem that this book will discuss: the process by which people move to violent radicalization.

It is important to note that violent radicalization is neither a "Muslim" phenomenon nor one limited to individuals or groups that happen to be Muslim. Canada and other countries have faced terrorist threats from groups across many ideological spectrums. Strictly speaking, prior to October 2014 the only *successful* terrorist attacks in Canada over the past half century have been carried out by groups *not* inspired by Al Qaeda or its affiliates (the October crisis in 1970 in which Quebec nationalists killed a provincial minister, the 1985 Air India bombing when Canadian Sikh terrorists carried out the largest single act of terrorism prior to 9/11, the EnCana gas-well bombings in 2008 and 2009 executed by possible environmental extremists, the 2010 RBC firebombing in which self-styled anarchists sought to protest the 2010 Winter Olympics in Vancouver, etc.). Nevertheless, according to Public Safety Canada's *2013 Public Report on the Terrorist Threat to Canada*, "Canadian authorities continued to investigate a range of potential domestic terrorist threats. The majority of these involved individuals influenced by the ideology of al Qaida."[14]

While chapter 4 of this book closely details planned acts of Al Qaeda–inspired terrorism in Canada since 9/11, it is worth underscoring that in 2013 alone two major plots were thwarted against a VIA Rail Canada passenger train in the Niagara corridor and a bomb plot on the grounds of the British Columbia legislature. Both attacks were Al Qaeda inspired. And of course the two tragic attacks in Montreal and Ottawa two days apart in October 2014 show all the hallmarks of Al Qaeda inspiration.

Self-Radicalization and Lone Wolves

Of late, the terms *self-radicalization* and *lone wolves* have become very popular in the mass media and in use by leading government officials (and sometimes even appear in the same sentence, like when US Secretary of Homeland Security Jeh Johnston noted in early February 2014 that "self-radicalized lone wolves" are the terrorist threat he is most worried about).[15] Remarks of this nature suggest we are faced with a new scourge of virtually undetectable individuals who are radicalized to the point of violence on their own and then go on to commit acts of terrorism. The problem, I believe, is that neither term is accurate, and therefore neither will be used in this work.

Self-radicalization is so rare as to be inconsequential. The term implies that an individual can sit alone with material that is extreme in nature and later engage in violence with no intervention or assistance. All publicly available case data in Canada and elsewhere suggest that radicalization does not occur in a vacuum and is critically dependent on input, affirmation, confirmation, and encouragement by others. In other words, radicalization to violence is an inherently social process.

It may be that for some the term *self-radicalized* as it is currently being used actually implies that the individual or group has no significant links to known or established terrorist groups. In this sense, it is undoubtedly true, as many individuals in the West do not appear to be tied to such groups. It is entirely possible to radicalize to violence without guidance or assistance from a more famous organization, and cases in Canada point to this (the Toronto 18 is, perhaps, the best example). But the process rarely, if ever, occurs in isolation.

Similar criticism can be raised for the term *lone wolf*. It is very rare for someone to act completely alone, with no support or input (materiel or ideological) from the outside. Anders Breivik, the Norwegian terrorist, planted a bomb outside government buildings and later killed sixty-nine youth on an island outside Oslo in July 2011. He was not a lone wolf but a "lone actor." The distinction is important and not merely semantic. The former exists in a vacuum and belong to no community, real or virtual, while the latter is part of a larger like-minded world but ultimately chooses to act alone. Breivik belonged to a virtual (i.e., online) anti-immigrant and Islamophobic universe but did not need assistance in executing his attacks.

If ever there were a true lone wolf, it is Ted Kaczynski, the "Unabomber," who carried out a campaign of bombings in the United States from the late 1970s to the mid-1990s. His actions and ideology do not appear to have benefitted from outside aid. He remains the rare exception, however; most people—the vast majority, even—exist in society and act in groups (even as small as the group of two responsible for the Canada Day plot in Victoria, British Columbia, in 2013). To speak of groups of "lone wolves" is incorrect. A paper in a 2014 issue of the journal *Terrorism and Political Violence* was titled "The Collective Nature of Lone-Wolf Terrorism"; the concept is absurd.[16]

It is interesting to note that in several cases individuals initially described as lone wolves are revealed, upon more careful examination, to have not been isolated. Mohammed Merah, a French citizen who killed several people in Toulouse in 2012, was immediately labeled a lone wolf and an example of a new and frightening phenomenon. In the end, it turned out that he had neither self-radicalized—he trained in Afghanistan—nor acted alone—he appears to have been aided in his attacks by his brother and possibly his sister.[17]

It is uncertain why the term *lone wolf* has become so popular. Perhaps it reflects a fear of the undetectable terrorist. Or it may simply be the fact that many in public office use the term, and so it perpetuates in usage. Interestingly, some extremist groups (IS, among others) have begun to use the term in their communications as they encourage individuals to strike at the West. Some critics have suggested abandoning the term (Brian Jenkins says we should use the phrase *stray dogs*), as it creates an almost romantic notion of a noble beast pursuing a worthwhile quest. In any event, the term is unlikely to be forgotten soon: it is thus perhaps best to insist that it be carefully defined. Much ongoing research examines the nature of lone-actor terrorism and whether it differs significantly from other forms (i.e., groups or small cells) of terrorism.[18]

ABOUT THOSE NUMBERS

At this point, we must consider a series of questions often raised in Canada and other countries: How many extremist (or radicalized) individuals are there? Are there enough to worry about? Or, to put it another way, do they represent a clear and present danger to Canada? The answer is not easy to determine. On one level, we could count the number of people arrested on terrorism charges or the number who leave for jihad abroad. That would give us, as of mid-2014, 28 people charged and 130 travelers.[19] But is this number accurate?

It is unlikely to be. A simple head count of those arrested or convicted Canadian citizens and a determination of how many people have become foreign fighters does not exhaust the total number of individuals known to have radical views supporting violence. CSIS has acknowledged that at any given time it has several hundred investigations on the go.[20] The Royal Canadian Mounted Police may have a similar or greater figure. It is probable that not all investigations lead to arrest or departure for a foreign war. So how many people should we worry about?

In my view, the number is unknowable. We do not—thankfully—have an East German Stasi–style security service that keeps files on all Canadians. We do not, therefore, have statistics on all extremists. But is it possible to determine the number using other methods?

That too is uncertain. There have been opinion polls in Canada and other countries that have asked whether participants support the use of violence for political ends—but an affirmative answer does not necessarily denote extremism. That said, a 2007 Environics poll in Canada did provide some noteworthy results; when several hundred Canadian Muslims were asked whether they thought that the goals of the Toronto 18 terrorist cell were justified (i.e., the execution of terrorist acts in Canada), 5 percent said they were "fully justified," 7 percent said they were "partly justified," and a further 15 percent were uncertain, answering, "It depends".[21] Extrapolated to the approximate Canadian Muslim population of one million, those percentages would yield fifty thousand, seventy thousand, and 150,000 individuals (or almost 270,000 in the aggregate) who did not categorically reject terrorism. Do we have tens (or hundreds) of thousands of potential extremists in this country?

Most probably not. One poll on a small sample does not tell us much. Environics did not pursue the question on terrorism, and thus further nuances are missing. It would be irresponsible, to say the least, to suggest that a quarter of Canadian Muslims would accept, condone, or actively contribute to the deaths of their fellow citizens at the hands of members of their own communities. In my dealings with Muslim communities across Canada, there has been a strong rejection of violent extremism and a desire to help authorities identify those that pose a threat to society.

It is most likely that a very small number of people in Canada think like the members of the Toronto 18 and other similar cells. Terrorism remains a low-probability event and will most assuredly remain so—at least in this country. Statements made in early 2015 by some government ministers not-withstanding, Canada is not about to become Somalia or Iraq, and the vast majority of Canadian Muslims have stately publicly and repeatedly that they would abhor an attack here. Extremism does not represent an existential danger to Canada, and it is highly improbable that it ever will. And yet, even if it is a rare occurrence, infrequent acts of terrorism do have a disproportionate impact on society. Those with violent intentions must be dealt with.

AN IMPORTANT NOTE

This book is the product of almost fifteen years of observations and analysis of individuals and groups radicalized to the point of violence through the Al Qaeda single narrative. These observations were drawn from actual cases and on information not publicly available but have been generalized, and public reporting in Canada and elsewhere has been included. In addition, everything discussed in this book is tied in some way to violent radicalization in Canada. All the concepts, behaviors, and beliefs presented are consistent with individuals who radicalize to the point of violence (committed or intended) and who can go on to plan acts in Canada, travel abroad to join terrorist groups, or support these activities. It is probable that some, if not many, of the topics and factors analyzed here will apply to other countries, especially those in the West with similar cultures, governmental systems, and societal structures. It should be stressed, however, that it is the intent of this study to look at what has happened, is happening, and will likely continue to happen in Canada. Nevertheless, open-source accounts of terrorist acts in the United States, United Kingdom, Australia, and other Western nations show remarkable parallels to those in Canada. It does bear stressing again, however, that each country has its own idiosyncratic conditions and that homegrown extremists are the product of those conditions.

The analysis in this book has benefitted from hundreds of presentations that I have delivered to a variety of audiences across Canada and around the world. Participants have included law-enforcement and security intelligence officers, community members, religious leaders, university students, and others whose input was invaluable in challenging assumptions and helping to refine both the content and the wording of the material in this book. It would have been much poorer without this feedback. I have also learned much from my interactions with my colleagues in Canada and around the world.

Everything I describe here is consistent with what I have seen—though I am no longer employed there—and experienced while working as an analyst at the Canadian Security Intelligence Service. It is not necessary to divulge secrets or classified material to make this book relevant. The increasing amount of very good material available in open source renders that need superfluous.

In intelligence brevity, accuracy, and timeliness are of the essence. Decision makers want information that is easy to digest and as current as possible. Writing a book is, of course, quite a different process. But thirty years of writing two- to five-page reports is a hard habit to break. I chose to write less rather than more to keep the book reasonably short but in a fashion that did not undermine its comprehensiveness. In addition, while I made every effort to include the most-recent information available, events will undoubtedly have surpassed some of the material presented by the time of publication. Nevertheless, it is highly unlikely that subsequent developments will affect the conclusions and implications of this book in a significant manner. Unfortunately, the phenomenon of Al Qaeda–inspired violent extremism is a threat that will not soon pass from Canada and the West. The information here is current as of the spring of 2015.

THE STRUCTURE OF THIS BOOK

There are five chapters in this book. In the first chapter I look at a number of frequently proposed drivers, causes, or risk factors for radicalization and show that they do not provide a very good set of explanations as to why some Canadians have engaged in Al Qaeda–inspired violence (the so-called "root causes"). I also present a number of elements that appear to be necessary for the violent-radicalization pathway to happen. In chapter 2 I present a number of key concepts drawn from Islam and Muslim history that crucially underlie the Al Qaeda narrative and make an important set of contributions to radicalization processes. These ideas are encountered every day, and it is important to understand what they really mean—at least to the extremist mindset. Chapter 3 is the heart of the book. It outlines twelve concrete, observable behaviors and attitudes often seen in those who are radicalized or on the path to violent radicalization. This chapter will be of most interest to those charged with detecting and dealing with violent extremism. Chapter 4 succinctly summarizes the major Canadian cases of Al Qaeda–inspired violence since 9/11. Prevention and counterstrategies are discussed in chapter 5. And the final chapter offers insight into where this phenomenon is headed and what we can expect in Canada over the short to medium term.

DISCLAIMER

The views and analyses presented here are not representative of CSIS or any other Government of Canada agency. Any error of fact or analysis is mine alone.

A NOTE ON SOURCING

I have had the opportunity to ponder many aspects surrounding the radicalization issue for almost fifteen years. My analysis is based on that thought process. More specifically, however, all of the examples cited come from three major sources:

1. Major Canadian newspapers, largely the *Globe and Mail*, the *National Post*, the *Ottawa Citizen*, and the *Toronto Star*, as well as the CBC website, were used to provide details on the case studies in chapter 5 as well as the narratives that begin each chapter.
2. Many of the quotations of extremist rhetoric were taken from the public website of the SITE Intelligence Group, an organization that locates, translates, and analyses postings in cyberspace.
3. Public Government of Canada websites greatly informed my writing, especially Public Safety Canada, which is responsible for articulating Canada's policy for countering violent extremism policy.

NOTES

1. I discuss Momin Khawaja's terrorist plans at length in chapter 4.
2. Veteran US–terrorism analyst Marc Sageman spoke of this gap with Max Taylor, coeditor of the journal *Terrorism and Political Violence*, in that journal's May 2014 podcast. See a transcript of their conversation at http://www.tandfonline.com/sda/4890/audioclip-transcript-ftpv.pdf, or listen to the original podcast at http://www.tandfonline.com/sda/4890/audioclip-ftpv.mp3.
3. Since 2001, Public Safety Canada and the Canadian Network for Research on Terrorism, Security, and Society have sponsored the Kanishka Project, a five-year initiative exploring issues related to terrorism and counterterrorism affecting Canada.
4. Tonda MacCharles, "Supreme Court of Canada Upholds Anti-terror Law; Khawaja's Appeal Rejected," *Star* (Toronto), December 14, 2012, http://www.thestar.com/news/canada/2012/12/14/supreme_court_of_canada_upholds_antiterror_law_khawajas_appeal_rejected.html.
5. See "Words Make Worlds: Terrorism and Language," the Royal Canadian Mounted Police's publication by Angus Smith, Officer in Charge, Alternative

Analysis, National Security Criminal Investigations, originally posted at http://www. rcmp-grc.gc.ca/pubs/nsci-ecrsn/words-mots-eng.htm, now removed (last modified September 11, 2009); a screen cap of the original article is available for review at http://pointdebasculecanada.ca/wp-content/uploads/2012/07/0%20org%20grc%20 jihad%20english.pdf.

6. A particularly venomous criticism was written by self-proclaimed Canadian terrorism expert David B. Harris on October 7, 2014: "Guest Column: Terror's Virus on the Northern Border," *The Investigative Project on Terrorism* (blog), http://www. investigativeproject.org/4602/guest-column-terror-virus-on-the-northern-border.

7. Peter Beinart, "Bill Maher's Dangerous Critique of Islam," Global, *Atlantic Monthly*, October 9, 2014, http://www.theatlantic.com/international/archive/2014/10/ bill-maher-dangerous-critique-of-islam-ben-affleck/381266/.

8. "Editorial: Speak the Truth," *Calgary Herald*, October 2, 2014, http://calgaryherald.com/opinion/editorials/editorial-speak-the-truth.

9. "RCMP Response: *United Against Terrorism* Handbook," Royal Canadian Mounted Police, last modified September 30, 2014, http://www.rcmp-grc.gc.ca/newsnouvelles/2014/09-30-uni-eng.htm.

10. The Islamic State, as they call themselves, is abbreviated alternately as IS, ISIS, or ISIL.

11. In chapter 2 I discuss on how violent extremists use the term *jihad*.

12. "Martin Couture-Rouleau, Hit-and-Run Driver, Arrested by RCMP in July," CBC News, last modified October 22, 2014, http://www.cbc.ca/news/canada/montreal/ martin-couture-rouleau-hit-and-run-driver-arrested-by-rcmp-in-july-1.2807078.

13. Royal Canadian Mounted Police, National Security Criminal Investigations, *Radicalization: A Guide for the Perplexed, June 2009* (Canada: Royal Canadian Mounted Police, 2009), archived online at http://publications.gc.ca/collections/collection_2012/grc-rcmp/PS64-102-2009-eng.pdf.

14. Last modified March 4, 2014, http://www.publicsafety.gc.ca/cnt/rsrcs/pblctns/ trrrst-thrt-cnd/index-eng.aspx.

15. Andrew Grossman, "Homeland Chief Says 'Lone Wolves' Biggest Terrorism Worry," Homeland Security, *Wall Street Journal*, February 7, 2014, http://blogs.wsj.com/ washwire/2014/02/07/homeland-chief-says-lone-wolves-biggest-terrorism-worry/.

16. Lars Erik Berntzen, "The Collective Nature of Lone-Wolf Terrorism," *Terrorism and Political Violence* 26, no. 5 (2014): 759–79.

17. Merah's brother was arrested and questioned regarding his role in the attacks. May 2014 reporting suggests that Merah's sister has traveled to Syria to engage in jihad. Joshua Melvin, "Terrorist's 'Proud' Sister Quits France 'for Jihad,'" *The Local* (Paris), May 23, 2014, http://www.thelocal.fr/20140523/mohamed-merahsister-disappear-syria.

18. In this regard, I particularly recommend Emily Corner and Paul Gill, "A False Dichotomy? Mental Illness and Lone-Actor Terrorism," *Law and Human Behavior* 39, no. 1 (2015): 23–34.

19. These numbers per the Canadian Security Intelligence Service. The Canadian Press, "CSIS Says Some 130 Canadians Support Foreign Extremists," *Global News*, February 3, 2014, http://globalnews.ca/news/1126694/csis-says-some-130-canadians-support-foreign-extremists/.

20. Ian MacLeod, "Former CSIS Boss Had Warned about Domestic Terrorism," *Hiiraan Online*, August 30, 2010, http://www.hiiraan.com/news2/2010/aug/former_csis_boss_had_warned_about_domestic_terrorism.aspx.

21. See "Special Theme: Muslims and Multiculturalism in Canada," section 3 of Environics, *Focus Canada: The Pulse of Canadian Public Opinion; Report 2006-4* (Ottawa and Ontario: Environics Research Group Ltd., 2007), 59–122.

Chapter 1

What Do We Know about the Basic Causes and Drivers of Al Qaeda–Inspired Radicalization and Violence in Canada?

THE FIGHT OF HIS LIFE

At the 2013 Boston Marathon, Tamerlan Tsarnaev and his younger brother, Dzhokhar, planted several pressure-cooker bombs, killing three and maiming scores. While Dzhokhar went on trial in Boston in early 2015,[1] Tamerlan died in a shootout with police shortly after the attack. The elder Tsarnaev had been an aspiring Olympic boxer.

So too was Vilyam (William) Plotnikov, an immigrant to Canada from Russia. Plotnikov's dad, Vitaly, had enrolled him in a boxing club in Thornhill, Ontario, in an effort to ease his son's integration into Canadian society. Despite Vilyam's lankiness, his coach immediately saw his talent: with the right training and experience, the younger Plotnikov could be an Olympian boxer for Canada.

Plotnikov began winning fights in Ontario—a silver medal at the 2006 Brampton Cup and a second silver at the 2007 Ontario Provincial Championships in Windsor. The victories did not, however, dispel his struggles with adjusting to life in Canada. By 2008, when he and his family gained Canadian citizenship, he was already drifting away from the boxing arena.

After high school, he enrolled in the international tourism and travel program at Seneca College in Toronto. He became intrigued by the "big questions" in life and sought meaning in a number of religious traditions. He eventually settled on Islam and converted.

In 2010, Vilyam Plotnikov disappeared from his parents' home. He was killed by Russian forces fighting Islamist insurgents in Dagestan in July 2012.[2]

CHAPTER ABSTRACT

In this chapter I will list and analyze the many drivers put forward by the media, academics, and lay people to explain why terrorists are the way they are. I will try to demonstrate that the factors they name neither sufficiently explain nor predict terrorist behavior. I will then list a few items that appear to be necessary for the terrorist trajectory to begin and continue. I will also briefly discuss where violent radicalization can occur (hint: anywhere!).

WHAT MAKES A TERRORIST?

A great deal has been written in recent years about the factors and causes behind why people radicalize to the point of violence. Political scientists, psychologists, sociologists, anthropologists, criminologists, and others have theorized on the circumstances and drivers that contribute to the transformation of "normal" individuals into terrorists. Some divide these factors into micro (i.e., at the individual level) and macro (group and societal levels) in an effort to understand the nature of this transformation. Journalists and opinion makers have also weighed in, as have average Canadians. I always ask audiences what they think drives terrorism before I begin my talks, just to see what preconceptions they bring to the issue.

It is not the intent here to discuss the merits and downsides of these theories. Based on my knowledge of the literature, it appears that most published works do not use large datasets. Furthermore, it is not always obvious that these theoretical frameworks can easily be translated into practice for security intelligence, law enforcement, or policy makers—let alone the general public—to assist in identifying those at risk of violent radicalization or help deal with these individuals or groups once identified. While there may be elements of value in some of these theories, specific frameworks will not be discussed here.

Perhaps the question that has to be asked is whether there is substantial benefit from or need to continue looking for "root causes." Cases of violent radicalization appear to be so diverse that it is unlikely we will ever find a concise, neat set of drivers that can be even slightly predictive. Every case appears to be distinct, in that each individual who radicalizes will bring his or her own set of characteristics (personality, psychological state, education, family background, sociopolitical views, economic situation, etc.) and makes a series of decisions unique to that case, such that any attempt at generalization is impossible. We are certainly very far from a model that can be used to predetermine potential violent radicalization. Can we ever hope to predict decision making at the individual level? (I'll leave that question to the psychologists and cognitive scientists.) Will the world of *Minority Report* (a future created by US writer Philip K. Dick in which police can make "precrime" arrests based on the predictions made by psychics) ever be a reality?

I was struck by an article Roger Cohen wrote for the *New York Times* in September 2014.[3] He wrote of an incident in a German concentration camp during World War II in which a prison guard was asked by an inmate why the guard was acting so cruelly. He replied, *"Hier gibt es kein warum"* ("There is no why here"). Perhaps there is no *why* for radicalization either. In an October 2014 interview with *Vice*, renowned terrorism scholar John Horgan said that "we may never fully crack the code, but we won't make any progress at all by continuing to obsess over the question of *why*. Truth be told, it's probably unanswerable. A better starting point is to answer the *how* questions: how do people become involved in terrorism?"[4]

Maybe a better statement would be, *There are too many whys.* If the underlying causes and drivers are so numerous, looking for a predictive set is perhaps a fool's errand. To date, the wide range of backgrounds and circumstances of those who have embraced violence for ideological reasons defies simple categorization. People choose to act for reasons sometimes known only to themselves—or maybe not even to themselves. It is possible that in some cases individuals cannot put their finger on exactly why they acted as they did. If these individuals are clueless, how can we (anthropologists, sociologists, psychologists, etc.) impose our causal factors?

An interesting analogy can be found in the study of aging. Scientists who have looked into why certain people live longer have learned that studying centenarians to gain insights into whether a particular drug or lifestyle modification leads to longevity (i.e., root causes) has not been particularly useful. Counterintuitively, some are heavy smokers; others drink a lot. There are apparently few vegetarians among the lot. As an article on aging in the October 2014 edition of *The Atlantic* noted, "nothing jumps out as a definitive cause of their long lives."[5]

As it stands, a fairly large number of reasons have been put forward to account for why individuals become violent radicals. Some of the reasons appear, at least on the surface, to be unhelpful. One of the more mundane causes I have encountered is boredom.[6] A Norwegian extremist stated that his country's lack of morality drove him to violence.[7] One Canadian scholar even argued that the violent jihad practiced by Al Qaeda–inspired extremists has nothing to do with religion.[8]

I will argue throughout this book that there is perhaps much more benefit in helping to identify what violent radicalization looks like rather than extend the debate over drivers and root causes. The overt indicators and signs will be dealt with in chapter 4. Nevertheless, it is worth looking at some of the factors put forward, if only to show that they are not representative of the Canadian reality.

Why do we care about why people radicalize to violence? Why not just locate them and shut them down (through kinetic action or incarceration or deprogramming)? What is the benefit in gaining a better understanding of the process? Simply stated, we cannot make responsible choices about action if we do not understand why something is happening. As the classic Chinese strategist Sun Tzu wrote, "Know your enemy, and know yourself, and you can fight a hundred battles without disaster." I am not advocating a purely military response to violent radicalization, but a lack of accurate knowledge will lead to bad decisions.

It is also important to not engage in what is called *mirror imaging*. This is an analytic practice in which the analyst believes that the subject studied shares the same biases and thought processes as he or she does. Perhaps a few examples will help to illustrate what I mean.

- "Suicide bombers must be crazy, because I wouldn't kill myself for a cause (I think doing so is crazy)." In actual fact, as we shall discuss later, suicide bombers are not crazy.
- "Terrorists engage in senseless violence, and their actions are unreasonable." In fact, there is an internal logic to their acts, as horrific as these acts might be.

Just because *I* think so doesn't mean that the person I am studying shares my views. Mirror imaging is as damaging as lack of understanding in trying to manage the violent-radicalization phenomenon.

With the previous points in mind, let us turn to what have been proposed as the critical drivers behind violent radicalization. Based on what we have learned from the cases in this country, it is possible to state that a number of factors and influences commonly put forward as important drivers are, in fact, not so useful—at least, not in Canada. Let us look at what I would call *nonfactors*—or perhaps *unsatisfactory factors* might be a better turn of phrase. They are drawn from accounts in media as well as comments made to me during my presentations (I assume many of these comments reflect what people had read in the media).

Gender and Age

Most terrorists and violent extremists are young males. Full stop. This should not come as a surprise to anyone. It is also consistent with data from criminologists: most criminals are young men. There are exceptions, of course. There has been an uptick in women seeking to join causes, such as that of the

Textbox 1.1

JIHOTTIE

Not all alleged terrorists are men.

Amanda Korody had a pretty good early life. Adopted by a dentist, she seems to have enjoyed a privileged upbringing in St. Catharines, Ontario, but was described as a "chameleon" by some. She sang and played the guitar and won a ribbon at the local Kiwanis music festival. She appeared to be a follower, however, changing her looks to suit those she was with. Amanda wrote in a blog that she suffered from an anxiety disorder. She eventually moved out to British Columbia and converted to Islam, choosing to wear the niqab (a face covering in which only the eyes show—very rare in Canada).

Korody became a drug addict and then began taking methadone in an effort to kick the habit. She met John Nuttall, another convert in similar straits, and the two exhibited "odd" religious behavior before a Surrey mosque kicked them out. They were described as street punks before they had found Islam and were "really, really nice people," according to a friend in British Columbia.

In January 2015 both Korody and Nuttall pleaded not guilty in a preliminary hearing, and they were found guilty in June 2015 for their attempt to carry out a bombing on the grounds of the British Columbia legislature on Canada Day 2013 (see chapter 4 for more on this plot).

Islamic State in Iraq and Syria. But it is unlikely that the trend will change significantly.

Does the knowledge that most violent extremists are young males help us find them before they radicalize or commit acts of terrorism? Not really. For one, it does not substantially narrow the data set (assuming we've eliminated women—which we cannot do—that takes our population sample from 7 billion to 3.5 billion humans). Furthermore, looking exclusively at young men could create a situation in which potential extremists are eliminated from consideration based on preconceived notions.

Poverty

It is often said that poverty drives some people to acts of terrorism. Renowned sociologist Ted Gurr put forward another theory—what he called *relative deprivation* (i.e., "You have more than I do, I deserve to have as much as you, and if necessary I will use violence to get it").[9] Perhaps to the average person this driver evokes the example of an impoverished Palestinian terrorist living in the West Bank who blows up a café in Tel Aviv, or a member of the Taliban who attacks a foreign embassy in Kabul.

The poverty argument suffers from two serious shortcomings. First, the vast majority of impoverished people do not become terrorists. If we take the poverty level in Canada alone, statistics show that approximately one in ten Canadians as of 2013 falls below the poverty line,[10] equating to more than three million individuals. We clearly do not have three million terrorists or potential terrorists in Canada—or, at least, there is no evidence to suggest that we do.

Second, many terrorists are not poor, by any stretch of the definition of poverty in Canada. A few examples suffice:

- Momin Khawaja, currently serving a life sentence in Quebec for his role in a 2004 terrorist plot in the UK, worked as a well-paid contractor with the Canadian Department of Foreign Affairs at the time of his arrest in March 2004.[11] Furthermore, Khawaja came from a solidly middle-class family in Ottawa.
- Shareef Abdelhaleem, serving a sentence for his role in the Toronto 18 plot, worked as a computer programmer in Toronto, where he earned a "six-figure" salary.[12]
- Misbahuddin Ahmed, convicted in the 2010 Operation Samossa plot, worked as a diagnostic-imaging technician in Ottawa.[13]
- The "Jihadi John" suspect who has featured in several Islamic State beheading videos is Mohammed Emwazi from London. Born into a well-to-do family, Emwazi grew up in West London and graduated from college with a degree in computer programming.[14] According to Maher Shiraz, senior fellow at the International Centre for the Study of Radicalisation in the UK, Emwazi "is middle class and well educated, which chimes with a lot of our research. Radicalisation is not principally driven by poverty or social deprivation."[15]

It is true that some of those who have radicalized to violence in Canada through the Al Qaeda narrative may be in financial distress, but it is unclear how or why poverty contributed to the process of radicalization. Furthermore, many of the ideological leaders of terrorist groups were anything but poor: Al Qaeda's Osama Bin Laden (the son of a wealthy Saudi construction magnate) and Ayman al Zawahiri (an Egyptian doctor) immediately come to mind. A 2014 UK study found, interestingly, that poverty and social inequalities were *not* relevant to violent radicalization.[16]

Marital and Family Status

Some propose that single men are more prone to violence.[17] This may be true for more general criminal behavior but is likely irrelevant in the radicalization process—at least in Canada. Many radically violent individuals are married or are in stable relationships:

- Both Zakaria Amara and Fahim Ahmed were married with children. Interestingly, their wives were supportive of their extremist ideology.[18]
- Hiva Alizadeh, who pleaded guilty to his role in the RCMP's Project Samossa, was married with two children.[19]
- Momin Khawaja was once engaged to be married.[20]
- A UK extremist arrested in October 2014 and charged with seeking to fight in Syria was a married high school chemistry teacher with children.[21]

Young, single men are inclined to violence, it is suggested, partly due to sexual frustration. The theory suggests that pent-up sexual urges find their outlet in outward aggression. Some have said that the sexual conservatism in Muslim and Arab cultures can make its adherents particularly sensitive to this urge. I think this is vastly overexaggerated and will revisit this theme when I look at martyrdom in chapter 3. It does not appear that marriage plays the same protective role against violent radicalization that it may have in cases of general criminals.[22]

Furthermore, many violent extremists are not only married but also have children. The notion that an individual with "something to live for" (i.e., children) would not choose to become a terrorist is demonstrably false.

Alienation and Lack of Integration

By *alienation* some mean a psychological state in which the subject is unable to function or feel a part of society. Some (notably, Lorne Dawson of the University of Waterloo) have suggested that a number of the Toronto 18 suffered from what can be called *immigrant syndrome*—the difficulty in living between two worlds, that of one's parents' background and that of the new life in Canada.[23] This conflict includes a clash of cultures and what appear to be irreconcilable differences between the old and new. It follows that those in the midst of such a conflict may themselves be conflicted and perhaps be vulnerable to others who implant violent ideas. This vulnerability can lead to what is called a *cognitive opening*—a time in which an individual is receptive to new concepts.[24]

There is little doubt that some new immigrants struggle in trying to balance two (or more) competing worldviews. In fact, it would be strange if such conflicts did not occur in Canada, which is known to be particularly open to immigration. I grew up in London, Ontario, in the 1960s and saw many of my friends and classmates deal with the duality of their Canadian and Polish, Italian, or Portuguese backgrounds. As a third-generation Canadian of Polish-Ukrainian extraction, I personally, however, did not feel the tension of living between two worlds. And so, evidently some feel the tension of multiple cultures while others do not (this probably is influenced by how close the ties are to the "homeland"—linguistic, cultural, political, etc. In my case they were nonexistent).

But do alienation and lack of integration serve as drivers or precursors to radicalization? Does the length of time in Canada matter (i.e., first, second, third generation—or the hybrid generation, 1.5)? I am uncertain on that point. Most people likely pass through a stage where they have doubts or uncertainties regarding their lot in life or the society in which they find themselves. And alienation does not have to be caused by immigration alone or a clash of cultures. Youth of varying backgrounds found their high school years anything but happy, for example. And, yet, if alienation or a lack of belonging leads to radicalization, we should see much higher levels of extremism, and we do not (at least, not as far as we know).

But what does *integration* actually mean, and how can we measure it? A colleague of mine who is knowledgeable in this regard once provided a simple yet useful definition of what it means to be integrated into Canadian society. According to him, individuals can be considered integrated within Canada if

- They have a command of English and/or French (both of which are official languages in Canada—it is hard to function fully without a solid knowledge of either).
- They carried out all or a large part of their education in Canada (thus assuring that they would be surrounded by Canadians from all walks of life and would have been exposed to what it means to be "Canadian").
- They have held some sort of employment in Canada.

Even if we acknowledge that language, education, and employment do not guarantee full adaptation into Canadian society—demonstrating all three may amount to no more than "surface" integration, for instance—using this general and undoubtedly inexhaustive definition as a starting point we see that the vast majority of immigrants, especially those who came to this country as children, would qualify as integrated. More importantly, the vast majority of those that went on to radicalize to the point of violence also fit this description.

More crucially, saying that lack of integration leads to radicalization cannot easily account for those who convert to Islam. Assuming that converts were born here, were once adherents to a faith that has a longer presence in Canada (Christianity, Judaism, etc.), and belonged to a nonminority community (usually white and either Francophone or Anglophone), it stands to reason that prior to their conversion they were integrated, at least by the simplistic definition cited above. They may have had "issues" or crises (but who doesn't?) that led to their decision to embrace Islam, but it would be a stretch to imply that they were poorly integrated into larger Canadian society.

Converts appear on the surface to have played a disproportionate role in terrorist plots in the West:

- One of the four perpetrators of the July 2005 attacks on the London subway was a convert (Germaine Lindsay).[25]
- Three of the Toronto 18 were converts (Nishanthan Yogakrishnan, Steven Chand, and Jahmaal James).
- Both of the July 2013 Canada Day plotters in Victoria, British Columbia, were converts (John Nuttall and Amanda Korody).
- Xristos Katsiroubas, who died in the January 2013 attack in Algeria, was a Greek Orthodox convert to Islam who lived in London, Ontario.
- Both Martin Couture-Rouleau and Michael Zehaf-Bibeau, the men who perpetrated attacks two days apart in October 2014, were converts.

Again, it is possible—if not probable—that issues linked to integration and alienation may contribute in some cases to an individual's radicalization process. It is clear, however, that neither phenomenon leads inextricably to the decision to embrace the use of violence to effect change. And so it remains unclear how these can be used as predictive elements. And recent thought challenges the role alienation plays in radicalization.[26]

A lot of attention has been dedicated of late to the matter of converts and violent extremism. The link between the two is fascinating and has led to suggestions that converts are particularly vulnerable to adopting extremist views for a number of possible reasons:

- the need to please
- a desire to prove they belong
- a poor understanding of their new faith, opening them up to manipulation by extremists
- or any number of contributing factors (depression, unhappiness, etc.) that lead to their conversion decision.

The convert-extremist link is one that requires much further study. Even so, it is not possible to say at this point that converts are more prone to embracing extremism than born Muslims.

Criminal Background

In some countries (notably France and the UK, according to available literature) there appears to be some correlation between criminal behavior or activity and violent radicalization. Obviously, terrorism is a crime, as it involves the use of violence. But is a criminal background a necessary driver of radicalization? In other words, does correlation equal causation?

Clearly not—at least, not in Canada. Few of the individuals that have engaged in terrorist activity appear to have had any previous brushes with the law. And even those who did engage in criminal activity (e.g., Ahmed Ressam, the infamous millennial bomber who targeted the Los Angeles Airport in 1999, had committed fraud and petty theft in Montreal[27]) had usually not been violent. In any case, it's unclear how we would convincingly argue that fraud or drug use or addiction leads to radicalization. We can, therefore, tentatively eliminate the causal relationship between violent criminality and radicalization in Canada.

The role of criminal behavior does lead to an interesting question, however. Is there a risk of radicalization among those who live in environments where such behavior is considered normal? In other words, might Canadian prisons be hotbeds of radicalization? There have been incidents of radicalization in prisons in Europe (both Richard Reid in the UK, the "Shoe Bomber," and Mehdi Nemmouche, the alleged 2014 killer of Jews in Belgium, may have been radicalized in prison).[28]

In my experience, the answer for Canada appears, at the present, to be no. I think that there are several reasons for this.

- There are to date very few prisoners incarcerated in Canada for terrorist offenses who can use their circumstances to radicalize others.
- Historically, those incarcerated under the Canadian Anti-Terrorism Act have been kept isolated from the general prison population.
- Canadian officials were ahead of the curve in looking into the signs of radicalization in prison well before the problem could have gotten out of control.

Of course, if additional people end up in prison on terrorist offenses, the possibility of violent radicalization among a "captive audience" grows. There are several individuals currently awaiting trial, and there will undoubtedly be other cases in the future. It is thus possible that violent radicalization in the prison environment may increase. It is thus imperative to remain aware of the signs of violent radicalization, and Correctional Services Canada is studying the issue. On the positive side, there does not appear to have been a single case to date of anyone who has committed an act of terrorism after being radicalized in whole or in part in a Canadian prison.[29] A January 2015 claim that prison radicalization was a significant threat in Canada was hugely overblown.[30]

Interestingly, a disproportionate percentage of recent cases in Canada—including several "foreign fighters" and both individuals who launched successful attacks in October 2014—appear to have had criminal records. Whether or not this is indicative of a new trend remains to be seen.

Lack of Education and Employment (Lack of Opportunity)

Similar to the poverty argument, one could posit that individuals with poor education or poor (or no) employment could feel disenfranchised and lash out at society or be open to the ideas of those that promote violence. A lack of education could, for example, result in poor critical thinking skills that would otherwise provide a layer of protection or resilience against violent ideologies. Similarly, a lack of employment could create a surplus of free time that could be filled by those seeking to exploit others. Perhaps, we might posit, these conditions facilitate violent radicalization.

There are enough counterexamples in Canada to show that this is not the case. I have already noted how some terrorists have had good jobs. Here are some examples of those with higher levels of education.

- Saad Gaya of the Toronto 18 was an honors student and enrolled at McMaster University in Hamilton, Ontario.[31]
- Chiheb Esseghaier, convicted in the Via Rail plot in 2013, was registered in a biology PhD program at the Institut National de la Recherche Scientifique at the time of his arrest.[32]
- Khurram Sher, alleged to have aided the Project Samossa perpetrators but acquitted in 2014, is a pathologist.[33]
- Several of the 9/11 hijackers were engineers.

So, while some extremists do suffer from a lack of education or high-paying employment, it should be obvious that neither is necessarily a precursor to violent radicalization.

What about too *much* education? Are particular fields more conducive to terrorism? A few years ago two UK scholars, Diego Gambetta and Steffan Hertog, published *Engineers of Jihad*, in which they claimed that graduates from the hard sciences (engineering, medicine, etc.) were overrepresented in Al Qaeda terrorism.[34] They hypothesized that engineers may have a "mindset" for terrorism. I find the argument interesting but not convincing. There are far too many educational disciplines found among terrorists. The statistical blip involving engineers is curious but likely correlational and not

Textbox 1.2

THE UNLIKELIEST TERRORIST?

Terrorists are all wild-eyed shabby men with scraggly beards and nothing to live for, right? Wrong. Meet Khurram Sher.

It would be hard to imagine a more bizarre alleged terrorist than Khurram Sher, who was arrested along with two others in August 2010 in conjunction with the RCMP's Project Samossa, a plot to build and detonate improvised explosive devices in Canada.

Sher was born in Montreal and is bilingual. He graduated from McGill's medical school and had just accepted a position as pathologist at St. Thomas Elgin General Hospital in Ontario and had moved with his wife and three children there.

A doctor with a clear humanitarian streak, Sher had traveled to Pakistan with an aid group to assist earthquake victims in 2006 and helped the local mosque distribute food to needy families on Montreal's South Shore.

In what has to be a first for an alleged violent extremist, Sher auditioned for Canadian Idol. Dressed in a traditional Pakistani shalwar kameez, he belted out a rendition of Canadian pop star Avril Lavigne's "Complicated" while dancing something like an intended moonwalk. Not too surprisingly, he failed to advance.

Sher was acquitted in August 2014 of terrorism charges. Presiding judge Charles Hackland cited Sher's "impressive" professional and academic record but noted he had "jihadist" sympathies.

For his association with extremists, Sher lost his job, his family, and his reputation.

causational. It is also possible that terrorist groups may seek out individuals with certain technical backgrounds.

Psychological Predisposition

This is one of the more interesting aspects of modern terrorism research. For most people living in a Western society, the fact that someone willingly puts on a suicide vest and dies in the course of an attack is a certain indicator of mental illness. Why would a sane person do such a thing? Is not the drive to stay alive stronger than any cause? (Interestingly, some terrorists have claimed, "As you love life, we love death."[35] The Islamic State has a variation on the popular meme YOLO—You Only Live Once—which they have termed YODO, substituting *die* for *live*).

In actual fact, it has been proposed that very few if any terrorists are "crazy."[36] They make choices based on a number of factors, but the available evidence suggests that they are psychologically normal. Little published evidence shows a preponderance of psychopathy or mental disorder. It must be noted, however, that very few studies have had recourse to actual data, and researchers have rarely had access to successful terrorists. Furthermore, it is undoubtedly a challenge to interview a successful suicide attacker!

I am not aware of any large data studies demonstrating that violent extremists suffer from mental illness to an extent greater than society in general. According to the Canadian Mental Health Association, 20 percent of Canadians suffer at some point from a mental illness (broadly defined). Do extremists suffer from analogous conditions at a rate disproportionate to the general population? That remains to be determined.

On occasion people associated with a terrorist (family, friends . . .) have stated that they believed the extremist suffered from mental illness. It should be stressed that these are *not* professional assessments: they are impressions. It is unlikely that lay people are in a position to determine true mental illness.

It may be that the rush to label extremists "mentally ill," which we saw in the wake of the October 2014 attacks in Canada, serves as a sort of "phew" moment. By this I mean that if we dismiss extremists as mentally ill, we separate them from "normal" people, putting a distance between us and them. Furthermore, if they are ill we can ignore other characteristics or influences, since the illness would become an overwhelming factor. Finally, we could conclude that mental illness renders them not responsible for their actions and thus perhaps minimizes the role of ideology (which must be present in some form for violence to be terrorism). Perhaps, also, a diagnosis of mental illness excuses our security and law-enforcement agencies from failing to detect and neutralize them (mentally ill people being hard to analyze and whose actions are impossible to predict).

In addition, overt signs of what appear to be illness may not be so. Talking of the devil or spirits is not necessarily indicative of an underlying mental problem. Believing that one sees jinn (spiritual beings in Islam) does not imply that one is suffering from hallucinations (how many people believe in angels in Western society?). John Nuttall, one of the convicted Canada Day terrorist, described seeing jinn and the "angel of death."[37] Interestingly, the Victoria plot strikes me as the most likely case in Canada where the possibility of mental illness may have played a role.

If mental illness is not a factor, are there personality prototypes that are more susceptible to violent radicalization? The simple answer is that we do not know. It may be that there are as many personality types as there are individuals. For example, do extremists score high on the thrill-seeking scale? What about narcissism or attention deficit hyperactivity disorder or sociopathy? More evidence-based research is needed. From a detection perspective, however, the likelihood of being able to devise and administer a psychological test to predict possible violent behavior is probably something in the distant future, if it's even feasible at all.

Again we have to distinguish correlation from causation. Some individuals who engage in violent extremism may in fact suffer from one mental issue or another, but it is very difficult, if not impossible, to determine that this illness caused that person to act. It is also not helpful to suggest that security and law-enforcement agencies focus their efforts on the mentally ill to uncover future actors before they strike. Mental illness is already greatly stigmatized in society: adding the extremist layer would worsen this situation.

I find it interesting that the popular view has swung from an initial belief that "They're all crazy" to "None of them is crazy" back to "They're all crazy." Surely the truth is somewhere in between. It is probably possible to be "mad" *and* "bad," as I have seen it described in several media reports.

Discussion

So, where does this leave us? Simply stated, there is no profile or checklist of factors or drivers that can be used to predict who is at greater risk of radicalization. It would be much easier to locate and deal with this phenomenon if there were such a set. Individuals who radicalize to violence may come from any environment and any set of inputs.

We do not need simplistic explanations for radicalization to violence. Putting forward baseless generalizations does not help our understanding of the phenomenon, and neither does it give us useful suggestions on what to do about it. Such overly general accounts may satisfy a heightened need to comprehend the incomprehensible—why otherwise normal Canadians are turning to terrorism here or abroad—but ultimately do more harm than good. The assumption that terrorism "must" be caused by factor X can lead, and probably has led, to practices and actions that are not only wastes of time and counterproductive but also may worsen the situation, not to mention generate false leads and time-consuming, wrong-headed investigation or inquiry.

Getting these drivers wrong can produce serious errors and counterproductive results. In early 2014, as reported by Al Jazeera,[38] the UK government attempted to provide indicators to first responders, including health sector workers, in order to identify radicalization at the earliest possible stage. This is a good and potentially very useful approach. Unfortunately, some of the indicators were overly general—for example, unemployment was a possible sign of radicalization—and led to severe criticism of the UK government's attempts to roll out what is a worthwhile and needed program. By not providing better explanation of the nature of the indicators, the government may have harmed its chances to gain a large number of eyes and ears on the ground. Unemployment is clearly not a valid or useful indicator, and it is unclear why it would be seen as such. Many unemployed young Muslims in the UK do not radicalize to violence, while many of those who have engaged in acts of terrorism were in fact employed full time. (For example, the 7/7 attacks in London in July 2005, perhaps the most serious attack in the UK post–9/11, and one that led to many changes in the UK's counterterrorism policies, was led by Mohammad Sidique Khan, a primary school teaching assistant[39]). So, in the end, how useful is "unemployment" as an indicator?

Note that some of the drivers discussed may be present in some cases (i.e., a certain percentage of extremists may be financially destitute, for example). The presence of a given factor does not, however, necessarily imply causation. It may simply be present (correlation). A particular driver may help to establish the conditions for violent radicalization to develop in a particular case. It remains very unclear how or why—or whether—these factors are crucial elements in one's pathway to violent extremism. Correlation does not imply causation.

In presentations to Canadian audiences, I have frequently been asked to provide violent-radicalization checklists and have had to inform my colleagues that I cannot. One example might illustrate the conundrum better.

Assume that you are a border agent working at a major Canadian international airport. During a given shift, you may process hundreds of people. You usually have a few minutes to determine whether the person before you requires a more detailed examination (known as *secondary* in the industry). On what do you base your decision to send to secondary?

From a terrorism perspective, the answer is unclear. Physical appearance is not a reliable indicator, as we shall discuss in more detail later. Travel patterns could be useful but aren't necessarily so. Address and occupation are of no value. In the end, without prior intelligence or a heads up, there is little to determine when and why (aside from random selection) someone should be sent for further examination to determine whether that person poses a threat to society.

Necessary and Sufficient Conditions

It is clear that none of the factors discussed above appears to be an either necessary or sufficient explanation as to why people radicalize to violence. But what do I mean by *necessary* and *sufficient*? There are detailed philosophical treatises on whether conditions are necessary and/or sufficient for another condition to occur; I will depart here from a purely philosophical usage. From a layperson's perspective, by "necessary *and* sufficient" I mean both that something (or a set of things) must be present for something to happen and that the presence of this thing (or these things) is enough to explain why something happens.

Using the list of drivers analyzed above, it is clear that feelings of alienation are not necessary for violent radicalization. Many radicalized individuals do not appear to suffer from alienation, and yet they radicalize. Similarly, there are undoubtedly many alienated people in Canadian society who never venture down the radicalization path. Relying on any given factor would lead to a problematic series of false positives and false negatives. For instance, if alienation were seen as a necessary condition, alienated people who do not radicalize would hence be false positives, while "normal" people who do radicalize would be false negatives. The same applies to the other conditions (poverty, lack of opportunity, etc.) discussed above.

Consider the following statement:

Terrorists are blond.

If this were so—and were the only clue on which to base a suspicion—security and intelligence agencies would investigate blond—and only blond—individuals if they suspected terrorist activity were taking place (or may even profile blonds in their investigations). What would it take to prove this statement wrong? Well, there are two possibilities.

A blond exists who is not a terrorist.

This is an example of a false positive.

A redhead commits an act of terrorism.

This is an example of a false negative.

Please note that I am not suggesting that blonds are any more likely to be terrorists than others (the same goes for redheads)! This is a very oversimplified example.

What about *sufficient* conditions, as I am using the term here? It appears again that there are no easily identifiable sufficient conditions for violent radicalization. The process is so individualized and idiosyncratic that it is not possible to determine which factors, if any, are enough to account for violent radicalization. It is uncertain that a tipping point can be generalized at which an individual is primed to act with violence.

So, returning to necessary conditions, is there anything useful that can be used to explain and possibly predict those people that radicalize to violence, other than the ones just outlined (and which I have shown not to be generally helpful)? It is difficult to say. The following drivers appear to me to be necessary and have been seen in most cases of violent radicalization in Canada, but it is still possible, though perhaps unlikely, that an individual or group can radicalize in the absence of any of the following factors. It would only take one exception, however, to show that any one of these is not necessary.

Association with Like-Minded People

One of the most important aspects of violent radicalization is that of association. As discussed in the introduction, violent radicalization rarely, if ever occurs, in a vacuum. Most people are social and live in a variety of small or large social networks. These networks serve as groups of people with whom an individual shares some aspect of their lives. We tend to have different social circles for a particular interest at hand—for instance, family, work environment, pickup hockey team, neighbors, friends, and so on.

The same goes for those who radicalize to violence. They too have multiple interests and circles. But what is interesting is what happens once the radicalization process matures. People tend to abandon circles that do not share these new feelings and beliefs and increasingly limit themselves to those circles that share this particular interest. This limiting of one's environment is often overt and observable. These people will leave employment and shun the company of their families and former friends.

This new, narrower, circle serves several purposes: It allows for the confirmation of ideas and the resolution of doubts or questions. It provides avenues for further exploration of the ideology. And, perhaps most importantly, it establishes a barrier that shields the individual from outside ideologies that could compete with the new one. In a sense, the individual on the path to radicalization is immunized and isolated from both former beliefs and from efforts to convince them to return to previous moderate ones. This barrier has serious implications for efforts by those from the individual's original circles to bring them back from the brink.

I already addressed the recent overblown fear of self-radicalization and "lone wolves" in the introduction. As noted, it only takes one example to disprove the theory. In this instance, the 2010 attack by Roshonara Choudhry on her member of parliament in East London, England, would fit the bill, as it appears that she radicalized and acted on her own.[40] So, should we worry about these kinds of attacks in Canada? I think not, for the following reasons:

- There has yet to be a lone-wolf attack in Canada (the October 2014 attacks by Martin Rouleau and Michael Zehaf-Bibeau are not examples[41]).
- These kinds of radicalization processes are rare, and not all bad things can be prevented from happening.

• A true case of self-radicalization would be next to impossible to detect anyway, so it is unclear how devoting resources to ferreting it out would help.

There are usually indicators, even if they are subtle. There are people in a position to observe the changes (i.e., family and friends). Scholars like the United States' Reid Meloy talk of *leakage*, where lone actors demonstrate their intention to do something violent.[42] These changes will be the subject of chapter 3. I would suggest that, without a group of similarly-motivated contacts, few if any people would radicalize to violence in Canada.

Presence of a Charismatic or Spiritual Mentor or Leader

If it is true that self-radicalization is rare to nonexistent, then it follows that a person being radicalized is likely in an environment where other people share similar views. Some of these people may be more radicalized and have the right mix of personality, charisma, knowledge (historical, current, religious, etc.), and skills to exert an influence over others. These people may be satisfied with passing inspiration and motivation on to others without taking any other action themselves. These people are called *radicalizers*.

Radicalizers can be present in person or in virtual environments. They can use the spoken or written word or use visual images to pass their ideas on and convince others of the need—or obligation—to act in a violent manner to achieve an ideological (political or religious) goal. Radicalizers are particularly challenging to security and law enforcement, as their actions rarely cross the line of criminal behavior (at least this is the case in Canada, where we do not have laws prohibiting the glorification of violence, although the Harper government was considering legislation after the October 2014 attacks). Generally, an individual or group has to engage in an act of terrorism, or plan to do so, before criminal charges can be made.

There is almost always the presence of a charismatic or spiritual guide that enables and furthers the radicalization process. Most people are neither experienced nor intelligent enough to understand the complications of the ideology surrounding Al Qaeda–inspired violence. The narrative contains elements of history, political science, and religion that can be very hard to follow. In particular, an appreciation and grasp of the religious justification or obligation for violence in the name of Islam as described by Al Qaeda and other groups is probably beyond the understanding of the majority of people. Most people are followers and not leaders and require the presence of someone to guide them to certain conclusions.

Radicalizers and charismatic or spiritual mentors provide that explanation and context. Who are they? In essence, anyone. A radicalizer can be a family member (father, brother, mother, uncle, cousin . . .), a friend, a religious mentor, an online contact, and so on. There are many occasions in recent years where radicalizers have been identified. I identify several types in the following.

Family

For Canadian readers, there is probably no better example of the role played by family members in the radicalization process than that of the Khadr family. It is not a stretch to posit that the Khadr children were radicalized in whole or in part by Ahmed Said Khadr, who was killed in a shootout with US forces in Afghanistan in 2003.[43]

In the United States, some reports suggest that Dzhokhar Tsarnaev, convicted in 2015 in Boston for his role in the 2013 Boston Marathon bombings, was radicalized by his elder brother, Tamerlan.[44]

Friends

Many have suggested that radicalization to violence is a young person's phenomenon. If true, then it stands to reason that the opinions and influence of friends is important. Given the amount of time young people spend with their friends, the presence of a radicalized individual can have a significant influence on others.

In Canada the role played by friends and acquaintances was evident in both the Toronto 18 plot (specifically for Fahim Ahmed and Zakaria Amara[45]) and in London, Ontario, among Xristos Katsiroubas, Aaron Yoon, and Ali Medlej, who were involved in the In Amenas, Algeria, gas plant attack in 2013.[46]

Religious Leaders

Religious motivation is important for Al Qaeda–inspired extremists. Individuals radicalizing need access to those with religious knowledge and an ability to seamlessly pass on that knowledge. Most religious leaders are neither radical nor violent. Nevertheless, a charismatic individual with the requisite background in Islam can be dangerous. One of the best examples of a religious leader's exhortation to jihad was Abu Hamza at the Finsbury Park mosque in London, England, in the 1990s and early 2000s.[47]

Online Figures

Given the nature of the Internet and claims that it has contributed significantly to the radicalization process, it should not surprise us that there are radicalizers online. The late Anwar al-Awlaki (also rendered *Aulaqi*), a Yemeni-American citizen, is probably the best recent example.

Textbox 1.3

SCARBOROUGH BLUFF

The Salaheddin Islamic Centre is a mosque on Kennedy Road in Scarborough, a district in Toronto. It is famous (infamous?) for being the religious center attended by several members of the Toronto 18. It is also known for its imam, Aly Hindy.

It is safe to say that Imam Hindy is controversial and even radical (recall, in my introductory remarks, that radicalism does *not* imply violence). He calls himself a "fundamentalist."

Among his more *interesting* statements are the following:

- Homosexuality was invented, and it is "nonsense and garbage" to believe that anyone could be born that way.[1]
- It does not matter that Canada accepts homosexuals, because Islam does not.
- 9/11 was a CIA operation.[2]
- The Toronto 18 terrorists were "good people."[3]
- In justifying his active participation in blessing polygamous marriages in Canada, Hindy said, "This is in our religion, and nobody can force us to do anything against our religion. . . . If the laws of the country conflict with Islamic law, if one goes against the other, then I am going to follow Islamic law, simple as that."[4]
- Fighting Canadian soldiers in Afghanistan was a jihad for Afghans.[5]

When Aly Hindy offered to act as a surety for Mohammed Mahjoub, subject of a national-security certificate in Canada, a judge rejected his application, stating, "[Hindy] is sympathetic to or at least defensive of the threats of Islamic terrorism towards Canada."[6]

Imam Hindy's attitudes and behaviors are consistent with some of those to be presented in chapter 4.

Sources:

1. Stewart Bell, "Toronto's Million-Dollar 'Radical Mosque,'" February 16, 2012, http://news.nationalpost.com/news/canada/aly-hindy-salaheddin-islamic-centre.

2. Dag, "Imam Aly Hindy's Previous Job," No Dhimmitude (blog), June 4, 2006, http://nodhimmitude.blogspot.ca/2006/06/imam-aly-hindys-previous-job.html.

3. Bell, "Toronto's 'Radical Mosque.'"

4. Noor Javed, "GTA's Secret World of Polygamy," May 24, 2008, http://www.thestar.com/news/gta/2008/05/24/gtas_secret_world_of_polygamy.html.

In my opinion, it is not an exaggeration to state that no single individual has had a greater influence on individuals in Canada—or in the Western world for that matter—than Awlaki. The US-born son of Yemeni students studying in the United States, Awlaki, who was killed by a US drone in 2011, was a charismatic scholar who used his fluency in both English and Arabic to inspire people, including many in Canada, to violence. Convicted member of the Toronto 18 Saad Khalid admitted in a series of letters to the CBC in early 2014 that during his radicalization process he was under the sway of Awlaki.[48]

Outside of Canada, both Roshonara Choudhry, who stabbed MP Stephen Timms,[49] and Major Hassan, who shot dozens of his colleagues at Fort Hood in Texas in 2009,[50] were in direct contact with Awlaki and received inspiration, if not direction, from him.

Interestingly, despite his death, Awlaki's influence is likely not in itself dead. Through the never truly deleted reality of the Internet, Awlaki's presence will live on for some time. Inevitably, one would think, someone else will come forward and carry the torch. We must remember, however, that even in the twenty-first century several ideologues who died long ago still resonate with extremists (Sayyid Qutb and Abdullah Azzam died decades ago, while Abdul Wahhab and Ibn Taymiyyah, centuries ago).

Awlaki's influence was spread through his writings and videos and his contributions to *Inspire*, an online magazine that serves as a how-to manual for the aspiring terrorist. In 2011, the UK's International Centre for the Study of Radicalisation and Political Violence published a paper by Alexander Meleagrou-Hitchens, titled *As American as Apple Pie: How Anwar al-Awlaki Became the Face of Western Jihad*. This paper provides an excellent overview of Awlaki's influence on (primarily) Al Qaeda–inspired extremists.[51]

Access to Confirming Information

It follows that in order to subscribe to an ideology one must have access to material that outlines that ideology. And for extremists, there is no lack of material available.

The host of media used to promote and explain the Al Qaeda ideology is truly impressive. Not only do the groups use every available method to spread the news (websites, chat rooms, blogs, Twitter, audio files, videos . . .), but there is also a long history of textual material going back to the beginning of Islam, in the seventh century CE. It is not uncommon to see exhortations to violence quoting the thirteenth-century *Ibn Taymiyyah* (a particular favorite of the late Bin Laden[52]), as well as others across the centuries. For extremists and those on the path to radicalization and violence, this material is ubiquitous. Whether online, in person, or on paper, inspiration is readily available for those looking for it.

One of the most common claims is that radicalization is happening on the Internet and via social media. While this may be true, it needs some clarification. A great deal has been written about the Internet and its role in terrorism and violent radicalization. There are frequent accounts about individuals "radicalized by the Internet." Is this an accurate description of what is happening?

It goes without saying that the Internet is everywhere and is used by almost everyone in the West. People do their banking, shopping, social connecting, and information searches online. Al Qaeda–inspired individuals also use the Internet for similar purposes.

The Internet should perhaps not be seen as the invincible game changer for violent radicalization. While it does allow a much larger pool of people to access information that traditionally would have had to be passed in person or via more mundane means (tapes, photocopies, etc.) and allows for some anonymity, it might be preferable to see it as a *force multiplier* of what would have happened anyway. Terrorism predates the advent of the Internet, and, in the event a new technology comes along, terrorism will adapt. In summary, everyone these days seems to use the Internet; so do extremists.

The notion that someone was "radicalized by the Internet" requires comment. The Internet does not radicalize anyone. While the process of radicalization may occur in part—or even primarily—online, it still requires interaction and contact with like-minded people. The Internet merely provides some with the opportunity to communicate with those who share their ideas but who may be living far away. The Internet is a vehicle or vessel, not an actor.

In addition, extremists seek affirmation of their views and contact with others of similar mindset on the Internet. There are probably thousands of such sites, which provide the following:

• texts that provide religious justification for jihad and violence
• media (video, audio, text) that provides glorification of violence
• ways to engage in personal contact (blogs, chat rooms, etc.)
• advice on how to travel to conflict zones
• and the possibility of planning attacks (this is probably rare).

All in all, many in government and academe recognize that extremists are making very efficient use of the Internet. Robert Hannigan, director of Britain's signals-intelligence agency, Government Communications Head-quarters, stated that the Islamic State of Iraq and the Levant is the first terrorist group whose members have grown up on the Internet.[53] According to Jamie Bartlett of the UK think-tank Demos, it should come as no surprise that extremist groups like the Islamic State are using social media very effec-tively, as many members are young people who have never lived without the Internet. He also argues that governments and opponents of extremist groups can use the same technology to challenge the message of violence.[54]

A Belief in the Narrative

To paraphrase a real estate saying, there are three things necessary—but not sufficient—for radicalization to violence: narrative, narrative, and narrative. As noted in the introduction, the narrative weaves a compelling story that spans centuries and provides what some see as a legitimate solution to a problem set. The narrative is flexible and adaptable and doesn't require years of study to be easily comprehensible. Without the narrative, there would be no Al Qaeda–inspired extremism. Nevertheless, belief in the narrative, or parts of it, does not necessarily lead to violence, as millions probably think that aspects of the narrative are true but do not act in violent ways.

VENUES OF RADICALIZATION

It is worth discussing briefly where radicalization is unfolding in Canada. While it may sound trite, radicalization can occur wherever people get together. It does not have to take place in a formal setting and, contrary to popular opinion, does not happen in all mosques across Canada and the world. I believe that the people involved are much more important to the process than the setting, but in the following I briefly discuss where radical-ization has been detected in Canadian cases.

Religious Institutions

Mention has already been made to the Finsbury Park mosque in London. Mosques could be seen theoretically as hotbeds of radicalization, since they are places where people gather and where topics of interest, including con-flict zones, may be discussed. Nevertheless, mosques and Islamic centers in Canada do not appear to be particularly useful as radicalization hubs. In fact, there have been cases where imams and mosque officials have prevented radicals from using their spaces to promote violence and hatred. A recent example in Canada was brought to light after the April 2013 arrests of the Via Rail plotters, when it was published that one of the alleged extremists, Raed Jaser, was reported to authorities by an imam who believed he was negatively influencing youth.[55] In other cases, extremists have been kicked out of mosques because their activities were seen as inconsistent with Islam.[56]

This is not to say that individuals cannot use, and have not used, mosque spaces for radicalization purposes. It is unlikely that all imams or mosque boards of directors are aware of the purposes for which their facilities are being used. In Ottawa, where I live, the local school boards rent out classroom and gymnasium space to a number of groups. How much scrutiny is given to those renting that space? A number of Calgarians who went on to fight with extremist groups in Syria attended the same storefront mosque, where they likely reinforced one another's beliefs.[57]

Schools

Radicalization has occasionally germinated in educational institutions, both secondary and postsecondary. In Canada, the two leaders of the Toronto 18, Fahim Ahmed and Zakaria Amara, began their journey to extremist violence at Meadowvale Secondary School in Mississauga.[58] The paths of Xristos Katsiroubas, Aaron Yoon, and Ali Medlej of London, Ontario, first crossed when they were fellow students at London South Collegiate Institute.[59] I am not suggesting that schools actively played a role in sponsoring or supporting radicalization. Rather, they are simply the venues where violent radicalization can occur. Interestingly, there is little to no public evidence that Islamic schools, which function somewhat in parallel to the provincial school systems in Canada, have served as fertile ground for extremism.

The Internet

If we consider the Internet as a "space," then it is certain that it is quickly becoming an incubator for extremist thought and propagation. Again, however, it is important to put the use of the Internet in context. Terrorism predated the advent of the Internet and would survive its (improbable) demise. It is perhaps useful to see the Internet as a force multiplier for Al Qaeda–inspired violent radicalization and not its irreplaceable generator.

Another way to see the use of the Internet is to compare how earlier pre-Internet movements used different technologies to spread their propaganda.

The Internet does provide a very large space to share ideas, methods, justifications, and other aspects of radicalization and will likely continue to do so for a very long time. Nevertheless, it is important to remember that apps

Table 1.1 Technology and Radicalization

Movement	Technology
Soviet dissidents, Cold War	samizdat press
Iranian revolutionaries, 1970s	cassette tapes
Saudi dissidents, early 1990s	fax machines

like Twitter play a limited role in the actual radicalization process (although they are being used to promote violent jihad in conflict zones such as Syria). As one female jihadi tweeted, "140 letters cannot define the Deen [religiosity] and Akhlaq [morals] of anyone on Twitter."[60]

Foreign Conflict Zones

Those that travel for violent jihad do not only engage in training activities or fighting. They also find themselves among dozens or hundreds of like-minded individuals who can share their experiences and views on jihad. This environment concentrates and probably accelerates the radicalization process (it must be remembered, however, that the travelers are already radicalized to a point upon arrival). Some groups build in ideological sessions during the training regime.

SUMMARY

There still appears to be an appetite for identifying the root causes of Al Qaeda–inspired terrorism, since articles and books on the subject continue to be published. Dozens of op-ed pieces were written about what drove Michael Zehaf-Bibeau to kill Nathan Cirillo and storm Parliament in the days and weeks following the attacks. Perhaps more useful generalizations will be proposed, tested, and validated in the months and years to come. I look forward to those results should they occur. Nevertheless, I believe it is highly unlikely that a set of drivers or factors with predictive value will be proposed and validated in the near future.

It is entirely possible that, given enough information, the real drivers of violent radicalization for a specific case may be determined. This would be a significant finding and would add to our knowledge base. It is unlikely, however, that one could extrapolate to more cases, as exceptions would always be found. From a security or law-enforcement perspective, theories of causal relationships are currently of little value. I prefer to identify and examine indicators of violent radicalization.

Is there anything to be learned from study of other types of violent extremism? Are there risk factors associated with those?

Researchers at the Intelligence Report, a journal on hate groups published by the Southern Poverty Law Center in the United States, studied one hundred murders by racist extremists over a two-year period and found that the typical murderer drawn to Stormfront.org (a white supremacist Web forum) was

- frustrated
- a white adult male
- living with his mother or an estranged spouse or girlfriend
- and not interested in seeking employment or furthering education (in fact, all one hundred were unemployed at the time they killed).[61]

This is indeed a fascinating finding and could be useful in identifying and stopping individuals keen on this particular type of violent extremism. As we have seen, however, it is rarely applicable to Al Qaeda–inspired extremists.

At the end of the day, all cases of violent extremism are probably not predictable—the vicissitudes of human behavior render a watertight model impossible. People of similar backgrounds exposed to similar stimuli and in similar environments will act differently. Maybe violent radicalization is a "perfect storm" of factors and conditions and environment: any change in one of the variables might lead to a very different end.

Throughout this book I will try to demonstrate that the people who have radicalized to violence are average Canadians and Westerners. Some are from privileged backgrounds, others have struggled. Most are more or less "normal," while a few have had mental issues. It is also my belief that anyone—and I do mean anyone—could embrace a violent ideology given the right circumstances. Let me cite a personal anecdote.

When I was in grade ten (second year of secondary school in Ontario) I was exposed in history class to the plight of migrant farm workers in Southern California and the efforts of Cesar Chavez to organize them for better working conditions. The suffering of these workers and the exploitation by the agribusinesses got my blood boiling. I wanted to do something to help. In the end, I did nothing (I was fourteen at the time). Besides, I am not sure I could have found California on a map!

What were the circumstances behind my "radicalization"? I was a young male, third-generation Canadian, from a solidly middle-class home (intact—my parents were together). I was the youngest of three boys, was academically gifted, and had begun to get into great physical shape through jogging. I was popular and had lots of friends. The person responsible for the information on the farm workers was a Catholic nun heavily into social justice issues. I was beginning to develop some minor "anti-American" sensitivities (not atypical in Canada), although I was from a very pro-US family.

The conditions were there for me to become very involved in this social outrage, and yet I did not. It could have gone either way: had the right person (or the wrong person, depending on your viewpoint) come into my life at the right time, I could have entered into a spiral that might have led to extreme action.

Furthermore, what if people join these movements because they really believe that they are doing the right thing? We assume that personal issues leave them vulnerable to manipulative recruiters who convince them to do things they normally would reject. But what if that is not the case? I think we have to consider the possibility that what we call *terrorism* is seen by some as legitimate action. If so, it will have implications for how we deal with these individuals. On the surface, it certainly appears that many ordinary Canadians living ordinary lives are opting for this kind of action.

As Pogo, the eponymous opossum of Walt Kelly's sardonic cartoon strip, famously said, "We have seen the enemy, and he is us." Violent extremists in this country come from our midst. They are us.

NOTES

1. In April 2015, he was found guilty on thirty counts.

2. Adapted from reporting by the *National Post*'s Stewart Bell. For more on Plotnikov's story see chapter 4.

3. Roger Cohen, "Here There Is No Why: For ISIS Slaughter Is an End in Itself," *New York Times*, September 29, 2014, http://www.nytimes.com/2014/09/30/opinion/roger-cohen-for-isis-slaughter-is-an-end-in-itself.html?module=Search&mabReward=relbias%3As%2C%7B%221%22%3A%22RI%3A9%22%7D&_r=0.

4. John Horgan, "Don't Ask Why People Join the Islamic State—Ask How," *Vice News*, September 10, 2014, https://news.vice.com/article/dont-ask-why-people-join-the-islamic-state-ask-how.

5. Greg Easterbrook, "What Happens When We All Live to 100?" *The Atlantic,* October 2014, http://www.theatlantic.com/features/archive/2014/09/what-happens-when-we-all-live-to-100/379338/.

6. Tim Stanley, "ISIL's Western Converts Are Not Motivated by Islam. They Are Motivated by Boredom," *Telegraph* (London), September 4, 2014, http://blogs.telegraph.co.uk/news/timstanley/100285161/isils-western-converts-are-not-motivated-by-islam-they-are-motivated-by-boredom/.

7. Amund Bakke Foss, "Norsk Syria-kriger i stort VG-intervju: Derfor kjemper jeg i Syria «Døden henger over deg hele tiden, og du må se på når gode venner blør sakte i hjel»," *VG* (Oslo), last modified September 9, 2014, http://www.vg.no/nyheter/utenriks/syria/derfor-kjemper-jeg-i-syria/a/23298934/.

8. Tom Quiggan, "Jihad Isn't about Religion," *Ottawa Citizen*, September 20, 2007, available online at http://www.canada.com/ottawacitizen/news/opinion/story.html?id=4b36d26c-e129-4fad-b645-d734d911fa07.

9. Ted Robert Gurr's seminal work *Why Men Rebel* is worth reading in this regard (Princeton: Princeton University Press, 1970).

10. Citizens for Public Justice, *Poverty Trends Highlights: Canada 2013* (Ottawa: CPJ, 2013), http://www.cpj.ca/sites/default/files/docs/Poverty-Trends-Highlights-2013.pdf.

11. "Momin Khawaja: The Road from Fun-Loving Teen to Terror Suspect," *Ottawa Citizen*, June 23, 2008, http://www.canada.com/ottawacitizen/news/story.html?id=61d14370-d12d-47f0-8e69-23722cc5f663.

12. Michael Friscolanti, "It Comes Down to These Four: The 'Toronto 18' Terrorism Case Rests on a Core Group of Suspects," *Macleans*, June 9, 2008, available online at http://www.thecanadianencyclopedia.ca/en/article/the-toronto-18-terrorism-case/.

13. "Trial of Ottawa Hospital Technician Accused of Terror Plot Begins," CBC News (Ottawa), last updated May 14, 2014, http://www.cbc.ca/news/canada/ottawa/trial-of-ottawa-hospital-technician-accused-of-terror-plot-begins-1.2643226; and Chris Cobb, "Second 'Operation Samosa' Terrorist Trial Gets Underway," *Ottawa Citizen*, last updated May 20, 2014, http://ottawacitizen.com/news/national/second-operation-samosa-terrorist-trial-gets-underway.

14. Thomson Reuters, "'Jihadi John' Identified as Mohammed Emwazi of London," CBC News, last updated February 26, 2015, http://www.cbc.ca/news/world/jihadi-john-identified-as-mohammed-emwazi-of-london-bbc-says-1.2973079.

15. "Islamic State: 'Jihadi John''s Background Typical yet Distinct," BBC News, February 26, 2015, http://www.bbc.com/news/world-middle-east-31646999.

16. Kamaldeep Bhui, Nasir Warfa, and Edgar Jones, "Is Violent Radicalisation Associated with Poverty, Migration, Poor Self-Reported Health and Common Mental Disorders?" *PLoS One* 9, no. 3 (March 5, 2014), doi:10.1371/journal.pone.0090718, http://journals.plos.org/plosone/article?id=10.1371/journal.pone.0090718.

17. Robert J. Sampson, John H. Laub, Christopher Wimer, "Does Marriage Reduce Crime? A Counterfactual Approach to Within-Individual Causal Effects," *Criminology* 44, no. 3 (2006): 465–508, available online at http://scholar.harvard.edu/files/sampson/files/2006_criminology_laubwimer_1.pdf.

18. Omar El Akkad and Greg McArthur, "Hateful Chatter Behind the Evil," *Globe and Mail* (Toronto), last updated August 22, 2012, http://www.theglobeandmail.com/news/national/hateful-chatter-behind-the-veil/article1203257/?page=all.

19. "Profile: Hiva Alizadeh," CBC News, last updated September 3, 2010, http://www.cbc.ca/news/canada/profile-hiva-alizadeh-1.938292.

20. "Terrorism Claims against Khawaja Stunned His Ex-Fiancèe," CBC News, last updated July 23, 2008, http://www.cbc.ca/news/canada/terrorism-claims-against-khawaja-stunned-his-ex-fianc%C3%A9e-1.710627.

21. Rosa Silverman, "'Breaking Jihad': Teacher Admits Syria-Related Terror Offences," *London Telegraph*, October 27, 2014, http://www.telegraph.co.uk/news/uknews/terrorism-in-the-uk/11189702/Breaking-Jihad-Teacher-admits-Syria-related-terror-offences.html.

22. Lauren Kirchner, "Marriage May Calm a Criminal Impulse in Men," *Pacific Standard Magazine*, July 15, 2013, http://www.psmag.com/navigation/health-and-behavior/marriage-may-calm-a-criminal-impulse-in-men-62504/.

23. CBC News, "Homegrown Terrorist: Toronto 18 Bomb Plotter Saad Khalid Recalls His Radicalization," Yahoo! News Canada, April 16, 2014, https://ca.news.yahoo.com/homegrown-terrorist-toronto-18-bomb-plotter-saad-khalid-223848260.html.

24. With regard to the world of Al Qaeda–inspired violent extremism, see the works of US academic Quintan Wiktorowicz, particularly his *Radical Islam Rising: Muslim Extremism in the West* (Lanham, MD: Rowman and Littlefield, 2005).

25. "7 July Bombings: The Bombers," BBC News, n.d., http://news.bbc.co.uk/2/shared/spl/hi/uk/05/london_blasts/investigation/html/bombers.stm.

26. Faisal Al Yafai, "Frustration and Alienation Alone Cannot Explain the Allure of Jihad," *National* (Abu Dhabi), last updated October 8, 2014, http://www.thenational.ae/opinion/frustration-and-alienation-alone-cannot-explain-the-allure-of-jihad.

27. PBS, "Trial of a Terrorist: A Terrorist's Testimony," *Frontline*, n.d., http://www.pbs.org/wgbh/pages/frontline/shows/trail/inside/testimony.html.

28. For reporting on Reid, see "Potential for Radicalization of U.S. Prison Inmates," Religious Tolerance: Ontario Consultants on Religious Tolerance (website), last updated August 20, 2005, http://www.religioustolerance.org/islpris.htm. For reporting on Nemmouche, see Steve Almasy and Shelby Lin Erdman, "Captured Jewish Museum Shooting Suspect Carried Weapons, Gas Mask," CNN, last updated June 2, 2014, http://www.cnn.com/2014/06/01/world/europe/france-belgium-jewish-shooting/.

29. Ali Dirie, a member of the Toronto 18, was alleged to have radicalized others while in prison. It is important to note that Dirie had been radicalized prior to his incarceration and that there is no evidence to suggest that individuals influenced by him have moved on to extremism. Michelle Shephard, "Toronto 18: Ali Mohamed Dirie, Convicted in Plot, Dies in Syria," *Toronto Star*, September 25, 2013, http://www.thestar.com/news/gta/2013/09/25/toronto_18_ali_mohamed_dirie_convicted_in_plot_dies_in_syria.html.

30. Kathleen Harris, "Radicalization a Growing Risk in Canadian Prisons, Experts Warn," CBC News, last updated January 22, 2015, http://www.cbc.ca/news/politics/radicalization-a-growing-risk-in-canadian-prisons-experts-warn-1.2928373.

31. Christie Blatchford, "Three Guilty Pleas—And Terror Case Is No Longer Near Collapse," *Globe and Mail* (Toronto), last updated September 6, 2012, http://www.theglobeandmail.com/news/national/three-guilty-pleas---and-terror-case-is-no-longer-near-collapse/article790989/.

32. Joseph Brean and Adrian Humphreys, "Two 'Religiously Strict' Men behind Foiled al-Qaeda-Supported Plot to Derail VIA Train," *National Post* (Toronto), April 22, 2013, http://news.nationalpost.com/2013/04/22/canadian-terrorist-plot-was-planned-by-chiheb-esseghaier-raed-jaser/.

33. Chris Cobb, "Khurram Sher Terror Case Hangs on Guilt by Association, Defence Lawyer Argues," *Ottawa Citizen*, last updated May 20, 2014, http://ottawacitizen.com/news/local-news/khurram-sher-terror-case-hangs-on-guilt-by-association-defence-lawyer-argues.

34. Diego Gambetta and Steffan Hertog, *Engineers of Jihad*, Sociology Working Papers, paper no. 2007-10, Department of Sociology, University of Oxford, http://www.sociology.ox.ac.uk/materials/papers/2007-10.pdf.

35. Charlotte Meredith, "'We Love Death More than You Love Life' Islamic Extremists Plead Guilty to EDL Terror Plot," *Daily Express* (London), last updated April 30, 2013, http://www.express.co.uk/news/uk/395897/We-love-death-more-than-you-love-life-Islamic-extremists-plead-guilty-to-EDL-terror-plot.

36. Andrew Giese, "The Mind of a Suicide Terrorist," ABC News, September 20, 2001, http://abcnews.go.com/Health/story?id=117233.

37. Ian Mulgrew, "Alleged Terrorist Accidentally Poisoned Himself Weeks before Planned Attack," *Vancouver Sun*, March 30, 2015, http://www.vancouversun.com/technology/Mulgrew+Alleged+terrorist+accidentally+poisoned+himself+weeks+before+planned+attack/10933053/story.html.

38. Matthew Cassel, "UK Uses Health Workers in Counter-Terror Plan," *Al Jazeera* (Doha), April 10, 2014, http://www.aljazeera.com/indepth/features/2014/04/uk-uses-health-workers-counter-terror-nhs-prevent-2014499261406691.html.

39. "7 July Bombings: The Bombers," BBC News, n.d., http://news.bbc.co.uk/2/shared/spl/hi/uk/05/london_blasts/investigation/html/bombers.stm.

40. Michael Seamark, "Curse the Judge, Shout Fanatics as the Muslim Girl Who Knifed MP Smiles as She Gets Life," *Daily Mail* (UK), November 5, 2010, http://www.dailymail.co.uk/news/article-1326208/Roshonara-Choudhry-knifed-MP-Stephen-Timms-smiles-gets-life.html.

41. See the fuller discussion of Rouleau and Zehaf-Bibeau in chapter 4.

42. J. Reid Meloy, Jens Hoffmann, Angela Guldimann, and David James, "The Role of Warning Behaviors in Threat Assessment: An Exploration and Suggested Typology," *Behavioral Sciences and the Law* 30, no. 3 (May/June 2012): 256–79, published online August 24, 2011, Wiley Online Library, doi:10.1002/bsl.999, available online at http://forensis.org/PDF/published/2012_WarningBehavio.pdf.

43. *Toronto Star* journalist Michelle Shephard's book *Guantanamo's Child* provides an excellent insight into the Khadr family (Mississauga, Ont.: John Wiley and Sons Canada, 2008).

44. "Lawyers for Boston Suspect Dzhokhar Tsarnaev to Pin Blame on Brother," *Guardian* (London), October 23, 2013, http://www.theguardian.com/world/2013/oct/23/lawyers-boston-suspect-dzhokhar-tsarnaev.

45. Doug Struck, "School Ties Link Alleged Plotters," *Washington Post*, June 11, 2006, http://www.ifpinc.com/Rage%20of%20the%20Random%20Actor%20-%20Live%20Addendum/Chapter%2023/School%20Ties%20Link%20Alleged%20Plotters.htm.

46. Greg Weston, "Canadians in Algerian Gas Plant Attack Identified," CBC News, last updated April 2, 2013, http://www.cbc.ca/news/politics/canadians-in-algerian-gas-plant-attack-identified-1.1325949.

47. In May 2014 Abu Hamza was found guilty on terrorism charges in New York after his 2012 extradition to the United States from the UK. Karen McVeigh, "Abu Hamza Found Guilty of 11 Terrorism Charges," *Guardian*, May 20, 2014, http://www.theguardian.com/world/2014/may/19/abu-hamza-found-guilty-terrorism-charges. For an excellent account of Hamza's story, read Sean O'Neill and Daniel McGrory, *The Suicide Factory: Abu Hamza and the Finsbury Park Mosque* (London: Harper Perennial, 2006).

48. Janet Davison and Janet Thomson, "Homegrown Terrorist: Toronto 18 Bomb Plotter Saad Khalid Recalls His Radicalization," CBC News, last updated April 16, 2014, http://www.cbc.ca/news/canada/homegrown-terrorist-toronto-18-bomb-plotter-saad-khalid-recalls-his-radicalization-1.2532671.

49. Vikram Dodd, "Roshonara Choudhry: Police Interview Extracts," *Guardian*, November 3, 2010, http://www.theguardian.com/uk/2010/nov/03/roshonara-choudhry-police-interview.

50. Thomas Joscelyn, "Missed Clues before Fort Hood Shooting," The Blog, *Weekly Standard*, July 26, 2012, http://www.weeklystandard.com/blogs/missed-clues-fort-hood-shootings_649008.html.

51. Alexander Meleagrou-Hitchens, *As American as Apple Pie: How Anwar al-Awlaki Became the Face of Western Jihad* (London: International Centre for the Study of Radicalisation and Political Violence, 2011), http://icsr.info/wp-content/uploads/2012/10/1315827595ICSRPaperAsAmericanAsApplePieHowAnwaralAwlakiBecametheFaceofWesternJihad.pdf.

52. Camille Mulcaire, "Assessing al-Qaeda from the Teachings of Ibn Taymiyya," student essay, E-International Relations: Students (website), written April 2013, published October 15, 2013, http://www.e-ir.info/2013/10/15/assessing-al-qaeda-from-the-teachings-of-ibn-taymiyya/.

53. Robert Hannigan, "The Web Is a Terrorist's Command-and-Control Network of Choice," November 3, 2014, Opinion, *London Financial Times*, http://www.ft.com/intl/cms/s/2/c89b6c58-6342-11e4-8a63-00144feabdc0.html#axzz3I6d3l0Vx.

54. Jamie Bartlett, "Why Terrorists and Far-Right Extremists Will Always Be Early Adopters," *The Telegraph* (London), November 4, 2014, http://www.telegraph.co.uk/technology/11204744/Why-terrorists-and-far-Right-extremists-will-always-be-early-adopters.html.

55. Stewart Bell, "Father of VIA Terror Suspect Came Forward with Concerns, Imam Says," *National Post* (Toronto), April 23, 2013, http://news.nationalpost.com/2013/04/23/toronto-iman-who-came-forward-with-concerns-about-al-qaeda-linked-terror-plot-wants-to-stay-anonymous/.

56. "Canada Day Bomb Plot Suspects Were Kicked Out of B.C. Mosque," CBC News, last updated July 3, 2013, http://www.cbc.ca/news/canada/british-columbia/canada-day-bomb-plot-suspects-were-kicked-out-of-b-c-mosque-1.1332874.

57. Stewart Bell, "The Path to Extremism: The Story of How One Young Man From Calgary Ended Up Dead in Syria," *National Post*, April 25, 2014, http://news.nationalpost.com/news/canada/the-path-to-extremism-the-story-of-how-one-young-man-from-calgary-ended-up-dead-in-syria.

58. Isabel Teotonio, "Toronto 18: The Brothers of Meadowvale," *Toronto Star*, n.d., http://www3.thestar.com/static/toronto18/index.1.html.

59. Adrian Humphreys, Stewart Bell, Maiya Keidan, and Tom Blackwell, "How Three Canadians Graduated from a Rebellious High-School Friendship to the World of Islamist Terrorism," *National Post* (Toronto), April 6, 2013, http://news.nationalpost.com/2013/04/06/how-three-ontario-school-friends-grew-up-to-become-islamist-terrorists-in-north-africa/.

60. Heba Saleh, "Western Female Jihadis Deploy 'Soft-Power' of Isis Online," *London Financial Times*, last updated October 28, 2014, http://www.ft.com/intl/cms/s/0/2d8b020c-5792-11e4-8493-00144feab7de.html?siteedition=intl#axzz3HWLnQ59b.

61. Heidi Beirich, "White Homicide Worldwide," *Intelligence Report* no. 154 (Summer 2014), http://www.splcenter.org/get-informed/intelligence-report/browse-all-issues/2014/summer/White-Homicide-Worldwide.

Chapter 2

Concepts Associated with Al Qaeda–Inspired Radicalization and Violence

DESIGNING THE "BASE"

Al Qaeda is an Arabic term that is loosely translated as "the base." This translation has been long debated (some even claimed—wrongly it turned out—that it described a huge database that contained details on all Al Qaeda members).

There is a real terrorist with experience in databases, however. His name is Shareef Abdelhaleem. According to the *Canadian Encyclopedia*,

> Before he was an accused terrorist, Shareef Abdelhaleem designed computer databases for drug companies. His salary was six figures, his car was a convertible BMW (metallic blue, with black leather seats), and his boss was everyone's dream boss: himself. "I had a successful career," says Abdelhaleem. "God blessed me with a little bit of talent."
>
> God also blessed him with a big heart, and not only because he shared his Mississauga home with seven stray cats rescued from animal shelters. Abdelhaleem was literally diagnosed with a growth on his heart, an unusual condition that required major surgery in the spring of 2006. He was still recovering a few weeks later when heavily armed officers stormed through his front door and pinned him to the floor. "To tell you the truth, I wasn't concentrating," he says now, recalling the raid. "I was looking to see if the cats were running out." Days after the bust—days after his name was forever linked to the Toronto 18—Abdelhaleem was still fretting about his felines. "Who knows where some of them are now," he says, shaking his head."[1]

CHAPTER ABSTRACT

In this chapter we will look at a number of religious and political concepts found frequently in extremist literature and online videos. We will see that it is impossible to fully understand this brand of extremism without first understanding the ideological and historical ideas upon which terrorism has been constructed.

THE CONCEPTS UNDERLYING AL QAEDA–INSPIRED TERRORISM

Individuals inspired by Al Qaeda tend to hold to and make use of a few principles drawn from Islamic history and theology. These principles are used to justify violence and are often written about and discussed in great detail. It is not possible to fully understand Al Qaeda–inspired violent radicalization without first having a solid understanding of how extremists see and rely on these principles. This chapter will discuss some of the more important ones and demonstrate how they have been used by Canadian and other Al Qaeda–inspired extremists in their radicalization and mobilization pathways.

There are those that state that we should not use the words explained in this chapter when talking about terrorism.[2] Terrorists misuse and abuse Islamic concepts and cast Islam in a bad light. While this is undoubtedly true, I prefer to follow the advice given by Sun Tzu, cited in the previous chapter: A doctor cannot treat an illness without using accurate terms. Since the word *cancer* frightens a lot of people, should doctors refrain from using it? An engineer cannot repair structural faults in a bridge without understanding the signs of stress. Dealing with terrorism is no different. Using and explaining the terms does not mean we agree with them. Recall that we are trying to understand a mindset. We need to explore the terms and meanings that extremists use before we can elect to act. In the end, we are trying to enter the mind of an extremist and see the world through his eyes: perspective is everything.

Jihad

There is perhaps no term more discussed and more controversial, and yet more central, than *jihad*. This word has entered the general Western vocabulary, often with the meaning of "holy war" or "terrorism." Extremist groups use it all the time, and some even incorporate it into their titles (e.g., the Islamic Jihad Movement in Palestine and the Islamic Jihad Union in Uzbekistan).

It is not my intent to reproduce the vast literature on jihad here. There are many excellent books on the subject (see appendix 1 for suggestions). *Jihad* has many different meanings, ranging from *personal struggle* to *improving one's nature* to *warfare*.[3] The intent here is to describe how Al Qaeda–inspired extremists see and use the term. To do that, it is useful to start with what are arguably the two most important extremist works of the twentieth century: *Defense of the Muslim Lands* by Abdullah Azzam and *The Forgotten Obligation* by Muhammad Al Faraj. Not only have these writings influenced Al Qaeda–inspired extremists around the world, they also contain most of the information necessary to understanding the extremist view of jihad. The following sections summarize the main points of both works.

Defense of the Muslim Lands

Abdullah Azzam was a Palestinian who was instrumental in the early days of the fight against the Soviets after they invaded Afghanistan in 1979. He was also in a way the spiritual founder of Al Qaeda before he died in a car bombing in Peshawar, Pakistan, in 1989 in what may have been an internal power struggle within Al Qaeda. Among his many writings is a tract known as *Defense of the Muslim Lands*.

This tract is subtitled *The First Obligation after Iman* (Arabic for "faith"), an indication of the importance Azzam placed on jihad. He notes that Islam has been victorious through the sword and spear but that many Muslims have neglected this obligation. It is because of this neglect that today's Muslim have become "like the rubbish of the flood waters."

Azzam differentiates between offensive and defensive jihad. The former is a *fard kifayah* (collective obligation) and occurs when the *kuffar* (infidels) are not gathering to fight Muslims. Under these conditions, it is sufficient to send an army at least once a year to "terrorize the enemies of Allah." All Muslims must assist those that fight.

Defensive jihad is, on the other hand, a *fard `ayn* (a compulsory duty on each individual) and arises when

- the *kuffar* enter a Muslim land
- an imam calls upon Muslims to fight and
- the *kuffar* capture and imprison a group of Muslims.

Azzam provides a number of supportive texts from the Quran and Islamic scholars for his views and stresses that, if a Muslim land is invaded, the obligation of *fard `ayn* negates the need for a wife to ask a husband's permission to fight or for a child to ask a parent or a debtor his creditor.

According to Azzam, it is unconscionable that Muslims are failing to obey the call to jihad in Afghanistan, Palestine, the Philippines, Kashmir, and other conflict zones. He prioritizes Palestine over Afghanistan and discusses the merits of both jihads. He notes that an amir (leader) is not necessary for jihad to be obligatory and that all must at least perform jihad with their wealth (i.e., finance mujahideen).

The Forgotten Obligation (Also Known as *The Absent Obligation*)

Muhammad Abd-al-Salam Faraj was an Egyptian extremist executed in 1982 for his role in coordinating the assassination of Egyptian president Anwar Sadat (seen as a traitor for his agreement to sign a peace accord with Israel). In his book *The Absent Obligation*, Faraj notes that those who do not go forth in jihad will be punished by Allah and that it is imperative that all Muslims abide by what Allah has ordained.

Faraj believed that jihad *fi sabil Allah* (in the cause of Allah) has been neglected by current Islamic scholars (hence the title of his book). He argues that Muslims must work to establish an Islamic state, since there is no such state today. Modern rulers have abandoned Islam and have been influenced by non-Muslim colonizers, he says. He uses the thirteenth-century conflict between the Mongols and Muslims as an example of how true believers must rise up against their infidel overlords. Faraj cites a Quranic verse used regularly by extremists: "Fighting [i.e., jihad] is prescribed upon you, but you dislike it." He advocates that fighting the "near enemy" (i.e., rulers seen as apostates) must take place before taking the battle to the "far enemy" (i.e., the West) and rejects the notion that jihad is defensive only in nature.

According to Faraj, those who believe that jihad is divided into stages (i.e., the struggle against oneself and against sin precedes fighting the enemy) are cowards. Scholars who advise that the "greater jihad" is more important than the "lesser jihad" (see below) have diverted Muslims from their true calling. He also contends that the use of the term *suicide operations* is inaccurate, since those that die in jihad are offering their lives for the cause of Allah in order to bring benefit and protection to Muslims.

Hadiths and Jihad

With this understanding of how two important extremist works have dealt with the issue of jihad, we now turn to an issue that has been raised on many occasions: the various types of jihad (Faraj had alluded to these, as mentioned above). The most famous reference to these can be found in one of the hadiths of the Prophet Muhammad.

One of the hadiths reads as follows:

> Upon his return from battle Muhammad said, "We have returned from the lesser jihad to the greater jihad [i.e., the struggle against the evil of one's soul]."

Textbox 2.1

WHAT IS A HADITH?

According to the website Peace with Realism,

> While non-Muslims often treat the Qur'an as if it were the only Islamic text, the literature of Islam is vast and spans many centuries. Next to the Qur'an in importance is the *hadith*, which refers to collections of oral traditions about what Muhammad said, what he taught, and what he did. These collections are also called *sunna* or "tradition"; hence the term *Sunni Muslims*, or "traditional" Muslims. Muslims naturally felt a need to preserve traditions about the Prophet from the time of the earliest witnesses. However, over the years since Muhammad's death, some of these traditions became embellished, and others were fabricated. In the ninth century, a number of Islamic scholars undertook the task of sifting the genuine traditions from the spurious and gathered the former in written collections. In Sunni Islam six of these collections in particular are considered *sahih* ("reliable").

Source: "*Jihad* in the *Hadith*," Peace with Realism (website), n.d., http://www.peacewithrealism.org/jihad/jihad03.htm.

This hadith has been the subject of much debate over the centuries: some say it is legitimate, while others say it is not. Suffice it to say that an individual can find approved or supported proponents of both sides.

An extremist will argue that a particular hadith is weak or not supported by the scholars. With that, he can ignore the advice in the hadith and go on to justify any action taken. Not surprisingly, the extremists deem the hadith on jihad as weak and hence believe that fighting is *not* less important than internal struggle.

The rejection of certain hadiths has serious implications for fighting radicalization. One oft-pronounced "cure" for radicalization (either as an intervention before someone radicalizes to violence or as a treatment afterward—i.e., as part of a "deradicalization" strategy) is the provision of "correct" Islam. Based on the assumption that these people actually have a weak understanding of Islam or one based on nonexpert views, the premise is that, by exposing that person to a "true" version, he will see the error of his interpretation and abandon violent thought.

While it may be true that most of these people have a poor or weak command of Islam (although this is probably not true in all cases), one cannot conclude that exposing them to a moderate, mainstream, or otherwise accepted version will be a sufficient antidote to radicalization and violence.

This is not to imply that a deep religious discussion is not useful as part of a larger strategy: it is simply to assert that it is likely insufficient.

I have been in meetings with Muslim communities where some state that it is enough for an imam or religious leader to engage a youth on the path to violent radicalization in order to dissuade that youth from going any further down the path. While I think that this desire to help is noble and potentially useful, it is also true that for some (many?) youth, the local imam is not the best placed to help. These youth would reject the imam's advice for a variety of reasons:

- The imam does not have good English language skills.
- The imam is too old or too "traditional."
- The youth is already too radicalized to listen to a community leader.
- The youth is receiving advice from another religious role model (possibly online).

Al Qaeda–inspired individuals believe that their version of Islam is correct. Furthermore, they are convinced that their interpretation is the only one worth having. Anyone who disagrees with them is no better than a nonbeliever (a *kaffir*).

If religious intervention is to have a positive effect, it is probably necessary to provide it as early as possible in the violent-radicalization process. In the first stages, individuals may have doubts or questions about the material they are reading or seeing and may be open to multiple interpretations. Inserting a moderate view at this point may be enough to provide a layer of protection should violent interpretations appear later.

Al Wala' Wal Bara'

This Arabic phrase translates awkwardly into English. The most common rendering is "Loyalty and enmity" (another is "allegiance and disavowal"). The underlying concept suggests that Muslims must engage in unswerving loyalty only to other Muslims and must consider everyone else an enemy. The idea is reflected in the Quran in several suras (chapters).

Extremists have used *Al Wala' wal Bara'* extensively in their works. Several well-known ideologues have penned lengthy treatises on the concept and its practice. For the sake of brevity, I will summarize the 2002 book by the current leader of Al Qaeda, Ayman al-Zawahiri, published in 2006 on the Al Sahab extremist website.

Al Zawahiri begins his book by noting that, in light of the "fierce conflict" between the forces of disbelief, tyranny, and arrogance and the *ummah* (Muslim nation), it is important to understand *Al Wala' wal Bara'*, especially as the West has undermined the concept by painting the enemies as allies and the pious as evildoers. Al-Zawahiri accuses the West of confusing the differences between righteousness and falsehood to the detriment of true Muslims. He notes that some Islamic states serve Western interests and customs, adding that imams are imposing secular constitutions on Muslims.

In his religious support for *Al Wala' wal Bara'*, al-Zawahiri cites the Quranic verse in which Allah states that the believers should not take the unbelievers as friends or allies. Specifically, he notes that the Quran also states that Muslims should not take Jews or Christians as protectors for fear of becoming like them; rather, a Muslim should only take fellow Muslims as friends. According to the Al Qaeda leader, those that assist the infidels will be punished in the afterlife.

In a later section, al-Zawahiri says that Allah has forbidden Muslims from befriending non-Muslims, because the latter have rejected him and his messenger (i.e., Muhammad). The infidels are said to hate Muslims and are seeking to have Muslims abandon their faith. Furthermore, Muslims should not honor non-Muslim religious rites and are forbidden to help them. Toward the end of the book, al-Zawahiri brings in the notion of jihad, adding that Muslims are commanded to wage jihad against the unbelievers—especially those who occupy Muslim lands—and against the apostate rulers who are in power in Muslim countries.

What are the implications of *Al Wala' wal Bara'*? Leaving aside al-Zawahiri's call for jihad, there are several aspects that could contribute to animosity and conflict within Canadian and other societies. *Al Wala' wal Bara'* creates an us-versus-them mentality in which one group is worthy of association and support while the other is to be viewed as the enemy. Differences are not to be embraced but shunned, and tolerance is not to be practiced.

This is, of course, highly problematic in a country like Canada that is both multicultural and multifaith. If one group is encouraged to reject the practices and beliefs of another, social cohesion breaks down. Outward vilification of one group's deeply held traditions could lead to similar reactions on the part of the offended group. Intercommunal relations would disappear, and an air of mistrust and hate could result.

Those that believe in *Al Wala' wal Bara'* could use this concept to justify a number of actions and convictions. Some of these could include

- the belief that it is okay to steal from or cheat non-Muslims
- the refusal to vote and encouragement for other Muslims to refrain from voting (this is discussed in much greater detail in the next chapter)
- a conviction that serving in a non-Muslim institution (government, the armed forces) is not permitted in Islam
- the rejection of any ecumenical dialogue among different faiths
- or the decision not to educate one's children in a public school system and to not expose them to non-Muslim friends.

Jahiliyyah

Jahiliyyah is an Arabic word that means "ignorance." In extremist literature it implies ignorance of Islam and of Allah's command. More specifically, the term is used to describe the world before the revelations received by the Prophet Muhammad beginning in 610 CE.

One of the more important discussions of *jahiliyyah* can be found in the seminal book *Milestones* (*Ma'alim fil Tariq* in Arabic) by the twentieth-century ideologue Sayyid Qutb. Qutb is a giant in the Al Qaeda–inspired extremist world, and a short summary of his life and works will help to place this section into perspective.

Qutb was born in 1906 in Egypt and became a teacher, working for the Ministry of Education. In 1948 he was sent to the United States to study and settled in Colorado. Qutb's years in the United States were an epiphany of sorts: he was appalled by much of what he saw—racism, sexual licentiousness, materialism, and a lack of spirituality. He summarized his experiences in a book titled *The America I have seen*.

Upon his return to Egypt, he joined the Muslim Brotherhood and became the editor of its weekly publication. The Muslim Brotherhood had been formed in 1926 by Egyptians opposed to the British-supported monarchy and believed that Egypt should return to its Islamic roots.

Following the 1952 military takeover by Gamal Abdel Nasser, Muslim Brotherhood members were harassed, and several were imprisoned, including Qutb, following an alleged Brotherhood coup attempt. Qutb was severely tortured and was bedridden in the prison's infirmary for many years. It was in prison that Qutb wrote *Milestones* and his lengthy exegesis of the Quran (*In the Shadow of the Quran*). He was ultimately hanged in 1966. It would be difficult to underestimate the importance of Qutb and his works (especially *Milestones*) to the modern Al Qaeda movement.

In *Milestones*, Qutb states that it is clear that the whole world is steeped in *jahiliyyah*, because by making some men rulers over others humans are rebelling against God's sovereignty (known as *hakimiyyah* in Arabic) on earth. He contrasts the original state of *jahiliyyah* (i.e., before the revelation of Islam) with the current one, implying that the latter is worse because mankind has received (through the Prophet Muhammad) but rejected God's message. Once the message of Islam was heard and embraced, believers had an opportunity and obligation to cut themselves off from the world of the ignorant. A new—and better—world had been created.

Qutb suggests the creation of a vanguard of true Muslims who would "march through the vast ocean of *jahiliyyah*" and pay attention to the landmarks and milestones (hence the title of the book) on the goal to reviving Islam. True believers should remove themselves from all *jahili* influences and return to the pure source of Islam. There is no room for loyalty to or compromise with *jahili* societies. Muslims are to follow in the footsteps of the first generations of believers who triumphed over the unbelievers.

The crucial part of *Milestones* is its recommendation to use violence to achieve the goal of reviving Islam and defeating the new *jahiliyyah*. This violence is to take the form of jihad. Qutb believed that it was only through jihad that Islam could annihilate all *jahili* systems that stand in the way of universal freedom.

What are the implications of a belief that much of the world exists in a state of ignorance? Similar to the previous discussion on *Al Wala' wal Bara'*, this concept sets Islam and Muslims against all others. Furthermore, it implies that Islam is the only way (this in itself is not that terrible, as many faiths teach that their followers are the "chosen ones"). Finally, and most worryingly, the *jahiliyyah* as described by Qutb, must be defeated by the use of violence.

Qutb's works have influenced Al Qaeda–inspired extremists around the world. His books are still read and discussed and will likely continue to provide guidance for generations to come.

Hijra

Hijra (or *hijrah*) is an Arabic word that refers to the Prophet Muhammad's escape from his enemies in Mecca and flight north to Medina in 622 CE where he and his followers regrouped before returning in triumph to Mecca a decade later. A related term—*hijri*—is used to refer to the Islamic lunar calendar, which began with the Prophet's flight to Medina.

Extremists use the term in two different—but ultimately linked—ways. The first is to describe the need for "true" Muslims to leave countries where Islam is not the majority religion and to emigrate to one where it is. These people believe that the temptations in non-Muslim lands are too much for the faithful and that it is thus best to eliminate exposure to such vices. Their views are also tied to the notion that Western ways are never suitable for Muslims. In addition, a Muslim must, in their view, live in a land where sharia (Islamic) law is in force. Extremists in this country believe that Canada does not allow Muslims to truly practice their faith.

There have been many references to hijra by Al Qaeda–inspired extremists.

- A French citizen who left to fight in Syria declared, "in our religion, there's a command called *hijra*—it's an obligation for all Muslims not to live in a non-Muslim country."[4]
- In October 2014 a UK extremist fighting in Syria called upon his fellow UK Muslims to join him: those that could not were encouraged to "cause terror" in the hearts of the kuffar.[5]

- A Canadian English–speaking extremist in Syria, Farah Shirdon (see more in chapter 4) threatened to attack Canada and the United States in April 2014, saying, "This is a message to Canada and all the American *tawagheet* [tyrants—plural of *taghut*]: We are coming and we will destroy you, with permission from Allah the Almighty. I made *Hijra* [emigration] to this land for one reason alone, I left comfort for one reason alone—for Allah, Glorified and Exalted be He—and Allah willing, after *Sham* [Syria], after Iraq, after the [Arabian] Peninsula, we are going for you, Barack Obama."[6]
- A terrorist group in Egypt, Takfir wal-Hijra, believed that Egyptian Muslims should reject countrymen who did not share their extreme interpretation of Islam and leave the cities, creating a utopian Islamic society in the desert.

In a second use of the term, extremists seek to hide their desire for jihad by claiming that they merely want to leave decadent Western societies by performing hijra. As we shall discuss later, the complete rejection of Western society is a potential indicator of violent extremism.

Many extremists sites have juxtaposed the terms *hijra* and *jihad*. Some examples follow.

- The German extremist/rapper Ruben Cuspert stated in April 2014 that after living for thirty-five years in the land of the *kuffar* he had attained "hijra and jihad" in Syria.[7]
- And the month prior, in March of 2014, a UK citizen claiming to be fighting in Syria advised British Muslims to "make hijra or attack those (oppressing you)."[8]

Hijra is thus not just an attempt to flee Muslim-minority and godless Western societies; it is also a precursor for engaging in jihad.

The Islamic State has written about hijra in its glossy online magazine, *Dabiq*. The group explicitly ties hijra to jihad and calls those Muslims who do not undertake hijra hypocrites. It even equates the terms, noting that hijra is the path to jihad. According to the Islamic state, "sincere" Muslims pray daily for an escape to the lands of jihad and dream of going to Iraq, Afghanistan, Yemen, Chechnya, Algeria, and Somalia, among other countries. Making hijra is, in effect, the first step toward jihad, and "there is no life without jihad (and there is no jihad without hijra)."[9]

Taghut

The Arabic term *taghout* (also spelled *taghut*) has a long history in Islam. The word has several meanings, among which are "tyrant," "rebel," and "sorcerer." Al Qaeda–inspired extremists use the word to refer to those they see as the enemies of Islam.

In the eyes of extremists, Islam's enemies include a wide range of people and institutions. We have already noted how the West is seen as the ultimate aggressor against Muslims. In addition, extremists view any state that is not sufficiently Islamic as run by a *taghout*. Among these would be found Saudi Arabia under the Al Sauds, Libya under Mu'ammar Gaddhafi, Egypt under Hosni Mubarak (or Nasser or Sadat), and Afghanistan under Hamid Karzai. *Taghout* governments must be overthrown and replaced with true Islamic leadership.

In the Quran, a *taghout* was anyone who led people astray—that is, away from Islam. Followers of a *taghout* were also associated with idol worship, a common practice prior to the advent of Islam.

Modern Al Qaeda–inspired extremists use other terms to describe Islam's enemies. These include

- *Hulagu*. Hülegü Khan was the grandson of Genghis Khan, the famous Mongol ruler of the thirteenth century. Hülegü is infamous for the sacking of Baghdad in 1257. During the US invasion of Iraq in 2003, then-US president George W. Bush was often compared to Hülegü Khan—the twenty-first-century reincarnation of the destroyer of Baghdad.[10]
- *Pharaoh*. The Quran contains many references to the pharaohs of Egypt— perhaps the most noteworthy being the story of Joseph and his dealings with the Egyptian ruler. Pharaoh is associated with arrogance, sin, dis-obedience, and cruelty. When extremists assassinated Egyptian president Sadat in 1980, one of the terrorists famously declared, "I have killed Pharaoh!"
- *Ferenj*. This Arabic word for "Frank" was used to describe the Christian Crusaders of the tenth to thirteenth centuries. Over the course of a few centuries, Crusader and Muslim armies fought for control of the Levant (modern-day Turkey, Lebanon, Syria, and Israel), and the Crusaders were accused of wanton slaughter and cruelty. Many Muslim observers thought that the invaders were Franks (the inhabitants of modern-day France and Germany), and the Arabic word *Ferenj* stuck. In modern-day Arabic, *Ferenj* refers generically to Europeans. The memories of the Crusades still resonate with Al Qaeda–inspired extremists, for whom the campaigns were proof of the West's intolerance of Islam and desire to destroy it. In the aftermath of 9/11, President Bush's call for a "crusade against terrorism" evoked these memories and underscored the belief that the "Crusades never ended."
- *Rome (also Rum)*. Similarly, Rome is seen as the embodiment of Islam's enemies. This term too appears to hearken back to the time of the Crusades.

The leader of the Toronto 18, Fahim Ahmad, called for the "destruction of Rome,"[11] even though he was referring to attacks in Canada.

All of these terms evoke powerful images for Al Qaeda–inspired individuals. They serve to divide the world into Muslims ("true" Muslims, as the extremists see themselves) and the enemy. In the face of such enemies, jihad is seen as a necessity.

It is interesting to note that all these terms are still widely used on extremist websites. A few examples are listed below.

- *Taghout.* A Facebook page in 2013 claimed that groups in Algeria and Mali were fighting (secular) *taghout* regimes.[12] The plural form, *tawagheet*, was used by the Canadian fighting in Syria, as noted above.
- *Pharaoh.* The leader of the Nigerian terrorist group Boko Haram stated in May 2014 that he was not afraid of the intervention of US armed forces that may have been sent to rescue kidnapped female students, adding, "Let even King Pharaoh himself be sent down here."[13] In 2006 Osama Bin Laden compared then-US president George W. Bush to the "pharaoh of the age."
- *Ferenj/Rome/Crusaders.* Osama Bin Laden issued a statement in 1998 in which he called for the creation of a group called the World Islamic Front for Jihad against Jews and Crusaders. In 2013 an Al-Shabaab commander described the conflict in Somalia as a war against "Crusaders."[14] In 2009, current Al Qaeda leader Ayman al-Zawahiri stated that the "Crusade had set its sights on Sudan."[15] And the Islamic State has portrayed the US-led bombing campaign in Iraq as part of a "Crusader war against Islam."[16]

The Al Qaeda–inspired extremists need a defined enemy to focus their violence. The variety of terms discussed here is used to enhance that focus.

In an interesting twist on using historical analogues, Asharq Al-Awsat published an op-ed piece in late December 2014 in which the Islamic State was compared to the "Tartars of our time" (a reference to the Mongol invasions of the thirteenth century).[17]

Takfiri Ideology (*Kuffar, Kaffir*)

Al Qaeda–inspired extremists divide the world into two irreconcilable camps: believers and nonbelievers. Not surprisingly, they see themselves as the believers and everyone else as nonbelievers. The practice of naming someone as an nonbeliever is called *takfir* in Arabic; an unbeliever is a *kaffir* (plural, *kuffar*). There are serious penalties for unbelief, ranging from paying a tax to slavery and death.

Extremists do not view non-Muslims only as *kuffar*. They see any Muslim who does not agree with their views as part of the world of unbelief and believe that the *kuffar* should be punished. It is worth noting that the vast majority of Muslims reject the *takfiri* view of the world.

Labeling someone a *kaffir* opens up the possibility of, and legitimizes, a series of acts and behaviors by the extremists. According to the extremists, the *kuffar* can be treated poorly, can have their property damaged or stolen, can be abused or lied to, and do not enjoy the same level of rights as the true believers. Calling someone a *kaffir* is a serious insult and leads to the impossibility of dialogue and interaction.

There are innumerable references to *takfir* and *kuffar* in extremist forums. A few examples will suffice.

- A Twitter user and supporter of the so-called Islamic State in May 2014 called for the beheading of *kuffar* in the UK in the wake of an "invasion" of a mosque in Bradford.[18]
- In April 2014 a member of an English language site called for the killing of the *kuffar* "everywhere" in response to an alleged US drone strike in Yemen.[19]
- Also in April 2014 a user of the Ansar al-Mujahideen English Forum wrote, "It is time to kill the *kuffar* where ever he is, in his bed, in his car, in his house, in his country!"[20]

During their 2005 training camp, members of the Toronto 18 imagined they were in a war to kill *kuffar*. An e-mail that was entered as evidence in the Momin Khawaja trial is reproduced below:

When the *kuffar* amreekans invaded Afghanistan that was . . . the most painful time in my whole life. . . . it would tear my hear [sic] knowing these filthy *kaafir* dog Americans were bombing our muslim bros and sisters. . . . Shaykh Usama bin laden is like the most beloved person to me in the whole world, after Allah.[21]

The simplistic division of the world into believers and nonbelievers mirrors the dehumanization of the enemy common to all wars and conflicts. If one sees another as inferior and not worthy of consideration, it is easier to contemplate using violence against them.

Bayat (Also *Bay'a, Bayah*)

Bayat is an Arabic word that means "pledge of allegiance." It describes the obligations and relationship between a ruler or authority figure and his followers or subjects. The agreement is based on the notion that individuals pledge binding allegiance to a person who will act in accordance with God's will. The only grounds upon which the pledge loses its binding nature are when the ruler no longer rules in keeping with God's law. Breaking a *bayat* incurs "dreadful punishment": the tie is personal and lifelong.[22]

There are many examples of the use of *bayat* by extremist groups.

- Attendees at Al Qaeda training camps in the 1990s were asked to pledge allegiance to Bin Laden.[23]
- In 2013 the leadership of the Syrian terrorist group Jabhat al-Nusra pledged allegiance to Al Qaeda.[24]
- In a similar vein, the leader of the so-called Al Qaeda in the Indian Subcontinent pledged allegiance to al-Zawahiri shortly after the group's creation in 2014.[25]
- UK authorities thwarted a terrorist plot in late 2014 in which the alleged extremists had pledged allegiance to the Islamic state.[26]

One of the Jabarah brothers of St. Catharines, Ontario,[27] Mohammed Mansour, pledged *bayat* to Bin Laden in Kandahar, Afghanistan, in July 2001.[28] He told the Al Qaeda leader that he was ready to join the group, that he had a "clean" Canadian passport and excellent English language skills, and that he had excelled at his training camp. Jabarah became a "living martyr" for Al Qaeda.

Even if he did not receive pledges of allegiance from his "followers," Fahim Ahmad was portrayed by the Canadian government as the original leader of the Toronto 18. He has been called the "Emir of Mississauga." It is noteworthy that his lieutenant and best friend, Zakaria Amara, split from Ahmad in the spring of 2006 when Amara decided Ahmed was not moving quickly enough with the terrorist plans.[29] This split could be interpreted as an indication that Ahmad had not fulfilled his part of the bargain required by a leader to whom *bayat* has been given.

Andre Poulin of Timmins, Ontario, who died fighting in Syria in 2014, claimed to have pledged allegiance to the Islamic State in a video released posthumously by the group.

The pledge of *bayat* should be seen as a critical phase in the radicalization process. An individual who offers allegiance understands the gravity of the act and its binding nature. He recognizes the authority of one above him who can issue commands and orders. Finally, the act of *bayat* is possibly indicative of a seriousness and final commitment to carry out acts of violence.

Shirk

In Islam Allah has no equal and no associates. The idea of a Trinity as found in Christianity is impossible (Jesus is a great prophet in the Quran but is human, not the Son of God). The Islamic notion of the indivisibility and oneness of Allah is known as *tawhid*. The first part of the Islamic statement of faith (known as the *shahada*) states, *La ilaha illallah*—"There is no God but Allah." Those who put anyone on the same level as Allah are accused of practicing *shirk* (association or, more generally, polytheism) and are known as *mushrikeen*.

Extremists use the term *shirk* in a variety of ways and situations. Some claim that Shia Muslims, for whom they exhibit a visceral hatred, are *mushrikeen* because of their special veneration for Ali—Muhammad's cousin and son-in-law and, according to the Shia, the first true successor to Muhammad (this contention led to the first great schism in Islam following the death of the Prophet)—and to a lesser extent Fatimah (Ali's wife and Muhammad's daughter). For extremists (and others), *shirk* is the worst possible sin.

Shirk has also been leveled at Christians for their belief in the Trinity, despite the acknowledgment in the Quran that Christians are People of the Book (i.e., share a prophetic tradition with Islam and Judaism) and are allowed to practice their faith within Muslim-majority lands. Not surprisingly, Hindus, Buddhists, and others are also *mushrikeen*.

Many Al Qaeda–inspired extremists use the allegation of *shirk* to justify attacks and violence:

- In his *bayat* to the extremist group Islamic State in Iraq and Levant, German rapper and convert Ruben Cusbert stated that lands should be cleansed of the stain of *shirk* and noted that his house in Germany had been soiled by visits from "cross-worshippers."[30]
- A Swedish national fighting in Syria praised the destruction of Sufi shrines since Sufis practice *shirk*.[31]

Fatwa

During the 1989 Salman Rushdie affair, when then Iranian spiritual leader Ayatollah Khomeini called for Rushdie's death for alleged insults to the Prophet Muhammad in his book *The Satanic Verses*, many in the West misinterpreted Khomeini's fatwa as a death threat. It is nothing of the sort.

A *fatwa* is a religious ruling given by a qualified scholar on a particular question of faith or Islamic law. The person giving the ruling is called a *mufti* (the word comes from the same Arabic root as *fatwa*). There is some debate on the validity and application of a fatwa. Islam is not a centralized religion like Catholicism where a recognized authority has the ability to make binding and universal laws and rulings. Any qualified scholar can issue a fatwa. Furthermore, it is uncertain whether a particular fatwa is binding after the death of the issuing mufti or beyond the person that asked the initial question.

Nevertheless, it is important to emphasize that, for extremists, it is not crucial that a mufti be recognized by the general population. There are enough scholars that support the extremist agenda to offer their opinions on the justification of violence. In addition, a fatwa is not required for an act of violence to happen. Some extremists may prefer to obtain one—perhaps to tick the last religious box on their list of preparations—but it is unlikely that a lack of a fatwa would cause them to abandon their plans.

It is also unclear what effect antiviolence fatwas have. While they are undoubtedly welcomed by the vast majority of Muslims and may help to assuage those who believe that Islamic scholars are not doing enough to condemn and stop terrorism, it is unlikely that committed extremists care what these scholars say or do. To an extremist, a scholar who states that violence is unsanctioned is seen as someone who kowtows to non-Muslims at best and is an enemy of Islam at worst.

There are two well-known instances where fatwas were issued to condone terrorism: one by a recognized scholar and one by an extremist. In 2003, Saudi sheik Nasir al-Fahd issued a fatwa, giving then-Al Qaeda leader Osama Bin Laden authority to use nuclear weapons against US civilians.[32] Bin Laden himself issued two fatwas—in 1996 and 1998. The first, "Declaration of War against the Americans Occupying the Land of the Two Holy Places," was in response to the presence of US troops in Saudi Arabia following the Iraqi invasion of Kuwait in 1990. The second called for the creation of the World Islamic Front for Jihad against Jews and Crusaders. The fact that Bin Laden was not a recognized mufti was not important to his followers and supporters.

According to testimony in the Toronto 18 case, a fatwa may have played a role in the decision making of one of the group's members. Shareef Abdelhaleem, currently serving a life sentence for his role in the plot, allegedly received a fatwa from his father, Tariq Abdelhaleem, stating that an attack in Canada was "acceptable." The ruling was seen as a confirmation by Shareef, as it clarified the Islamic correctitude of his plans. Mohamed Tariq has denied issuing the fatwa, claiming that the Crown witness made the statement because of a "personal disagreement."[33]

Dividing the World into Different *Dars*

Violent extremists have segmented the world we live in into different spheres. These spheres (or "abodes") are called *dar* in Arabic. A few are listed here:

- *dar al Islam*
- *dar al harb*

- *dar al jihad*
- *dar al kuffar*
- *dar al ahd* (a.k.a., *dar al sulh*)

Dar al Islam refers to those lands where Muslims are in the majority and sharia law is observed. *Dar al harb* ("house of war") and *dar al jihad* are more or less equivalent and describe areas with which "true" Muslims are in conflict. Extremists will also refer to non-Muslim lands as *dar al kuffar*—the land of the infidels and nonbelievers. They believe that "true" Muslims are always at war with those in these abodes.

It is with the term *dar al ahd* where things get interesting. In classic Islamic jurisprudence, Muslims are allowed to live in a non-Muslim land as long as they can freely practice their faith. Furthermore, countries that grant Muslims entry (through a visa or residency permit) are considered safe and there exists a "covenant of security" between a Muslim and the welcoming state. In such circumstances, Muslims must obey the local laws and cannot engage in violence against the state.

Not surprisingly, violent extremists reject any compromise or concession to nonbelievers.

- A member of the Ansar al-Mujahideen English Forum stated in April 2013 that any covenant was broken by the West when the Catholic kings retook Spain from its Muslim occupiers.[34] In any event, the covenant is used by the West to dominate Muslims.[35]
- A Twitter user asked UK Muslims to abandon the notion of a covenant between Muslims and the British government and to attack the UK.[36]
- Extremist cleric Omar Bakri Muhammad justified the brutal murder of a UK solider in May 2013 by claiming that *dar al ahd* did not apply to military personnel.[37]

The extremist website At Tibyan posted a paper titled "A Call to Migrate from the Lands of the Disbelievers to the Lands of the Muslims."[38] In this paper, Shaykh Abd al-Aziz bin Salih al-Jarbu states that Muslims who believe that they can live in the lands of the *kuffar* (disbelievers) have been misled and that the texts used to justify their misunderstanding are incorrect (this is a common tactic among extremists: they point to certain texts—those that support their views, of course—as true and state that other texts—those that do not support their views—are false). Muslims are commanded to fight and kill the nonbelievers at all times. Those that associate with the unbelievers are "simple-minded" and ignorant. They are incapable of understanding the true meaning of the Quran. The battle with the nonbelievers is one of the distinction between true and false belief.

Muslims must perform hijra in order to avoid adopting the beliefs of the enemies and to help those Muslims who are fighting. The paper goes on to explain the different *diyar* (plural of *dar*):

- *dar al Islam.* Every piece of land in which the rulings of Islam are in authority
- *dar al kufr.* Lands where the beliefs of the disbelievers are uppermost
- *dar al harb.* Any land in which there is a state of war between Muslims and non-Muslims
- *dar al ahd.* Any land that has made peace with Muslims by not fighting them.

Muslims outside *Dar Al Islam* who cannot practice Islam and can migrate to a Muslim country are obliged to do so, whereas for those who are free to practice, the scholars disagree on whether hijra is mandatory. The author provides a detailed explanation on what it means to be able to practice Islam in a non-Muslim country.

All in all, migration to a land where Islamic law and practices are the norm is preferable to living among the unbelievers.

Khilafa (Caliphate)

The *khilafa* (caliphate) refers to the office of leadership that was created after the death of the Prophet Muhammad in 632 CE. As Muhammad did not have a surviving son to whom he could pass on the mantle of leader, a debate arose within the nascent Muslim community. Some wanted his successor (the Arabic word for successor is *khalif*—caliph in English) to be chosen from among Muhammad's followers and those in the community. Others preferred that someone related to the Prophet (i.e., bloodline) should succeed him—namely, Ali, Muhammad's cousin and son-in-law through his marriage to Muhammad's daughter, Fatimah (this split led ultimately to the division of Islam into Sunni and Shia sects). Those in favor of selecting a worthy man to lead the community won the day, and Abu Bakr, a close companion of Muhammad, was ultimately chosen as the first caliph (Abu Bakr and the next three caliphs—Uthman, Umar, and Ali—are generally referred to as the *rashidun* (the rightly guided).

The caliphate morphed throughout the centuries as its seat swung from Arabia to Damascus to Baghdad and other locales within the Islamic empire. At one point, two areas vied for the honor at the same time: Cairo and Cordoba in Muslim-controlled Spain. The Ottomans moved the caliphate to Istanbul, where it was abandoned in 1924 following the defeat of Turkey as an ally of the defeated Germany and the Austro-Hungarian empire.

The caliph ruled over Muslims and ensured the proper application of sharia (Islamic law). In essence, the relationship between caliph and ordinary Muslims was in the form of a contract: Muslims pledged fealty (*bayat*) to the caliph, provided he upheld Islamic law and remained a good Muslim.[39]

To the extremists, the concept of the caliphate evokes the glory years of Islam, when it ruled over a vast empire and struck fear into the hearts of its enemies. Many still see the dissolution of the caliphate by Turkey in 1924 as a betrayal of Islam.

- In May 2013 an activist on a jihadi forum called upon Muslims in the Maldives to rise up and launch an Islamic revolution, stating that "Muslims have 'been living in this dark night for eighty-one years' since dissolution of the Caliphate on March 3, 1924."[40]
- A spokesperson for the Indonesian militant group Majelis Mujahidin Indonesia stated in 2006 that the fall of the caliphate allowed Islam's enemies to dominate.[41]

The militant group Hizb ut-Tahrir (HT—Islamic Liberation Party), considered by some countries as a terrorist entity, calls for the re creation of the caliphate. HT claims that it wants to do so through education and dialogue, although it does call for infiltration of a Muslim nation's armed forces in its bid to seize power. Some analysts have labeled the group a conveyor belt for terrorism.[42]

In recent years, of course, the notion of reestablishing the caliphate is associated with the group known variously as the Islamic State of Iraq and the Levant (ISIL), Islamic State of Iraq and Shams (ISIS), the Islamic State (IS), or by its Arabic acronym Daesh. IS leader Abu Bakr al-Baghdadi has declared himself caliph, and the group promises it will undo the 1916 Sykes-Picot Agreement (an entente signed between Britain and France in which they divided the remnants of the Ottoman Empire in the Middle East between them) and free Palestine.[43] According to IS, it is only through the courage of the mujahideen that the caliphate has been restored.

In the first issue of *Dabiq*, IS declared that the return of the caliphate had ushered in an era of dignity, might, rights, and leadership, a society where all are brothers. Muslims will "walk everywhere as master . . . anyone who dares to offend him will be disciplined, and any hand that reaches out to harm him will be cut off." According to IS, the time has come for the *ummah* (Islamic nation) to "wake up from its sleep, remove the garments of dishonor, and shake off the dust of humiliation and disgrace."

There is some evidence that the announcement of the reappearance of the caliphate has encouraged some individuals to volunteer to fight for IS.[44]

- British and Australians fighting for IS have cited the caliphate as one of the benefits of joining the group.[45]
- Authorities in Indonesia and Malaysia are worried that IS may inspire followers in their nations who want to establish a caliphate in Southeast Asia.[46]

Not surprisingly, most Muslims reject the new caliphate and the status of al-Baghdadi as caliph.

SUMMARY

The concepts discussed in this chapter provide an overview of the extremist mindset. They illustrate the lengths to which extremists go to understand and justify the use of violence and acts of terrorism. All of these concepts have been subject to debate and disagreement in the Islamic world for centuries, and all have a great deal of scriptural and scholarly backing. There is no universal understanding of any of these ideas. Extremists will take whatever interpretation fits their purpose.

It is best not to be flippant when dealing with these notions. It is not sufficient to say "Oh, that's wrong," or "Oh, that's stupid." Each of these concepts makes an important contribution to the radicalization pathway of an individual. If we are to stop more people from embracing violence, careful arguments have to be made to challenge these interpretations and demonstrate why they are either incorrect or not representative of Islam.

These concepts also serve as barriers between extremists and the larger community, both Muslim and non-Muslim. They are used to justify the idea that extremists are separate from greater society and are the only ones to truly abide by the teachings of Islam. It is not an exaggeration to state that these ideas help to create an us-versus-them conflict.

Furthermore, the horizontal nature of religious authority in Islam is conducive to those looking for answers and justification. There is no authority hierarchy in Islam, and individuals can seek and follow whichever religious leader or scholar they want. Extremists can easily locate people who will tell them that violence is necessary and that Allah calls for a specific action. Even if there were a hierarchical structure within Islamic practice, would it help? The Catholic Church, which is incredibly hierarchical (from priest to bishop to archbishop to cardinal to pope), has attempted to impose doctrine on the faithful for centuries. Has it always been successful? Well, the church outlaws artificial contraception, and yet the majority of Catholic women use some method or other of birth control.[47]

Muslim communities and leaders cannot pretend that these terms are not being used or simply dismiss their "misuse" as wrong, hoping that they will just go away. A more detailed examination of each term and a discussion of their origins and implications would be a much more effective argument against those that seek inspiration and justification for violence from Islam.

NOTES

1. Michael Friscolanti, "It Comes Down to These Four: The 'Toronto 18' Terrorism Case Rests on a Core Group of Suspects," *Macleans*, June 9, 2008, available online at http://www.thecanadianencyclopedia.ca/en/article/the-toronto-18-terrorism-case/.

2. Islamic Social Services Association, National Council of Canadian Muslims, and Royal Canadian Mounted Police, *United against Terrorism: A Collaborative Effort towards a Secure, Inclusive and Just Canada*, (Winnipeg: ISSA, NCCM, and RCMP, 2014), http://www.nccm.ca/wp-content/uploads/2014/09/UAT-HAND-BOOK-WEB-VERSION-SEPT-27-2014.pdf.

3. For a good summary of the multiple meanings of *jihad* see Adam L. Silverman, "Just War, Jihad and Terrorism: A Comparison of Western and Islamic Norms for the Use of Political Violence," *Journal of Church and State* 44, no. 1 (2002): 73–92, doi:10.1093/jcs/44.1.73.

4. "French Jihadist Defends Taking Baby to War-Torn Syria," France 24, last updated April 10, 2014, http://www.france24.com/en/20140410-france-syria-jihadist-baby-assia-nosra-war/.

5. Nadeem Badshah, "Jihadist Calls for British Terror Attacks," *London Times*, last updated October 4, 2014, http://www.thetimes.co.uk/tto/news/uk/article4226939.ece.

6. Stewart Bell, "Syrian Extremists Threaten to 'Destroy' Canada in Online Video," *National Post* (Toronto), last updated January 25, 2015, http://news.national-post.com/2014/04/14/syrian-extremists-threaten-to-destroy-canada-in-online-video/.

7. "German Rapper Turned Jihadist Ruben Cuspert (Deso Dogg) Pledges to ISIL," SITEIntelGroup.com, April 11, 2014, http://ent.siteintelgroup.com/Jihadist-News/german-rapper-turned-jihadist-ruben-cuspert-deso-dogg-pledges-to-isil.html.

8. "Jihadi Directs British Muslims to Attacks or Emigration," SITEIntelGroup.com, March 27, 2014, http://ent.siteintelgroup.com/Western-Jihadist-Forum-Digest/jihadi-directs-british-muslims-to-attacks-or-emigration.html.

9. *Dabiq* no. 3 (July/August 2014): 25–27.

10. Hmida Ben Romdhane, trans. Amélie Filliatre "The Falls of Baghdad," *La Presse* (Tunisia), April 11, 2010, available online at http://watchingamerica.com/News/52238/the-falls-of-baghdad/.

11. Megan O'Toole, "Toronto 18 Ringleader Fahim Ahmad Faces Up to 12 Years in Prison," *National Post* (Toronto), September 28, 2012, http://news.nationalpost.com/2010/09/28/toronto-18-ringleader-fahim-ahmad-faces-12-years-in-prison/.

12. The page, now deleted, was originally found at https://www.facebook.com/stand.up.muslims/posts/401052100004164.

13. Patrick Goodenough, "Boko Haram Video Showing Captured Schoolgirls Features al-Qaeda Banner," CNS News, May 12, 2014, http://cnsnews.com/news/article/patrick-goodenough/boko-haram-video-showing-captured-schoolgirls-features-al-qaeda.

14. "Shabaab Claims Attacks on Locations of Somali President in Kismayo," SITEIntelGroup.com, December 11, 2013, http://ent.siteintelgroup.com/Jihadist-News/shabaab-claims-attacks-on-locations-of-somali-president-in-kismayo.html.

15. Caroline Clowney, "Ayman al-Zawahiri Audio Message 'The Crusade Sets Its Sights on the Sudan,'" Global Terrorism Research Project (blog), http://gtrp.haverford.edu/aqsi/aqsi-statement/189.

16. Oren Adaki, "AQAP Continues to Portray US-Led Bombing Campaign as 'Crusade,'" *The Long War Journal*, November 1, 2014, http://www.longwarjournal.org/archives/2014/11/aqap_continues_to_po.php.

17. Mshari Al-Zaydi, "Opinion: Jordan's ISIS Dilemma," *Asharq Al-Awsat* (London), December 28, 2014, http://www.aawsat.net/2014/12/article55339834.

18. "Jihadi Calls for Beheadings in UK," SITEIntelGroup.com, May 13, 2014, http://ent.siteintelgroup.com/Western-Jihadist-Forum-Digest/jihadi-calls-for-beheadings-in-uk.html.

19. "Jihadi Suggests White House Target for Yemen Revenge," SITEIntelGroup.com, April 23, 2013, http://ent.siteintelgroup.com/Western-Jihadist-Forum-Digest/jihadi-suggests-white-house-target-for-yemen-revenge.html.

20. "Jihadi Calls to Target Enemies in Home Countries, Assassinate Leaders," SITEIntelGroup.com, April 21, 2014, http://ent.siteintelgroup.com/Western-Jihadist-Forum-Digest/jihadi-calls-to-target-enemies-in-home-countries-assassinate-leaders.html.

21. "Canada's Anti-terror Legislation vs. Ottawa's Momin Khawaja," *Ottawa Citizen*, June 21, 2008, available online at http://www.canada.com/ottawacitizen/news/observer/story.html?id=1bc4587f-748c-45be-8668-116fdb57619b.

22. "Bayat (Allegiance)," Al Muntazar (online Islamic course), n.d., http://www.almuntazar.com/?p=163.

23. See Jason Burke's *Al-Qaeda: The True Story of Radical Islam* (London and New York : I. B. Tauris, 2003), 6.

24. Kavkaz-Center, December 21, 2013, kavkazcenter.com/eng/content/2013/12/21/18718.shtml.

25. Thomas Joscelyn, "AQAP Endorses New Branch of Terror Network in the Indian Subcontinent," *The Long War Journal*, September 8, 2014, http://www.longwarjournal.org/archives/2014/09/aqap_endorses_new_br.php.

26. Sean O'Neil, "Terror Attack Is Inevitable, Says Security Chiefs as Plots Escalate," *London Times*, November 10, 2014, http://www.thetimes.co.uk/tto/news/uk/article4262905.ece.

27. See chapter 5 for a summary of their story.

28. Stewart Bell, *The Martyr's Oath* (Mississauga: J. Wiley and Sons Canada, 2005), 20.

29. "Last Two 'Toronto 18' Defendants Found Guilty," *Canadian Press*, June 23, 2010, available online at http://toronto.ctvnews.ca/last-two-toronto-18-defendants-found-guilty-1.525506.

30. "German Rapper Turned Jihadist Ruben Cuspert (Deso Dog) Pledges to ISIL," SITEIntelGroup.com, April 11, 2014, http://ent.siteintelgroup.com/Jihadist-News/german-rapper-turned-jihadist-ruben-cuspert-deso-dogg-pledges-to-isil.html.

31. "Alleged Swedish Jihadi in Syria Reports on ISIL Activities," SITEIntelGroup.com, March 7, 2014, http://ent.siteintelgroup.com/Western-Jihadist-Forum-Digest/alleged-swedish-jihadi-in-syria-reports-on-isil-activities.html.

32. Rolf Mowatt-Larssen, "Al Qaeda's Religious Justification of Nuclear Terrorism," excerpt of forthcoming research report, available online at belfercenter.hks.harvard.edu/files/aq-religious-justification.pdf.

33. Megan O'Toole, "Bomb Plotter's Dad Tells Court There Was No Fatwa," Canwest News Service, January 30, 2010, available online at http://www2.canada.com/windsorstar/news/story.html?id=e93156de-b760-43ac-ad82-042538a04398.

34. The vast majority of Spain was occupied, beginning in 714 bce, by Muslim forces invading from northwest Africa (modern-day Morocco). By 1492, the Muslim presence had been eradicated by the Catholic monarchs (Ferdinand and Isabella). At the time, Spain was known as "al-Andalus" (modern Andalusia). Al Qaeda–inspired extremists still use the term.

35. "Jihadists Deny Security Agreements in West Call for Cleansing," SITEIntelGroup.com, April 22, 2013, http://ent.siteintelgroup.com/Western-Jihadist-Forum-Digest/jihadists-deny-security-agreements-in-west-call-for-cleansing.html.

36. "Jihadi Incites British Muslims to Violence against State," SITEIntelGroup.com, March 19, 2010, http://ent.siteintelgroup.com/Western-Jihadist-Forum-Digest/jihadi-incites-british-muslims-to-violence-against-state.html.

37. Kim Sengupta, "Exclusive: Woolwich Killings Suspect Michael Adebolajo Was Inspired by Cleric Banned from UK after Urging Followers to Behead Enemies of Islam," *Independent* (London), May 24, 2013, http://www.independent.co.uk/news/uk/crime/exclusive-woolwich-killings-suspect-michael-adebolajo-was-inspired-by-cleric-banned-from-uk-after-urging-followers-to-behead-enemies-of-islam-8630125.html.

38. See appendix 4 for a much closer analysis.

39. Tiziana Corda, "The Caliphate and Its Followers," Geostrategic Forecasting (website), n.d. http://www.geostrategicforecasting.com/the-caliphate-and-its-followers/.

40. "Media Group Incites for Revolution in Maldives," SITEIntelGroup.com, May 10, 2013, http://ent.siteintelgroup.com/Western-Jihadist-Forum-Digest/media-group-incites-for-revolution-in-maldives.html.

41. SITEIntelGroup.com, http://ent.siteintelgroup.com/Search.html?searchphrase=all&searchword=1924.

42. Zeyno Baran, "Fighting the War of Ideas," *Foreign Affairs* 84, no. 6 (November/December, 2005), https://www.foreignaffairs.com/articles/europe/2005-10-01/fighting-war-ideas.

43. Mark Tran and Matthew Weaver, "ISIS Announces Islamic Caliphate in Area Straddling Iraq and Syria," *The Guardian* (London), June 30, 2014, http://www.theguardian.com/world/2014/jun/30/isis-announces-islamic-caliphate-iraq-syria.

44. Patrick Cockburn, "ISIS Caliphate Has Baghdad Worried Because of Appeal to Angry Young Sunnis," *The Independent* (London), June 30, 2014, http://www.independent.co.uk/news/world/middle-east/isis-caliphate-has-baghdad-worried-because-it-will-appeal-to-angry-young-sunnis-9574393.html.

45. Sharona Schwartz, "Militant Recruitment Video: Fighters Tout 'Imminent' Caliphate and Jihad as 'Cure' for Depression," June 23, 2014, TheBlaze, http://www.theblaze.com/stories/2014/06/23/militant-recruitment-video-fighters-tout-imminent-caliphate-and-jihad-as-cure-for-depression/.

46. http://khabarsoutheastasia.com/en_GB/articles/apwi/articles/features/2014/10/16/feature-02.

47. Glenn Kessler, "The Claim that 98 Percent of Catholic Women Use Contraception: A Media Foul," *Washington Post*, February 17, 2012, http://www.washingtonpost.com/blogs/fact-checker/post/the-claim-that-98-percent-of-catholic-women-use-contraception-a-media-foul/2012/02/16/gIQAkPeqIR_blog.html.

Chapter 3

Twelve Indicators of Al Qaeda–Inspired Radicalization and Violence

DAMIAN'S DILEMMA

We have already discussed the prevalence of converts in extremist plots in an earlier chapter, as well as some of the reasons why they may gravitate to violent interpretations of Islam.

Damian Clairmont was born in Nova Scotia to an Acadian family and at the age of six or seven moved with his parents, who later separated, to Calgary. Damian had issues with depression—he was diagnosed as bipolar—dropped out of high school, and attempted suicide by drinking antifreeze. Then converted to Islam, and he appeared to put his life back together; his family noted that it helped to calm him down.

According to Damian's mom, her son "did seem to find some peace. Then he changed." He moved into a boarding house and became "very secretive, very angry, and very political."

Damian Clairmont died fighting in Syria in 2013.[1]

CHAPTER ABSTRACT

In this chapter, I present and discuss twelve tangible, observable behaviors and attitudes of violent radicalization. I describe each indicator and provide examples illustrating the behavior or attitude.

FROM CAUSE TO INDICATOR

In this book, I have discussed many aspects of the process of radicalization and have attempted to demonstrate how difficult, if not impossible, it is to list the factors and influences that lead people to accept and promote the use of violence. Throughout, I have stressed that there is no single pathway to Al Qaeda–inspired terrorist violence. The lack of a single pathway has been recognized in many journal articles and books.

Despite this lack of certitude or ease of identification, there are nevertheless common traits in the Al Qaeda–inspired violent-radicalization process. Individuals and groups *tend* to exhibit certain behaviors and attitudes that are indicative of this process. In this chapter I present these behaviors and attitudes.

It is *extremely* important to emphasize that the following indicators are *not* always present in violently radicalizing individuals; that said, the indicators are nonetheless very frequently seen among the radicalized population in Canada. Equally important to bear in mind is the fact that some individuals or groups that demonstrate some or all of these characteristics may never move to the violence stage (false positives). Similarly, it is possible (but probably unlikely) that individuals or groups may show no signs of any of these indicators and yet ultimately engage in terrorist violence (false negatives).

I believe that these indicators are concrete and observable and could prove useful to those on the frontlines of detecting and thwarting terrorist violence. Still, as with most things in life, context is critical. No single indicator should be taken in isolation. Furthermore, these characteristics are only indicators— not proof—of a particular violent radicalization process. They should be considered as part of a greater tool kit used by agencies and individuals tasked with, or interested in, stopping people from engaging in terrorist violence.

Each indicator is followed by a discussion of its meaning, its significance, and concrete ways it manifests itself. While there is no overall weighting to the list, the indicators tend to be more serious and worrisome as the list continues. Furthermore, some of these indicators may not be tied to any intent to engage in terrorist violence but may still contribute to an overall negative effect on Canadian society (i.e., on community resilience, intercommunity harmony, violation of Canadian law, etc.). The debate as to whether or not these indicators should be challenged is probably one we need to have in Canada. What kind of country do Canadians want—a nation of inclusivity and variety or of rejection and animosity?

Indicator #1: Sudden Increase in Intolerant Religiosity

This is undoubtedly the most controversial indicator. I by no means am attempting to suggest that finding or enhancing one's faith is a problem in Canada. Radicalization does *not* refer to a person's return to the roots of faith (despite the fact that the word *radicalization* is derived from the Latin word "radix," or root). There are many reasons for which increased religiosity can be seen as a net benefit for Canada. It is also true that for many, especially parents of Canadian Muslims, a return to Islam is seen as a very positive development, as it could lead the subject away from activities of which the parents disapprove (inappropriate mixing with members of the other sex, for example) or that are dangerous or illegal (gang activity, crime, drugs, etc.).

This indicator should be seen in the following context: An individual or small group suddenly abandons activities and relationships, some of which may be long-standing, and migrates to a religious sphere that sees itself as superior and is intolerant and rejectionist. Once in this stage, the individual sees himself as better than others in the community (including family members) and seeks to impose a particular brand of Islam on others. As noted earlier, violent radicalization is an inherently social process, and people at this stage will dissociate themselves from people who are not like-minded. The subject will avoid or even abandon altogether activities seen as inconsistent with a narrow interpretation of Islam (sports, games, gender mixing).

A quotation from Columbia University scholar Bernard Lewis describes this attitude: "I'm right, you're wrong, go to hell."[2] Individuals at this stage brook no argument or difference of opinion, as they are completely convinced that their interpretation of Islam is the only one. Even if these individuals do not move on to terrorist activity, their attitudes and sense of superiority contribute to acrimony and unease within the Muslim community. I liked the term suggested to me by a community leader in Calgary in March 2015: *arrogance*. Extremists see themselves as the only interpreters of Islam and do not care what others think, say, or believe.

Among the concrete manifestations of this characteristic, we *may* see

- an overt challenge of authority in the religious community (as when, for example, an individual stands up in the mosque or Islamic community and yells at the imam or other Muslims, accusing them of false practices or calling them *kuffar*)
- an attempt to sabotage any sign of intercommunity contact by ripping down posters or announcements posted on mosque or community billboards
- criticism of the family's faith and practices and aggressive attempts to force change (as when, for example, men attempt to shame their mothers and sisters into wearing the hijab or niqab and resort to calling them sluts or whores if they resist)
- and rejection of any attempt to engage in civil dialogue on religious difference (which has implications for attempts by leaders or scholars to lead individuals away from the path to violent radicalization).

I have elected to *not* include "a sudden change in physical appearance" as an indicator. Some who have radicalized to the point of violence *may* adopt a certain type of clothing (e.g., short pants of the Salafi style, long beard, etc.), but this change is too general to be a helpful indicator. Many people alter their physical appearances to emulate what they see or feel to be more genuinely "Muslim" and yet have nothing to do with violent radicalization. I would caution not using these changes as an indicator. If a change in physical appearance is accompanied by other indicators, however, it could be worthy of consideration.

Indicator #2: Rejection of Different Interpretations of Islam

Within Islam there are several interpretations or sects that have developed over the faith's fourteen-hundred-year history. This book will not present an overview of these differences, as there are many useful accounts already available. Suffice it to say that individuals and groups on the path to violent radicalization *tend* to belong to a particular strain of Islam known as *Salafism*.

Salafism (from the Arabic phrase *Al Salaf Al Salih*—the righteous ancestors) is a school of Islam (although not one of the four "classic" schools) that believes the Islam practiced in the early years of the faith (embodied by the Prophet Muhammad and the first four successors, lasting from 610 to 660 CE) represented the glory years of the faith. Much of what has happened since that time is seen as unwanted adulteration. Salafis are particularly concerned with what they call *bida'*—innovations to the practice of Islam. They look to the Quran and the hadith (sayings of the Prophet Muhammad) as the only texts worthy of consideration and reject everything else. Salafis tend to be intolerant of other interpretations of Islam.

This intolerance is particularly strong when it comes to the Shia. Shiism is an alternate sect within Islam with an overall minority status (10 percent worldwide), although it is the majority sect in some countries (Iran, Iraq, and Bahrain). The basic difference between Shia and Sunni Islam (the majority of Muslims) concerns the question of succession to the leadership of the Prophet Muhammad. There are also minor differences in practice.

To an individual on the path to violent radicalization, Shiites are *kuffar*—apostates. Their interpretation of Islam and their practices are utterly rejected. Radicalized individuals do not believe that Sunnis and Shiites should mix. This could be particularly problematic in some smaller Islamic communities where both sects share the same places of worship.

In some instances, radicalized individuals believe that the Shia should be killed. There is a lot of rhetoric on jihadi websites that label the Shia as greater enemies of Islam than the regular *kuffar* (Christians and Jews). Conflicts in which Sunnis and Shiites are engaged in violence (Iraq, Syria, Afghanistan, and Pakistan) serve to fuel this hatred.

To a lesser extent, radicalized individuals express an intolerance and hatred for Sufis and Ahmadis. Sufism is a sect in which outward displays of spirituality are important and music and dancing are part of worship. Radicalized people reject the use of music and dance common to Sufism: both practices are seen as haram (forbidden in Islam). Ahmadis are persecuted worldwide because they claim that their eponymous founder was an eighteenth-century prophet. Muslims see Muhammad as the final "seal of prophethood"—the last prophet sent by God to earth—and reject any further prophecy.

In Canada, there is little public information that Sunni-Shia tension (or Sunni–Sufi/Ahmadi tension, for that matter) is a problem, although I have learned that many in the "mainstream" Muslim communities in this country do not consider Ahmadis true Muslims. It should be stressed, however, that intrafaith animosity could contribute to community rancor, even where violence is not used or implied.

Indicator #3: Rejection of Non-Muslims

Judaism, Christianity, and Islam are among the world's largest monotheistic faiths. The three share much of what is known as the Abrahamic tradition. Many of the stories found in Judaism are also found in Christianity, and many found in both the former make their way into the Quran of Islam.

Islam sees Christianity and Islam as special and treats them as such within its faith. Christians and Jews are known as *'Ahl al-Kitāb*—literally, "People of the Book"—in acknowledgment of this shared history. In Western societies where Islam tends to have a minority status, the communities usually have positive interactions. There are many places in Canada where the leaders of religious communities will invite members of the other faiths to their places of worship on special occasions. This is not to say there are not issues of disagreement, but the situation in Canada is generally peaceful.

To radicalized individuals and groups, however, the situation is markedly different. They advocate no contact whatsoever with Christians and Jews. They view non-Muslims through the lens of *Al Wala' wal Bara'*.[3] Reliable signs of an intolerant view of non-Muslims among those who have been radicalized include

- a refusal to deal with businesses owned by non-Muslims
- parents forbidding children from having non-Muslim friends
- parents forbidding children to attend non-Muslim schools and resorting to home schooling
- aggressive denunciation of interfaith contact or dialogue
- refusal to greet non-Muslims with religious messages ("Merry Christmas," "Happy Easter," "Happy Chanukah," etc.)

- viewing all non-Muslims as *kuffar*
- and believing that it is okay to cheat, lie, or steal the property of non-Muslims (as it is sometimes stated that the "blood, wealth, and honor" of the nonbelievers can be taken).

In Western societies this animosity is most usually expressed toward Christians and Jews. In other countries, other non-Islamic faiths are targeted. In India, for example, relations with the dominant Hindu population are viewed as haram. In Sri Lanka, Myanmar, and other Asian countries, relations with the majority Buddhists are viewed with suspicion and even scorn. Conflicts in which Muslims are fighting Hindus (India) or Buddhists (Sri Lanka and Myanmar) add to the hatred. It is probable that these conflicts will in turn contribute to the call for jihad. It is noteworthy, however, that in May 2014 a group of "self-styled jihadists" attacked a Catholic prayer meeting in Yogyakarta, Indonesia.[4]

Refusal to acknowledge the rights of non-Muslims does not lead inexorably to violence. Within Canadian communities, however, this attitude could detract from our long-standing policy of multiculturalism and intercommunity dialogue and coexistence.

Indicator # 4: Rejection of Western Ways

The "West" is known for a variety of concepts and institutions that have developed over centuries to become a canon of sorts. These include democracy, the rule of law (man-made), the equality of the sexes, liberal secularism, a degree of capitalism, and, increasingly, recognition of sexual preferences. All these are enshrined in laws or constitutions, and they are likely among the reasons why so many outside the West are seeking entry into it through immigration or the refugee stream.

To radicalized individuals, however, everything the West stands for is wrong. A sample of the above aspects of Western society will be treated individually here.

Democracy

The Egyptian extremist ideologue Sayyid Qutb believed that democracy was an unnecessary and arrogant attempt by humans to govern themselves.[5] Democracy to him was a part of *jahiliyyah*—a state of ignorance that existed before the advent of Islam. By holding elections and placing people in positions of government, went Qutb's thinking, humans were placing people on the same level as God—in effect, equating themselves with God (a practice known in Islam as *shirk*). In Qutb's view, the only government was that of God himself.

Abdulwahhab Al Humayqani a Yemeni individual described by the United States as an Al Qaeda–affiliated extremist, has stated that Al Qaeda doesn't believe in participatory politics. Al Qaeda, he said, "believes in jihad as a means to establishing an Islamic state, and it believes that joining the political arena is a form of infidelity, or a non-Muslim goal."[6] In May 2014, members of the UK extremist group Need4khilfah described voting as "un-Islamic."[7] A former official in the extremist Libyan Islamic Fighting Group stated in April 2015 that "There is no doubt that democracy contradicts the principles of Islam."[8]

A paper published by At Tibyan Publications,[9] "The Doubts regarding the Ruling of Democracy in Islam," is worth citing at some length:

> Therefore it [democracy] is a system [that] is at odds with the very essence of Allah's exclusive right of legislation, and as such it steps outside the mere disobedience of Allah into the realm of shirk, in that it seeks to elevate mankind to the level of the Legislator [Allah]
>
> And because the people are the ones who select the laws, by means of their representatives, these laws are based upon what the people wish, and they are in accordance with the desires of the majority, rather than what Allah has revealed.

The paper also notes that it is not only the representatives making laws who are working against Allah's will but also the voters who put them in legislative positions. By participating in the democratic system, they are facilitating a system inimical to Allah's law and judgment.

Whether or not to vote in an election at any level is still a matter of personal choice in Canada. There are no mandatory voting laws as there are in some Western countries (Australia, for example). Municipal elections generally show low voter turnout (less than 40 percent turned out for the 2014 Ottawa civic elections), and there has been a marked decrease in voter participation in Canadian federal elections since the mid-1980s. Not voting out of laziness, disinterest, or a belief that one's vote does not count ("The politicians will do whatever they want anyway") is different, however, than not voting because an extremist has convinced you that to vote makes you an infidel. Furthermore, mainstream Muslims do not see democracy as incompatible with Islam, and many Muslims have been elected representatives at all levels of government in this country (presumably, the extremists would consider them non-Muslims).

Western Laws

Within Islam, a body of law (called *sharia*) governs all aspects of Muslim society. In this respect, sharia is analogous with Jewish law or the Catholic canon. In some Muslim-majority countries sharia forms the basis of national laws. In Muslim-minority countries, like Canada, sharia does not enjoy equal status with civil law (recall the acrimonious debate over the institution of Muslim family law in Ontario in 2004 that resulted not only in the over-turning of the original decision to allow Muslim law in certain prescribed instances but also the ouster of certain aspects of long-standing Jewish and Catholic family law[10]). Muslims are obliged to follow the laws of the country of residence while still endeavoring to live a Muslim lifestyle within the confines of that society. The vast majority of Muslims in the West accept this obligation.

Al Qaeda–inspired extremists, however, reject non-Islamic law for the same reasons they reject democracy: neither comes from God, they believe. As a result, extremists justify flouting the law, as they do not believe it applies to them.

There have been extremists that have condoned cheating, stealing, and lying in situations where it is seen as harmful to the *kuffar*. They do not see the refusal to obey local law as inconsistent with mainstream Islam (which they do not follow in any event).

One of the more obvious examples of this attitude was seen during one of the preliminary appearances before the court by Chiheb Esseghaier, who was convicted in early 2015 of conspiring to derail a passenger train in the Niagara Peninsula in 2013. Choosing to represent himself, Esseghaier told the court that, because the Canadian Criminal Code was not a "holy book," he required a lawyer who would help him be judged by the Quran and not according to "a book written by humans."[11] Not surprisingly, this position is untenable under Canadian law.

Both the rejection of democracy and the refusal to recognize the applicability of Canadian law are aspects of *Al Wala' wal Bara'*.[12]

Homosexuality, Prostitution, and Drug Use

In February 2011, dozens of stickers appeared across the London Borough of Tower Hamlets, proclaiming it a "gay-free zone" and promising that "verily Allah is severe in punishment" of those who transgressed.[13]

Al Qaeda–inspired extremists believe that the West is a den of vice and iniquity. They cite the acceptance of gay marriage, high rates of drug abuse, and prostitution as signs that the West has lost its way and is not governed by God's law. (Though many Muslim-majority countries suffer from similar problems, extremists would also view these states as non-Muslim). In response to these societal ills, radicalized individuals call for draconian punishments (stoning, lashing, beheading), as is prescribed in some Islamic canons.

During an interview with CBC's Brian McKenna in 2004, Maha el-Samnah, the widow of former Al Qaeda lieutenant Ahmed Said Khadr, stated "that she didn't want to raise her children in Canada because they would have become involved in 'drugs and homosexual relationships.'"[14]

At a Friday khutbah (a stylized pulpit address) at the Salaheddin mosque, Imam Aly Hindy told his followers that homosexuality was "invented," calling it "nonsense" and "garbage" to believe anyone could be born that way.[15] He went on to talk about "illegal sexual acts" but added a qualifier: "*Illegal* means *illegal in Islam*, not *illegal in the Canadian law*, because everything is legal in the Canadian law except children. Other than that, they allow everything."

Extremists also call for hijra (flight) to remove Muslims from temptation and sin.[16] They are especially adamant that they do not want to raise their children in a permissive environment but want to live in a society that practices true Islamic law.

Gender Equality

Al Qaeda–inspired extremists are misogynists. They do not believe that women should enjoy the same benefits and rights as men and would prefer that women remain in the background. Examples of this misogyny in Canada include

- forbidding one's spouse from leaving the home alone
- forbidding female family members from answering the phone for fear that a male may be calling
- and refusing to work in an environment where women are present.

In 2014, a student enrolled in an online course at York University informed his instructor that he would be unable to participate in mandatory sessions if women were present.[17] This led to a national outcry over what constitutes reasonable accommodation in a multicultural Canadian polity. Although the individual was later identified as a fundamentalist Christian, his beliefs are consistent with the attitudes of those radicalized in the Al Qaeda narrative. At the same time, the fact that this individual was not an extremist with ties to Al Qaeda's ideology is an important reminder that no indicator should be taken in isolation as proof that violent radicalization is brewing; context is everything.

Chiheb Esseghaier, convicted in the Via Rail plot, once had become so enraged upon entering his university laboratory and seeing a United Way poster depicting women that he tore it off the wall.[18]

It should be acknowledged that many Canadian Muslims are conservative when it comes to the role and status of women. This book does not attempt—and is not the place—to debate this issue. For our purposes, suffice it to say that extremists tend to react more vehemently than mainstream conservative Muslims on this matter.

That said, this general misogyny does not preclude women's becoming extremists. While it is true that the vast majority of extremists are male, a few women have participated in jihad. There has also been a lively online debate whether women can fight.[19]

Summary

Many of the behaviors and lifestyles discussed here are still subject to debate even within Western society. The growing acceptance of homosexuality and gay marriage, for example is still upsetting to some, especially fundamentalist Christians. Concerns over alcoholism and drug use are also widespread. Many are distressed by much of celebrity culture—the explicit nature of song lyrics and dance moves, perceived immodesty, materialism, hypersexualiza-tion, and so on. Yet there is a long stretch between disapproval and calling for the death of those who do not think like you. Once again, radicalized individuals and groups are not interested in debate and compromise but in imposing—violently, if necessary—their worldview.

Indicator # 5: Rejection of Western Policies (Domestic, Military, Foreign, Social, etc.)

The Al Qaeda narrative mixes elements from history, politics, and religion to justify its call for violence. Among the grievances outlined by Al Qaeda and like-minded groups is a series of events and policies interpreted as inimical to, or targeting, Islam and Muslims.

Al Qaeda–inspired individuals believe that the West is engaged in an anti-Islamic crusade or campaign. They view Western action (or inaction, in some cases) as evidence that the West hates Islam and is working actively to destroy the faith and kill its adherents.

For example, Western military action that occurs in Muslim-majority nations or regions is seen as a deliberate attempt to take over Muslim land, steal its resources, and, in some cases, force Muslims to convert to Christianity or Judaism (or Hinduism or Buddhism in parts of Asia).[20]

Jihadist websites often refer to the presence of Western (non-Islamic) forces in Muslim countries as a reason to engage in jihad. Among the con-flicts frequently cited are between Iraq and the United States and the coali-tion forces, Afghanistan and the International Security Assistance Force, Chechnya and Russia, Kashmir and India, Xinjiang province and the People's Republic of China, Somalia and Ethiopia, Kenya, and the African Union, and Palestine and Israel.

Western governments are damned if they do and damned if they don't get involved in Muslim lands. They are criticized for the policies in each of the countries listed in the preceding paragraph as well as for not doing anything to stop atrocities and the deaths of Muslims in others (Syria, for example).

Extremists have been critical of Canada's decision to send forces to Afghanistan in the aftermath of 9/11, for example. The Toronto 18 is the most obvious group that sought to punish Canada and its citizens for the presence of Canadian soldiers in a Muslim-majority nation. One of the accused (charges were later stayed), Abdul Qayyum Jamal, gave a speech at the Ar Rahman Islamic Center in Mississauga (west of Toronto) in which he claimed that Canadian soldiers were sent to Afghanistan to "rape Afghan women."[21]

In 2011 Canadian prime minister Stephen Harper was roundly criticized when in an interview with the CBC he claimed that the biggest threat to Canada came from "Islamicism."[22] His comments elicited outrage from those who felt he was equating Islam in general with terrorism, and extremists saw the remark as confirmation that the Canadian government was against Islam.

Debates within the Quebec government on "reasonable accommodation" and the wearing of religious clothing or signs in the workplace has also led to anger over a perceived attack on Islam. Despite the general nature of the proposed restrictions (i.e., that they would apply equally to Sikh turbans and kirpans and to Jewish yarmulkes), extremists see them targeted explicitly at Muslims.[23] A young Montreal woman cited Quebec's racism against Muslims for her decision to join the Islamic State.[24]

The fact that Canada has alliances with other nations also raises ire among extremists. In particular, the perceived shift in the Harper government toward an overtly pro-Israel position on Middle East issues is seen as not only a rejection of a long-standing Canadian middle position but also indicative of the power of the so-called "Jewish lobby" in Canada.[25]

Differences and disagreements about Canadian government policies are not uncommon in this country. The decision to remain involved in the ongoing war in Afghanistan—particularly in light of the large number of Canadian troop casualties—was a divisive issue across Canadian society. The more recent decision to aid air strikes against the Islamic State in Iraq and Syria has also led to much debate. The threat lies not in the differences of opinion but in the belief that Canada has an overt animosity toward Islam and therefore must be punished through acts of terrorism. Extremists seem to believe that by carrying out attacks in Canada and killing Canadian civilians they will force the government to alter its policies. It is one thing to register one's opposition to a particular policy and quite another to plan a terrorist attack to impose one's views and force a change.

Indicator # 6: Association with Like-Minded People

As noted throughout this book, violent radicalization is a social process and does not occur in a vacuum (no man is an island). It is through one's network of family, friends, and acquaintances that violent radicalization can happen (or can be prevented from happening, in the right circumstances). While this topic was broached in chapter 2, I expanded upon it here.

We are all generally liable to listen to people and sources of information that support our view of things. This propensity is known in psychology as *confirmation bias*. This is true for average people as well as for extremists.

People at risk of violent radicalization will often remove themselves from contexts where messages inconsistent with their newly found "truth" are found. They will expose themselves almost solely to like-minded people and sources of knowledge (e.g., websites) that confirm their beliefs and will reject any other views. This isolation can contribute to a lack of "competition for ideas": by refusing to consider contrary viewpoints, a person can consolidate their own outlook, which remains unchallenged.

Signs that an individual or group may be on the path of violent radicalization may include

- a sudden change in circles of friends or associates and a complete rejection of a previous lifestyle (sports, activities, clubs etc.)
- association with individuals aggressively pushing an intolerant view of issues (religious, political, social, etc.)
- refusal to acknowledge the possibility that differences of opinion are valid and healthy
- an obsession with maintaining a small circle of friends to the exclusion of all others
- and a level of secrecy in the activities of the new circle of friends.

It is true that such changes in group association may occur for a variety of reasons, both legitimate (e.g., discovery of a religious group) or illegal (gangs or criminal sets). Again, it is important to place these indicators within the context of what else is happening within the life of the individual or group of concern.

Indicator # 7: Obsession with Jihadi and Violent-Extremist Sites and Social Media

While the role of the Internet was discussed at length in chapter 2, a few additional comments are necessary here.

First and foremost, visiting jihadi sites is not necessarily a sign of violent radicalization (if that were the case, many scholars and security and law-enforcement officials would be subject to investigation!). In several cases in the UK, the accused have claimed that their possession of downloaded jihadi material was for research purposes.

Problematic use of the Internet would include

- obsessive browsing (hours and hours per day)
- sharing violent videos (beheadings included)
- posting violent material
- efforts to hide browsing of jihadi sites from family, friends, teachers, etc.
- and attempts to join closed, password-protected sites that expound violence.

Indicator # 8: Obsession with the Narrative

The single narrative was discussed at great length in the introduction. What is important to ascertaining a burgeoning violent radicalism is noting an individual's obsessive belief in the narrative.

The narrative has a number of strengths that render it difficult to undermine or counter (although this has not stopped several think tanks and governments from attempting to develop counter-narratives).[26]

A Note on Conspiracy Theory

To the average reader, the Al Qaeda narrative may seem to have much in common with what are known as *conspiracy theories*. There are many conspiracy theories that surround acts of terrorism and are prevalent on extremist websites (and nonjihadist websites, for that matter). Some of these theories include the belief that the attacks of 9/11 were carried out by the Israeli Mossad, by the CIA, or even by the Bush administration itself to justify an invasion of Iraq.

Another interesting set of conspiracy beliefs on jihadi sites involves a shadowy cabal of leaders and groups that seek to control the world. These actors include the Freemasons, the Zionists, and even the Bilderberg Group (a club for international bankers and businessmen). Stranger agents that have been identified include the Illuminati and the Knights Templar.

The single narrative is *not*, however, quite the same type of belief as these conspiracy theories. While the notion that the West is at perpetual war with Islam may strike many—particularly those in the West—as incredible, it is not that far-fetched for many in the Muslim and Arab worlds. Opinion polls in these regions have consistently shown that many believe in certain aspects of the narrative and see support for it in the actions (and inactions) of the West in their countries.[27]

It is important to remember that the perspective or filter through which an individual or society sees events (past, present, and future) determines one's outlook. The filters and experiences common in one part of the world do not have to be the same as those in another. The narrative remains an elegant and simple way of interpreting the world—and one that has some hold on a large number of people.

Indicator # 9: Desire to Travel to Conflict Zones

The belief that Islam is under attack and that true Muslims must rush to its defense often means that individuals are keen to travel to areas where that attack is seen as most crucial. Given the number of conflicts in which Muslims are involved—either as perpetrators or as victims—it is not surprising that Canadians have left this country to fight and possibly die in what they see as *fi sabilillah* ("in the cause of Allah").

Many different countries have been end points for extremists. This list is constantly changing as conflicts change and as appeals for aid shift. It is thus not possible to provide a single list of destinations, though such a list would be incredibly helpful. There are of course a number of countries that—together with other information (intelligence)—could be helpful in this regard. Should information or intelligence on specific countries become available, a useful list could be (temporarily) constructed. This core group would include places such as Afghanistan, Somalia, Yemen, and increasingly Syria. The obsession with travel is tied to several factors, including

- the urgency of the situation ("Muslims are dying now, and there is no time to lose")
- an easier justification, perhaps, for action (for example, it being one thing to say that Canada is to blame for the actions of its soldiers in Afghanistan but quite another to look at the brutality of Assad's forces against Syrian Muslims)
- a sense of thrill and adventure
- a desire to join a "band of brothers" in a good cause
- and, in some cases, a link with a cosmic historical end-time jihad (particularly applicable in Syria, as shall be shown below).

The Canadian Security Intelligence Service has stated publicly that it is aware of at least 145 Canadians who have fought abroad (a figure released in early 2014).[28] There are undoubtedly more, since some may not have come to the attention of CSIS or the Royal Canadian Mounted Police. The cases discussed in chapter 4 are probably the tip of the iceberg. More cases will likely come to light in the months and years to come.

Why is foreign travel seen as a threat and a concern to Canada? I believe there are three primary reasons.

1. Canadians have left this country to join terrorist groups and have killed people. A few examples have been discussed in earlier chapters. Suffice it to say that Canada does not want its citizens or landed immigrants to kill foreigners, especially those from closely allied countries, as happened in the January 2013 attack on a gas plant in Algeria. We do not want to be seen as a "net exporter" of terrorism. Recall 1999's Millennium Plot, which saw Ahmed Ressam travel from Quebec to California with plans to bomb Los Angeles International Airport. Had he been successful, Canada's relations with the United States would have undergone a dramatic turn. There are still US politicians who point to that incident as evidence that Canada's efforts against terrorism are weak.

2. Canadians who go abroad may be convinced by extremist leaders that their talents and enthusiasm would be better served by returning to Canada and carrying out action here. This has clearly happened in other countries: both Faisal Shahzad (the failed Times Square bomber) and Najibullah Zazi (another failed New York terrorist) had gone abroad but were trained and told to do something in the United States. Terrorist groups must see Westerners as ideal candidates to strike at the heart of the enemy, given their easy access as citizens and their familiarity with Western societies.

3. Those that fight and survive may eventually return to Canada and act as vectors of radicalization for others. These individuals command a level of respect with some—particularly the youth—because they have "walked the walk." The passing on of adventures and stories, some of which may be a little embellished, serves as source of inspiration. In addition, returnees have practical experience covering travel patterns and evading government detection, as well as contacts abroad and perhaps a variety of skills (small arms and explosives training) to pass on. In essence, these people can become the radicalizers of others in Canada.

Concrete Signs of Travel to Conflict Zones for Jihad

A number of warning indicators point to the possibility of travel for terrorist purposes, including

- keeping travel plans secret
- leaving travel itineraries to the last minute
- paying cash
- odd travel routes (possibly in an attempt to avoid obstacles such as US airspace)
- traveling one way only
- seeking travel to an area inconsistent with one's background or interests (e.g., a white convert traveling to Somalia—odd at best)

- inordinate interest in a specific area (it being one thing to be upset and angry over the situation in Syria, for example, but perhaps a little strange to talk of nothing else)
- and severe criticism of those who do not share this passion for foreign jihads.

Given the importance of travel in the overall radicalization process, ranging from skill acquisition and battle experience to increased ideological commitment, it is important to pay attention to this indicator.

Indicator # 10: Obsession with Violent Jihad

While the ideology and central position of violent jihad was discussed at great length in chapter 2, it is perhaps worth emphasizing the obsessive nature of the need for violent jihad in radicalizing individuals. They will speak of little else and will chastise others for not sharing their zeal.

Seeking permission to engage in action is another important aspect of violent jihad. In classical Islam, a child has to seek his parents' permission to engage in jihad. Modern extremist ideologues, however, claim that as violent jihad is *fard `ayn* (obligatory act for a Muslim) and that it is incumbent on each individual to engage in it. Hence, they would say, permission is not required. This also applies to the few cases of women extremists, who historically would have had to obtain their father's or husband's permission before leaving.

Indicator # 11: Obsession with Martyrdom

Christian and Islamic notions of martyrdom have a lot in common, starting with the words themselves. The English word *martyr* comes from the Greek word for "witness." Martyrs are those who die while witnessing and living their faith. The Arabic word for martyr is *shahid* and is linked to the Arabic word for "witness."

Much has been written about martyrdom and Islam, and there is a long history of theology behind this tradition. Unfortunately, in the popular sphere some misconceptions have arisen that, while very compelling, are not accurate. The most obvious one involves the virgins.

According to collective wisdom, Muslim men blow themselves up in some kind of sexual frenzy in order to sleep with black-eyed virgins who will do the martyrs' bidding for all eternity. Some even claim that sexual repression in the Islamic world leads men to commit violent acts in hopes of sexual reward.

There is some truth to this theory, and the availability of the houri—these virgins who tend the righteous in paradise—is a feature of extremist websites.

The word *houri*, incidentally, does really mean "black-eyed virgin" and not "white grapes" as claimed by self-professed Muslim refusenik Irshad Manji. She believes that jihadists have misinterpreted an old Semitic word and would be disappointed to find bowls of grapes waiting for them in the hereafter rather than the expected virgins. This is highly unlikely. In any event, extremists do not think it refers to white grapes. It is difficult to determine what role if any the belief in an eternity of sex with virgins has on an extremist's decision to sacrifice his life. There are, nevertheless, a few more important and enticing promised rewards that could push someone toward martyrdom, including

- the forgiveness of one's sins
- an opportunity to intercede on behalf of seventy of one's relatives in paradise
- hero treatment on earth
- the ascent to heaven of one's soul in the form of a green bird (green being the color of Islam)
- and having one's body remain intact forever without corruption (there are analogies here to Christian saints).

Do those considering martyrdom exhibit overt signs or behaviors? Those thinking of becoming a *shahid* may

- seek forgiveness for all the wrongs done to their family and friends before the "big day"
- leave a letter outlining their plans, to be opened only after departure
- and suddenly repay debts (an interesting tell, as extremists will also abuse credit and loans, claiming that they do not have to repay money owed to *kuffar*, and yet advice can be found on the Internet stating that a martyr with outstanding financial debts will not enter paradise).[29]

Clearly, not all extremist actions are suicidal in nature. To date, none of the planned attacks in Canada appears to have been suicidal, but several Canadians have died as martyrs abroad. Extremist groups extolled the deaths of Martin Couture-Rouleau and Michael Zehaf-Bibeau in their attacks in Canada in October 2014. It is best to keep some of these points in mind when looking at radicalized individuals.

Indicator # 12: Obsession with End-Times

Islam is similar to Christianity in that it has a series of scenarios that will transpire at the end of time and history. It is not necessary to go into excessive detail about these scenarios, as several books provide excellent explanation.[30] Suffice it to say that at the end of the world as we know it, three figures— Jesus (*Issa* in Arabic, who returns to earth), a mythical figure called the Mahdi, and the Dajjal (a type of Islamic Antichrist) will engage in a cosmic battle of good versus evil (with the former two victorious), followed by an era of truth and justice.

What do these events have to do with radicalization to violence? Many jihadi websites will speak of the signs of the end-times and call upon true Muslims to join Jesus and the Mahdi in this battle of all battles.

More importantly, in some of the narratives, signs of the impending end-times include a conflict in Syria, the deaths of hundreds of thousands of civilians, and a clash between large armies. Websites have portrayed the civil war and associated atrocities in Syria through this lens, with the roles of the armies played by the Islamist extremist (Sunnis) and the Assad regime (Shiites). Participants in the war on the extremist side are actors in the "great battle." Some analysts believe that the Islamic State is aiming for an apocalyptic battle in Iraq and Syria.[31] Its online magazine *Dabiq* is full of apocalyptic references. A French extremist charged with preparing a suicide attack stated in court that he went to fight in Syria because he had seen that the "signs of Day of Resurrection are coming soon."[32]

CSIS has publicly noted that at least thirty Canadians have traveled to Syria to fight the Assad regime, some of whom joined groups such as the Islamic State of Iraq and Syria and Jabhat al-Nusra. In addition, thousands of foreign fighters have entered Syria from dozens of countries. It is not unreasonable to posit that some have been driven to do so by their views of fighting jihad at the side of the Mahdi. One mujahid has spoken of fighting the battle described by the Prophet Muhammad as a harbinger of the end of the world.[33]

While it is not clear how attractive this call for jihad is, it is not difficult to imagine the draw for an individual looking to engage in fighting and reading that his contribution will hasten an era of peace and justice.

SUMMARY

Note the preponderance of the words *obsession* and *intolerance* in this section. Al Qaeda–inspired extremists tend to see the world in black and white, right versus wrong. They do not see the value in debate and are convinced that their interpretation of events and issues is the only right one.

This obsessive stubbornness and arrogance does have implications for intervention and deradicalization. Some in the Muslim community, including religious leaders, believe that it is simply a matter of sitting these individuals down and explaining why their version of Islam is wrong. This may work for people at an early stage of the radicalization process but is less likely to be effective at a later stage.

It must be emphasized that these characteristics and observable behaviors, as with all things, must be placed in context. It is for this reason that learning to observe these indicators is presented as a tool and is *not* meant to serve as a checklist or be considered exhaustive, infallibly identifying a person on the edge of violence. It is nevertheless likely that Al Qaeda–inspired individuals and groups in Canada will manifest many if not all of the traits discussed here. We will see this time and time again in the next chapter's consideration of case studies in Canada. Again, I must caution that the presence of several of these characteristics and behaviors does not imply the presence of a dangerous terrorist.

Furthermore, I hope it is clear that when these traits are observed even in a nonviolent individual their implications ought to be taken equally seriously. Society should not tolerate individuals and groups that reject the rule of law, gender equality, and our system of democracy. While we may at times have differences of opinion, it is necessary to start with a common set of beliefs and thereupon build our society. Individuals who reject these founding premises should be challenged—at all levels of society. I am not advocating some sort of thought police but rather debate through which the ideas that probably the majority of Canadians see as valid and enriching can be shown to be vastly superior to extremism. We all have a vested interest in entering into this debate as we continue to build Canada.

Who is best placed to observe these indicators? Well, anyone. In fact, many of these behaviors will be noticed first by family, friends, religious leaders, and others close to the subjects *before* security and law enforcement could possibly note them. It is my hope that by learning what the indicators can mean, people best positioned to detect them in their early stages will be empowered to not ignore them but act.

NOTES

1. "Damian Clairmont Killed Fighting with al-Qaeda-Linked Rebels in Syria," CBC News, last updated June 19, 2014, http://www.cbc.ca/news/world/damian-clairmont-killed-fighting-with-al-qaeda-linked-rebels-in-syria-1.2497513. For more on Damian's story, see chapter 4.

2. Bernard Lewis, "I'm Right, You're Wrong, Go to Hell," *The Atlantic* (May 2003), http://www.theatlantic.com/magazine/archive/2003/05/-im-right-youre-wrong-go-to-hell/302723/.

3. See page chapter 2 for a more detailed discussion of the concept of *Al Wala' wal Bara'*.

4. "Self-Styled Jihadists Attack Yogya Catholic Prayer Meeting," *Jakarta Globe*, May 31, 2014, http://www.thejakartaglobe.com/news/self-styled-jihadists-attack-yogya-catholic-prayer-meet/.

5. See chapter 2 for a deeper analysis of Sayyid Qutb.

6. Abigail Hauslohner, "Yemeni 'Global Terrorist' Says He Has Counterterrorism Advice for Washington," *Washington Post*, February 16, 2014, http://www.washingtonpost.com/world/middle_east/yemeni-global-terrorist-says-he-hascounterterrorism-advice-for-washington/2014/02/15/c689f72a-8e51-11e3-878e-d76656564a01_story.html.

7. Originally posted at https://www.youtube.com/watch?v=wslRzZGuubo, now found at http://www.liveleak.com/view?i=556_1401378754.

8. The original video uploaded to YouTube has been deleted.

9. See appendix 4 for more on At Tibyan Publications.

10. James Sturcke, "Sharia Law in Canada, Almost," *The Guardian* (London), February 8, 2008, http://www.theguardian.com/news/blog/2008/feb/08/sharialawin canadaalmost.

11. Allison Jones, "VIA Terror Plot Accused Chiheb Esseghaier Tells Court He Was 'Forced to Show My Sex,' Rants about Gay Marriage," *National Post* (Toronto), last updated January 25, 2015, http://news.nationalpost.com/2014/01/29/via-terror-plot-accused-chiheb-esseghaier-tells-court-he-was-forced-to-show-my-sex-rants-about-gay-marriage/.

12. See chapter 2 for a more involved discussion of *Al Wala' wal Bara'*.

13. "Muslim Fanatic Fined £100 for 'Gay Free Zone' Stickers," *The London Telegraph*, June 1, 2011, http://www.telegraph.co.uk/news/religion/8550178/Muslim-fanatic-fined-100-for-gay-free-zone-stickers.html.

14. The Khadr family is infamous in Canada. "A Family in Conflict," *The Guardian* (London), March 9, 2004, http://www.theguardian.com/world/2004/mar/09/worlddispatch.annemcilroy.

15. Bell, "Toronto's 'Radical Mosque.'"

16. For a more detailed discussion of the possible implications of hijra, see chapter 2.

17. Graham Slaughter, "York U Student's Refusal to Work with Women Sparks Rights Debate," *The Toronto Star*, January 8, 2014, http://www.thestar.com/news/gta/2014/01/08/york_u_students_refusal_to_work_with_women_sparks_rights_debate.html.

18. Randall Palmer and Alastair Sharp, "Canadian Train Plot Suspects Caused Unease with Extreme Views," Reuters, April 25, 2013, http://mobile.reuters.com/article/worldNews/idUSBRE93O1F820130425.

19. For a debate on women fighters in Syria, see "Jihadists Determine Syrian Women Permitted to Fight," SITEIntelGroup.com, July 12, 2013, http://ent.siteintelgroup.com/Western-Jihadist-Forum-Digest/jihadists-determine-syrian-women-permitted-to-fight.html.

20. The role foreign-military invasions play in terrorism is well outlined in US political scientist Robert Pape's *Dying to Win: The Strategic Logic of Suicide Terrorism* (New York: Random House, 2005).

21. Isabel Teotonio, "As Suspect Waits in Jail, Wife Has Trials of Her Own," *The Toronto Star*, June 4, 2007, http://www.thestar.com/news/2007/06/04/as_suspect_waits_in_jail_wife_has_trials_of_her_own.html.

22. JustMediaWatch, "Muslim Response to Stephen Harper's Statement 'Islamicism' Biggest Threat to Canada!!" YouTube (video), September 14, 2011, http://www.youtube.com/watch?v=B3UyAN01ODI.

23. "Quebec's Debate on 'Reasonable Accommodation'—A Socialist View," Life on the Left (blog), December 16, 2007, http://lifeonleft.blogspot.ca/2007/12/quebecs-debate-on-reasonable.html.

24. *The Tornoto Star*, http://www.thestar.com/news/canada/2015/02/27/quebec-stunned-by-exodus-of-four-young-men-two-women-to-join-islamic-state.html.

25. Patrick Martin, "Nearly Half Canadians Say Ottawa's Policy on Israeli-Palestinian Conflict 'Strikes Right Balance,'" *The Globe and Mail* (Toronto), last updated September 6, 2012, http://www.theglobeandmail.com/news/politics/nearly-half-canadians-say-ottawas-policy-on-israeli-palestinian-conflict-strikes-right-balance/article554580/.

26. These strengths will be discussed in the section in chapter 5 on counter-narratives.

27. "Muslim-Western Tensions Persist: Common Concerns about Islamic Extremism," Pew Research Center (website), July 21, 2011, http://www.pewglobal.org/2011/07/21/muslim-western-tensions-persist/.

28. Tonda MacCharles, "RCMP Tracking 90 Individuals in Terrorism Probes," *Toronto Star*, October 8, 2014, http://www.thestar.com/news/canada/2014/10/08/rcmp_tracking_90_individuals_in_terrorism_probes.html.

29. Moulana Muhmmad A., "Will a Shahid (Martyr) Be Liable for His Debts?" Hadith Answers.com (website), March 22, 2014, http://www.hadithanswers.com/will-a-shahid-martyr-be-liable-for-his-debts/.

30. See Jean-Pierre Filiu's *Apocalypse in Islam* (Berkeley: University of California Press, 2011) and Timothy R. Furnish's *Holiest Wars: Islamic Mahdis, Their Jihads, and Osama bin Laden* (Westport, CN : Praeger Publishers, 2005).

31. Martin Chulov, "A Sledgehammer to Civilisation: Islamic State's War on Culture," *Guardian*, April 7, 2014, http://www.theguardian.com/world/2015/apr/07/islamic-state-isis-crimes-against-culture-iraq-syria.

32. Agence France-Presse, "French Jihadist Describes Lebanon Attack Plan," *The Local* (Paris), November 8, 2014, http://www.thelocal.fr/20141108/french-jihadist-describes-lebanon-attack-plan.

33. Mariam Karouny, "Apocalyptic Prophecies Drive Both Sides to Syrian Battle for End of Time," Reuters, April 1, 2014, http://www.reuters.com/article/2014/04/01/us-syria-crisis-prophecy-insight-idUSBREA3013420140401.

Chapter 4

What Do Radicalized Individuals and Groups Do?

FROM WINNIPEG TO WANTON DESTRUCTION

In the early part of the twentieth century, Winnipeg was touted as the "Chicago of the North." Once one of the continent's fastest-growing cities, the economic stagnation following World War I and the opening of the Panama Canal, which transformed North American trade, played some part in deflating this economic miracle.

Nevertheless, it was to Winnipeg that Hiva Alizadeh fled from Iran in the early 2000s. A Sunni Muslim—and a Kurd to boot—in largely Shia Persian Iran, he may have been subject to some kind of discrimination in his home country. So why did he choose to live in Winnipeg? He had an uncle already there.

Alizadeh soon married a local woman—a convert—and the couple had two children. He attended Red River College where he took English language lessons but dropped out. His pattern of not following through with education continued when he quit an electrical engineering program after only one semester.

He had difficulty finding work, in large part because of his poor English language skills. He ended up working at a halal meat store in Winnipeg. The owner said he worked long hours, "open to close, seven days a week."

In 2008, Alizadeh and his family moved to Ottawa. He and three others were arrested in August 2010 and charged with several terrorism offenses. Alizadeh pleaded guilty in October 2014 and received a twenty-four-year sentence.

According to his neighbor at the apartment complex in Ottawa's west end where he lived, Alizadeh and his wife "were nice people . . . they were my friends."

CHAPTER ABSTRACT

In this chapter I analyze several cases of individuals and groups in Canada who were either tried and convicted of terrorist offenses or left Canada to join groups or execute terrorism abroad. I examine each with an eye to determining how many, if any, of the indicators discussed in the previous chapter made an appearance.

FROM THOUGHT TO ACTION

Now that radicalization to violence has been discussed at length, it is necessary to look at what happens once radicalization is either well underway or complete. In this chapter I discuss a number of cases in Canada where individuals or groups have actually engaged in acts of violence or planned acts of violence.

The information I present here is drawn from a number of open sources, as all these cases are now public. There are excellent narratives on some of them (I particularly recommend the reporting of Isabel Teotonio in *The Toronto Star* on the Toronto 18, Stewart Bell of Toronto's *National Post* on Damian Clairmont and the London, Ontario, young men who went to Algeria in January 2013, as well as Bell's book on the Jabarah brothers, *The Martyr's Oath*). I will not, therefore, provide an exhaustive account of any particular case. Each one could be the subject of its own book.

In this chapter I use the case studies to underline the aspects of radicalization discussed in this book. I highlight the specific characteristics of radicalization found in each case, which may serve as useful illustrations for individuals or officials and agencies in positions to identify people at risk of radicalization. It bears repeating again, however, that every case is different and that frontline staff and first responders should not create inflexible templates that may not adequately transfer to future scenarios.

The cases are divided into three broad categories: people and groups who have planned or carried out acts of terrorism in Canada, those who have joined terrorist groups abroad and engaged in attacks, and individuals who have traveled to fight in foreign conflicts. Despite the differences in goals and intents, there are significant similarities in the particular paths to radicalization. In addition, there will be common indicators pointing to the radicalization process.

PLANNED ACTS IN CANADA

There have been four major foiled attacks in Canada since 9/11: the Toronto 18 in 2006, Project Samossa in 2010, and two plots in 2013—the Via Rail plot and the plan to bomb the British Columbia Legislature on Canada Day. There have also been two successful attacks in 2014: the October 20 killing of a Canadian soldier in Quebec by Martin Couture-Rouleau, a convert to Islam who had apparently wanted to fight in Syria, and the October 22 killing of reservist Corporal Nathan Cirillo at the National War Memorial in Ottawa by Michael Zehaf-Bibeau and Zehaf-Bibeau's subsequent unsuccessful attack on Parliament.

The Toronto 18

Canada awoke on June 2, 2006, to headlines announcing that seventeen men had been arrested (an eighteenth was arrested later) on allegations that they were planning a series of terrorist attacks in Toronto and elsewhere.[1]

All were Canadian residents, crushing the conviction that terrorism comes from "over there." Over the course of the following months and years, the Canadian public was made privy to a series of plots and intrigues, ranging from planned truck bombs to plans for the beheading of the prime minister. It is no exaggeration to say that this case is seen as the single greatest terrorist threat in Canadian history.

After a number of trials and hearings, eleven men were convicted or pleaded guilty to a number of terrorism charges: seven men were released when the Crown decided not to pursue their cases. Several of the eleven were granted time served and are now free. Five are still in prison, and one, Ali Dirie (whose story is told in greater detail below) served his sentence, was released, and left a year later for Syria, where he died in 2013.

Much of the story of the Toronto 18 is known, especially in Canada. One of the best synopses is that of Isabel Teotonio, a *Toronto Star* reporter who wrote an overarching piece in 2010. In view of the notoriety of this case, I will not rehash all aspects of the plot in the following but instead focus on the aspects of the case that address the radicalization process.

The original leader of the group was Fahim Ahmad, an Afghan immigrant who came to Canada at the age of ten. He had come to the attention of Canadian Security Intelligence Service in the early 2000s because of his extreme postings on websites such as ClearGuidance, IslamicAwakening, and At Tibyan Publications. His online moniker was "Soldier of Allah," and he admitted to CSIS agents that he did post the messages but added that it was not "the right time" for him to do jihad. At the time of his arrest, Ahmad was married with a baby girl.

Ahmad's co-conspirator was his closest friend, Zakaria Amara. The son of a Christian mother and a Jordanian father, Amara converted to Islam at the age of ten and came to Canada from Jordan when he was twelve. He and Ahmad attended the same high school outside of Toronto, in Mississauga, where they joined the Muslim Students Association. Another member of the association, Saad Khalid, would talk of jihad and martyrdom at school.

In December 2005, Ahmad led a group to a wooded area a few hours north of Toronto. Unbeknownst to Ahmad and the others, one of the attendees was a CSIS source, Mubin Shaikh. During a twelve-day period, the group marched and did some shooting, pretending they were mujahideen in Chechnya and killing *kuffar*. Their ad hoc camp served as a bonding experience for the group.

By the spring of 2006, Ahmad and Amara had suffered a falling out. Amara did not think Ahmad was serious about their plans, and the group split in two: Ahmad's group concentrating in the Toronto district of Scarborough, and Amara's meeting in Mississauga. Amara collaborated with Shareef Abdelhaleem, a software engineer who at one time was earning a "six-figure salary." Amara used the money from his part-time job at a Canadian Tire gas bar to work on his "project"—a remote-controlled detonator. He later ordered three tons of ammonium nitrate to be used in a truck bomb. Indications are that Amara's wife appeared to have been as extreme as her husband.

Other members of the group had their roles as well. Steven Chand, born in Fiji and a Hindu convert to Islam, helped with the training at the December camp. Ali Dirie and Yasin Abdi Mohamed traveled to the United States to acquire guns and were arrested at the Fort Erie border crossing in August 2005. Abdul Qayyum Jamal (charges were stayed in his case) worked at the Ar-Rehman Islamic Center in Mississauga where he was custodian and part-time *khatib* (one who gives khutbahs—sermons in Arabic); the youth viewed him as a father figure, and he told them that Canadian soldiers were raping women in Afghanistan. Four young offenders were also arrested, one of whom, Nishanthan Yogakrishnan, was tried as an adult and sentenced to time served—the first person convicted under Canada's anti-terrorism legislation.

The arrests took place when two members, Saad Gaya and Saad Khalid, were unloading into a storage shed what they believed to be ammonium nitrate (the Royal Canadian Mounted Police had substituted an inert substance). The group was planning to explode three truck bombs (these were not to be suicide attacks) against the CSIS offices in Toronto, the Toronto Stock Exchange, and an unnamed military base in Ontario.

Of the eighteen arrested, six had their cases stayed. The other twelve received sentences as follows:

Fahim Ahmad	16 years
Zakaria Amara	life
Shareef Abdelhaleem	life
Saad Gaya	12 years

Saad Khalid	20 years
Ali Dirie	7 years
Jahmaal James	7 years (equivalent to time served)
Steven Chand	10 years (given credit for 9 years, 4 months)
Yasin Mohamed	2 years (subsequently acquitted)
Nishanthan Yogakrishnan	30 months (equivalent to time served)
Amin Durrani	7 1/2 years (equivalent to time served)
Asad Ansari	6 years, 5 months (equivalent to time served)

The Toronto 18 sought to punish Canada for its decision to send forces to Afghanistan in the wake of 9/11. They wanted to cause catastrophic damage, cripple the economy, and unleash mass carnage. The members' trials unfolded over several years, and a degree of skepticism about the true nature of the threat entered Canadian society, and especially some parts of the Muslim communities, as time dragged on and some charges were dropped. Still today some see the group as amateurish, duped by a CSIS source (who later became an RCMP agent). They were "the gang that couldn't shoot straight," subjected to a sting operation.

Key Points

The group demonstrated a number of the indicators discussed in chapter 3, including (1) a belief that the West, including Canada, is at war with Islam (Ahmad referred to "Rome," a frequent extremist term for the West), (2) a belief that jihad is required to right this wrong and is *fard `ayn*, an individual obligation for Muslims, (3) severe angst over the suffering of Muslims worldwide, (4) a desire to punish Canada for its perceived anti-Muslim actions, (5) a belief in the principles of Al Qaeda, and (6) the rejection of Western culture (television, movies, etc.).

Project Samossa

In a project known by the RCMP as Project Samossa, three individuals were accused of planning to deploy explosives in Canada.[2] In May 2014 the Crown concluded the trial of one alleged extremist, Khurram Sher, who was found not guilty, though the judge did note that he had been naive and exhibited jihadist sympathies.[3] The trial of the second participant, Misbahuddin Ahmed, began in May 2014, and Ahmed was found guilty on two of three charges in July 2014 and sentenced to twelve years in prison.[4] The third participant, Hiva Alizadeh, pleaded guilty in September 2014 to explosives possession with the intent to cause harm and was later sentenced to twenty-four years in prison. In his statement Judge Colin McKinnon noted that Alizadeh was in effect guilty of treason and had embraced a "radical Islamist jihadist ideology." A fourth conspirator, Awso Peshdary, was arrested in August 2010, but the charges against him were dropped. It is worth noting that Peshdary was rearrested in February 2015, accused of having ties to the Islamic State.[5] His rearrest raises some very difficult questions regarding how long individuals continue to hold views consistent with Al Qaeda–inspired violent extremism before they may actually act.

The Canadian government had alleged that Ahmed and Alizadeh had amassed a large quantity of computer circuit boards that were to be used to create improvised explosive devices that they may have been planning to use against a repatriation ceremony for deceased Canadian soldiers who had fought in Afghanistan. Sher was a relative latecomer to the plot: he was present at a meeting in Ottawa where attacks were discussed in July 2010, one month prior to the arrests.

The Crown alleged that Alizadeh traveled to Pakistan for terrorist training (this was later confirmed in the agreed statement of facts). Ahmed was working as an X-ray technician in Ottawa, and the Crown alleged that he was Alizadeh's right-hand man and had trained in bomb making.

Key Points

The cell was preparing to carry out an attack on a military repatriation ceremony to punish Canada for its action in Afghanistan and believed that an attack in Canada would be justified. It is also worth noting that, as we have discussed, radicalized individuals are not all marginalized people: Sher was a successful doctor with an apparent humanitarian streak and was clearly integrated into Canadian life (he was born in Montreal), while Ahmed appeared to have a good job at a hospital in Ottawa. On the other hand, Alizadeh appeared to have difficulty adjusting to life in Canada, struggling with language and employment.

This case clearly illustrates how preconceived notions of radicalization to violence should always be challenged: Does economic status affect violent radicalization? Two of the three (Sher and Ahmed) were leading comfortable lives, while a third (Alizadeh) struggled. Does country of origin matter? The same two were born in Canada, while Alizadeh emigrated from Iran. Individual backgrounds vary, and it does not seem likely that we can draw generalized conclusions from these variations.

The Via Rail Plot

2013 was a banner year for counterterrorism in Canada.[6] Two sets of arrests of two individuals each were made in April and July for alleged plots—one to derail a Via passenger train and the other to set off explosives on the grounds of the British Columbia Legislature in Victoria on Canada Day.

The Via Rail plot is known to the RCMP as Project Smooth. The two individuals accused of planning to derail a passenger train somewhere in the Niagara Peninsula were Chiheb Esseghaier, a Tunisian PhD student of biology living in Quebec, and Raed Jaser, a Palestinian resident of Toronto.

On April 22, 2013, the RCMP charged the two in conjunction with an Al Qaeda–linked plot to carry out an act of terrorism. According to the RCMP, "directions and guidance" were sent from Al Qaeda "elements" in Iran. Esseghaier is alleged to have traveled to Iran where he received terrorist training. The accused are alleged to have had the "capacity and intent" to commit an act of terrorism.

Both men have been described as devout Muslims, and Esseghaier's faith in particular led to disputes with his colleagues at a high-tech research facility south of Montreal. A classmate described his hardline religious views as "troubling," and evidently Esseghaier once tore down a poster raising awareness for charity on which women were shown. He had issues with young people dating, calling it "crookedness."[7] Allegedly, Esseghaier's Facebook page had an image of a flag associated with an Al Qaeda–linked group in Iraq. At his preliminary hearing, Esseghaier stated that he does not recognize the authority of the Canadian Criminal Code, since the code is not a "holy book." He sought to have the court judge him against the Quran and not Canadian law. Not surprisingly, he was unable to find a Canadian lawyer to defend him on this basis and so elected to defend himself. During the trial he did not utter a word but, rather, issued a two-page statement after the Crown had finished its closing arguments. In the statement, he offered "advice" to the jury, begging them to repent for using Canadian law to judge him instead of the Quran. He added that as a man of science he knew that the Quran contains all scientific proofs. He asked the jury members to prepare themselves for Judgment Day.

Jaser immigrated to Canada with his parents in 1993 on fake French passports. The family's claim for asylum was rejected—they had lived in Germany where they claim a Molotov cocktail had been thrown into their house. Jaser was later convicted in Canada of fraud on five occasions, offenses for which he was later pardoned. An imam at a Toronto mosque claims that Jaser had spoken of the need to wage war against non-Muslims. Jaser's father had approached a religious scholar with concerns about his son's religious views. A second Toronto imam contacted the RCMP when he noticed Jaser trying to influence youth with extremist material.

For his part, Jaser believed that Islam was a conquering faith that forces itself on others. He saw himself as Allah's servant to defeat "wickedness," which he described as fornication and the consumption of alcohol. He did not believe in other faiths having the right to exist. In his words, Islam could "bulldoze the world."[8] He once discussed obtaining a sniper rifle to assassinate Canadian leaders.[9]

Esseghaier was believed to have had contact with a man living abroad known as "the responsible one." This individual reportedly suggested that Esseghaier hire a cook to poison a military base in Canada or the United States.[10]

In March 2015, both men were found guilty in a trial by jury on eight of nine charges (Esseghaier was found guilty on all five charges, Jaser on three of four).

Key Points

A number of elements in this case square with the indicators. Esseghaier and Jaser plotted against a target with little overt security and held intolerant religious views. Esseghaier showed a clear contempt for Canadian law and appeared to have ties to an overseas group. He was also misogynist and arrogant in his faith. Jaser arrogantly believed that his faith was superior to others.

The Canada Day Plot

On Canada Day 2013, the British Columbia division of the RCMP arrested two people in Abbotsford, British Columbia, on allegations of conspiracy to commit an act of terrorism. John Nuttall and Amanda Korody, both converts to Islam, were accused of preparing three pressure-cooker bombs on the grounds of the British Columbia Legislature in Victoria, timed to explode at 2 p.m., when the venue would be packed with those celebrating the national holiday. It is interesting that Nuttall and Korody's attack method was similar the Al Qaeda–inspired Tsarnaev brothers' at the 2013 Boston Marathon.

Nuttall had once been a heroin addict and was living on social assistance with Korody, his partner, who may also have had a drug addiction. There have also been allegations that Nuttall suffered from mental illness. The couple had been kicked out of a Surrey mosque for exhibiting "odd" religious behavior. Nuttall had been critical of his brother's time serving in the Canadian Armed Forces, believing that Canadian soldiers should not be "on Muslim soil." He further told an RCMP agent that he wanted to avenge what he believed was the Canadian military's mistreatment of Muslims abroad. He was active in paintball, posting on an online paintball forum as Muhajid. In response to an alleged online insult against the Prophet Muhammad, he called the person who had posted the comment a *kaffir* and a *mushrik* (one who practices *shirk*—idolatry) and tried to provoke a fight, saying he was ready to die as a *shahid* (martyr). A neighbor reported overhearing him yelling into a cell phone about jihad.

The two called themselves "Al Qaeda Canada" and mujahideen operating behind enemy lines. Nuttall believed he saw jinn (spirits) and the angel of death after mistakenly ingesting strychnine while trying to kill ants.

This case is the strongest one to date where aspects of mental health may be at play. John Nuttall appears to have had serious mental issues. His mother told reporters that he was suffering from post-traumatic stress disorder and had been certified under the Mental Health Act. Even if all this is true, it does not explain why the two radicalized; nor does it necessarily excuse them of the act of conspiracy to commit terrorism.

The pair was found guilty in June 2015, but the defense is planning to contest the finding on the grounds of entrapment.[11]

Key Points

This case underscores a number of elements: (1) the belief that Canadian soldiers are intent on killing Muslims and a desire to avenge these deaths, (2) a hardline view of Islam and intolerance for other belief systems, (3) a possible desire for martyrdom (it should be stressed that the terrorist act they are alleged to have planned was not a suicide mission), and (4) visions of end-times.

SUCCESSFUL ATTACKS IN CANADA

Martin Couture-Rouleau

On October 20, 2014, two members of the Canadian armed forces were struck by a vehicle in a parking lot in Saint-Jean-sur-Richelieu, Quebec (southeast of Montreal): one man, Warrant Officer Patrice Vincent, died of his injuries. The driver, Martin Couture-Rouleau, was chased by police, rolled his car into a ditch, emerged wielding a knife, and was shot, later succumbing to his wounds.

Couture-Rouleau was a convert to Islam who appeared to have an obsession with the Islamic State in Iraq and Syria. He was known to the RCMP and had even been designated a high-risk traveler—an individual who wanted to travel abroad to engage in violent jihad—and attempted to leave Canada in July 2014, only to have his passport seized (no charges were laid). Investigators later worked with his family and officials at a local mosque to try to divert Couture-Rouleau from his ideology and appeared to have succeeded (as recently as two weeks before the killing, Couture-Rouleau he indicated a desire to "change his life"). He owned a pressure washer company and owned a bungalow in Saint-Jean.

Friends described Couture-Rouleau as someone who used to like to party and play poker, extroverted and sociable. But this changed after his conversion, and he began spending a great deal of time online (likely on violent jihadi sites) and withdrew from his former associates. Other associates claimed that he wanted to die a martyr and even offered to finance the travel of friends to Afghanistan. On his Facebook page, Couture-Rouleau wrote that the Canadian military were pawns to be used in foreign policy.[12] He was allegedly angry that the Canadian government elected to participate in the campaign to bomb the Islamic State and had material praising violent jihad on Facebook. One post read, "Allah has promised the hypocrite men and hypocrite women and the disbelievers the fire of hell, wherein they will abide eternally. It is sufficient for them. And Allah has cursed them, and for them is an enduring punishment." There was also material that was anti-Semitic and anti-American in nature.[13]

Key Points

Couture-Rouleau is an excellent example of how the indicators can assist in identifying those on the pathway to extreme radicalization. Among the indicators we can see (1) anger at military policy, particularly Canada's decision to bomb the Islamic State, (2) an obsession with foreign conflict and attempt to travel, (3) dissociation from friends and acquaintances, (4) an unsuccessful attempt at deradicalization, (5) a desire for martyrdom, (6) an attempt to influence others to follow his ideology, (7) an obsession with violent jihad, and (8) clear anti-Semitism and denunciation of Christianity and Judaism.

Michael Zehaf-Bibeau

On October 22, 2014, Michael Zehaf-Bibeau of Montreal left a homeless shelter in Ottawa and fatally shot a Canadian reservist performing honor guard duties at the National War Memorial; he then entered the Centre Block of the Canadian parliamentary complex, engaging in gunfire before being killed by the sergeant at arms. Born in 1982, Zehaf-Bibeau was a convert to Islam who attended a private school where he "fit in" and was well liked; he was described by neighbors as a "sweet boy." He had a criminal record linked to drug possession, robbery, and uttering threats. He was allegedly a cocaine addict who sought help, at one point wanting to be incarcerated.[14] He was raised in Laval by a Francophone mother and a Libyan father who had allegedly fought against former Libyan leader Muʿammar Gaddhafi.[15]

Zehaf-Bibeau's passport had been taken away because of suspected jihadist sympathies[16]; he had allegedly told a friend that he wanted to go to Libya to study. It is alleged that he may have been mentally ill.[17] He also allegedly told a fellow resident at a downtown shelter in Ottawa to "pray because the world was ending" and made comments seen as "anti-Canadian."[18] It is important to note that this statement is not necessarily a sign of mental illness but could be an indication of Zehaf-Bibeau's belief in the end-time.[19] A psychiatrist in British Columbia assessed him to be "deeply troubled" but not mentally ill.[20]

Zehaf-Bibeau attended a mosque in Burnaby, British Columbia, where he was described as "rude." He allegedly was angry that the mosque was "open and welcoming." There were also unspecified "behavioral" changes.[21] He picked a fight over the mosque's outreach attempts, complaining that too many non-Muslims were visiting.[22] Mosque officials asked him to leave the premises over his behavior.[23]

The RCMP later found a video that Zehaf-Bibeau had made the day before his attack, in which he blamed Canada's foreign policy and praised Allah. He specifically stated that his actions were in retaliation for "Afghanistan and because Harper wants to send his troops to Iraq." Canada had become the enemy of the mujahideen, in his view, by "fighting and bombing us and creating a lot of terror in our countries and killing us and killing our innocents." Targeting soldiers in Canada was justified, he believed, to demonstrate that Canadians are not safe in their own country. Zehaf-Bibeau concluded his statement by warning that attacks would not stop until Canada and its allies ceased to occupy Muslim countries and stopped killing its citizens.

He angrily engaged an individual at a ServiceOntario outlet at an Ottawa mall, where he railed about the killing of civilians by soldier.[24] He allegedly used money he had made working in the Alberta oil sands to fund his plans. Zehaf-Bibeau's mother told officials that her son had claimed he wanted to travel to Saudi Arabia to study: it is unclear whether this statement was truthful, as it is possible it was his ruse to go to engage in violent jihad abroad. The RCMP also investigated his interactions with others prior to the attack to determine whether Zehaf-Bibeau was aided or encouraged to take action.[25]

It is uncertain whether Zehaf-Bibeau was a so-called "lone wolf."[26] He is alleged to have had online contact with Hasibullah Yusufzai, an Afghan-Canadian who left Canada for Syria in 2014 and who has been charged under the Combating Terrorism Act.[27] Yusufzai attended the same mosque in Burnaby as Zehaf-Bibeau, although it is unknown whether or not the two knew each other. Reports state that Zehaf-Bibeau followed the online postings of an Islamic State member from Canada, Abu Khalid Al-Kanadi, who calls for attacks in Canada.[28] As of the writing of this book, the RCMP investigation into Zehaf-Bibeau is continuing.[29]

The Islamic State, who lionized both Couture-Rouleau and Zehaf-Bibeau online for their actions,[30] later took credit for inspiring the attacks.[31]

Key Points

In a case that is strikingly similar to Couture-Rouleau's, Zehaf-Bibeau demonstrated a desire to travel to foreign conflict, an association with like-minded individuals, an obsession with online violence, apocalyptic views, and an intolerance for non-Muslims.

LEAVING CANADA TO FIGHT ABROAD

According to CSIS in 2014, at least 130 Canadians have left the country to engage in some form of violent Al Qaeda–inspired extremism or foreign conflict in which groups aligned with Al Qaeda ideology are involved. A few cases have been highlighted in the Canadian and international press.

Jabarah Brothers

Abdul Rahman and Mohammed Mansour Jabarah were Kuwaiti-born Muslims who had lived through the Iraqi occupation of their homeland in 1990 and 1991 and then moved to Canada with their parents in1994.[32] The family settled in St. Catharines, Ontario. The boys appeared to integrate well, learning English and associating with others in the small Muslim community in their new hometown. Their father raised them as observant Muslims.

Mohammed and Abdul Rahman made regular summer visits back to Kuwait, as their parents wanted them to maintain close links with their culture. During these trips, they would renew friendships, and on one visit they were introduced to Sulaiman Abu Ghaith, a cleric who taught that jihad was a duty for all Muslim men. Himself a veteran of the Bosnian War, Abu Ghaith used his battlefield experiences and propaganda videos to convince the Jabarahs of the need for action. Abu Ghaith was, in effect, a recruiter for Al Qaeda. Mohammed began to see others as infidels.

Back in Canada, the brothers' keenness for jihad only increased, and the Russian war in Chechnya appeared to galvanize them. They frequented online jihadi sites and watched extremist videos. In 2000, following a series of stopovers, they traveled to Afghanistan, where they received terrorist training. Mohammed pledged *bayat* to Al Qaeda leader Osama Bin Laden.[33]

Mohammed was then sent to Singapore to carry out a number of bomb attacks against Western targets. The plot was foiled, however, and Mohammed fled, first to Thailand and eventually to Dubai. Instructed by Al Qaeda to leave for Oman in 2002, Mohammed was arrested upon entry, eventually flown back to Canada and handed over to the United States. He was tried, convicted, and sentenced to life in prison. As of 2014 he is at the maximum-security prison in Colorado.

Abdul Rahman had a different fate. He traveled to Saudi Arabia in May 2002, joined an extremist group, and was accused by Saudi authorities of preparing attacks in the kingdom. He was killed in July 2003 by security forces in a shootout.

Key Points

The Jabarah brothers were obsessed with a foreign war (Chechnya), were recruited and manipulated by an extremist ideologue, pledged *bayat* to Osama Bin Laden, sought training in an extremist camp, and viewed the world as divided into believers and nonbelievers.

Vilyam (William) Plotnikov

According to the Canadian media, Vilyam (William) Plotnikov, a Russian immigrant to Canada, was killed in a battle with Russian security forces in Dagestan in July 2012.[34] Plotnikov had joined an Islamist extremist militia in the Caucasus. There are also unconfirmed reports that he may have met and associated with Tamerlan Tsarnaev, one of the two brothers accused of setting off the Boston Marathon bombs in April 2013.

We've already discussed some of Plotnikov's past. He converted to Islam in 2009, observed Ramadan, grew a beard, and eliminated pork from his diet. He withdrew from friends and family. Despite the family's Tatar origins (a largely Muslim group), Vilyam rejected his Christian baptism, stating that he had not asked to be baptized.

After returning to Toronto in 2010 after a vacation, Plotnikov's parents found a note their son had written, saying he had gone to France for Ramadan. Plotnikov ended up leaving France for Moscow, where, according to Russian officials, he was a self-professed mujahid, ready to fight. From Moscow he traveled to Dagestan, where he allegedly connected with extremists. His father contacted Russian security forces, who raided the house where Plotnikov was staying and ordered him to go back to Canada. Vilyam went to Moscow but soon returned to Dagestan, where he was subsequently killed. A jihadist site known as Kavkaz (Arabic for *Caucasus*) called Plotnikov a martyr.

Despite his lack of communication with his family, Plotnikov, it was learned, posed with assault rifles and called himself a terrorist who kills *kuffar*. He rejected the West as "garbage" and was confident that Allah would bless his plans.

Key Points

Plotnikov clearly demonstrated a complete rejection of non-Muslims, underwent an abrupt change in character, converted to Islam (possibly under the influence of an extremist preacher), had an obsession with foreign jihad, and ended up rejecting Western ways.

Project Darken

In 2010 Canadian media reported that three students from the University of Manitoba had dropped their studies without warning in the spring of 2007 and flown to Pakistan via Europe.[35] Maiwand Yar, Ferid Imam, and Muhanad Al Farekh—two Canadians and a Texan—were allegedly spotted in areas of Pakistan believed to house Al Qaeda extremists. The three were later listed on an RCMP wanted poster in conjunction with conspiracy to participate in terrorist activities in what is known as Project Darken.

Yar was born in Pakistan to Afghan refugees and immigrated to Canada with his family at the age of eight. He got into trouble at school, where he was allegedly a bully. He later became involved in drug trafficking and was arrested in 2013 for selling crack cocaine to an undercover police officer (the charges were later dropped). Yar was studying mechanical engineering at the University of Manitoba at the time of his arrest.

Imam had arrived in Winnipeg at the age of seven from East Africa and seemed to quickly integrate into a multicultural group of friends. He was apparently a devout Muslim but did not make an ostentatious display of his faith. Imam was in his final year of biochemistry at University of Manitoba in 2007. Al Farekh was a business student who grew up in the United Arab Emirates and was educated in Jordan. All three volunteered with the University of Manitoba Muslim Students Association.

After meeting Imam and Al Farekh, Yar grew out his beard, adopted traditional clothing, and appeared to have abandoned his wayward past. Imam became more forthcoming in his faith once at university, once posting online critical comments about those who made light of the Danish Muhammad cartoon affair.[36] In December 2006 the three jointly made the pilgrimage to Mecca.

Yar left a note for his brother, stating that he would not return and asking that his student loans be paid off.[37] His family filed a missing persons report. None of the three have since returned to Canada.

The RCMP has alleged that the three went to Pakistan for terrorist training. Information collected by US intelligence now publicly available states that Imam became a weapons instructor at a training camp in Peshawar. He is also alleged to have provided material support for terrorism and to have played a role in a 2009 plot to plant a bomb in the New York subway system, for which three US residents have been convicted.[38] In April 2015, Al Farekh was captured by Pakistani forces and flown to the United States for trial.[39]

The sudden and unexplained disappearance from Winnipeg has caused much distress within the Muslim community. Leaders have stated that the three showed no signs of radicalization. The trio appeared well integrated and involved in community events.

Key Points

The three Winnipeg residents departed Canada suddenly after a somewhat secretive radicalization process, criticized Muslims who disagreed with their views, were obsessed with a conflict zone (Pakistan), felt a desire to pay debts (in preparation for possible martyrdom), did not seek family permission to go for jihad, and left a letter (Yar) telling family of his decision to leave and noting that they would not see him again.

Canadian Somalis

A number of Canadians of Somali heritage are believed to have left Canada to join Al-Shabaab in Somalia. A few have died: Mahad Ali Dhore, a former student at York University, is alleged to have died in a suicide attack in Mogadishu in April 2013,[40] while Mohammed Elmi Ibrahim, also known as Canlish, was eulogized on an extremist site as having "died in battle" some-time in 2010.[41] Two Canadian Somali females are believed to have traveled to join Al-Shabaab in 2011.[42]

In what is proving a crucial test of new Canadian legislation makes it illegal to leave the country to join a terrorist group, Mohamed Hersi[43] was tried in a Brampton court in May 2014. He was accused of attempting to link up with Al-Shabaab. Hersi was arrested at Toronto Pearson International Airport in May 2011 as he was about to leave for London and Cairo. He had come to the attention of Toronto police in 2010 when a dry cleaner found a USB memory stick with bomb-making instructions in Hersi's security-guard uniform. The stick contained a copy of the *Anarchist's Cookbook* (a well-known guide to making explosives and other terrorist materials).

According to an undercover police agent, Hersi had admitted to befriending Canlish and the cousin of a man arrested for planning to bomb a shopping mall in Ohio. Hersi had advised the undercover officer on how to join Al-Shabaab and had allegedly spoken of the possibility of returning to Canada to "take care of" anyone who insulted the Prophet Muhammad. According to Hersi, a US woman who launched "Everyone Draw Mohammad Day" in response to a threat to kill the creators of a South Park episode in which the Prophet was depicted in a bear costume should be "taken down." He also provided advice on how to acquire guns and how to avoid raising the suspicion of authorities. Hersi was apparently a fan of Anwar al-Awlaki and Al-Shabaab leader Omar

Hammami, a US convert to Islam who lived in Toronto for a few years in the 2000s.

Hersi believed that it was "God's will" that he join Al-Shabaab and indicated that he wanted to make the "ultimate sacrifice." He wanted to leave Canada because he viewed it as anti-Islam and thought that all non-Muslims hate Islam. He described Canada as a "police state" targeting Muslims.

On May 30, 2014, Hersi was convicted of attempting to participate in terrorist activity and providing counsel to a person to participate in a terrorist activity.[44] In July 2014 he was sentenced to ten years in prison.[45]

Key Points

Hersi exhibited a hatred for Canada, held a strong belief in the narrative that non-Muslims hate Islam, may have had a desire for martyrdom, sought to punish those who insult Islam, wanted to perform hijra to get away from a non-Muslim land and was a big fan of Anwar al-Awlaki.

PARTICIPATING IN FOREIGN TERRORIST PLOTS

There have been three noteworthy cases in which radicalized individuals remained in Canada but contributed to plots abroad.

Momin Khawaja

Canada passed the Anti-Terrorism Act in December 2001 in the wake of the 9/11 attacks.[46] The first person arrested and charged under this act was Momin Khawaja, a contract computer programmer with the Canadian Department of Foreign Affairs, Trade and Development. Khawaja was accused of conspiracy to commit terrorism in conjunction with a UK cell that planned to detonate a six-hundred-kilogram bomb in London. He and his British coconspirators were arrested in separate operations in Canada and the UK in March 2004.

Khawaja traveled on several occasions to Pakistan, ostensibly to visit family. It has come to light that intelligence agencies in Canada and the UK believe that during these trips he attended a terrorist training camp, on one occasion with two members of the cell that carried out the London tube attacks on July 7, 2007. Khawaja returned to Canada and spent a lot of time online, reading and listening to material about the situation of Muslims in Chechnya and Palestine and the killing of innocent Muslim women and children. Together with a few friends he would play paintball in secluded spots, planning their outings under the code name *hockey*.

On one trip to Pakistan he met with the family of a woman he had met online and wished to marry. He was accompanied on that visit by Mohammed Junaid Babar, a Pakistani-American who would later plead guilty to terrorism charges but later cooperated with US and UK officials in the July 2005 terrorism investigations in London (the group that planned an attack similar to the July 7 bombers').

Khawaja traveled to the UK in February 2004, where he met with a UK terrorist cell headed by Omar Khyam. The cell was being monitored by UK security agencies, who witnessed Khawaja show his friends at an Internet café bombing materiel that he had created. The cell was broken up and its members arrested soon after that visit.

The trial for Khawaja was not held until 2008. He was found guilty on five of seven terrorism-related charges in October 2008 and sentenced to ten and a half years in prison in March 2009. Khawaja's defense lawyer claimed that his client had only wanted to fight allied soldiers in Afghanistan and knew nothing of the UK plot. Both the defense and the Crown appealed the verdict, and in December 2010 the Ontario Court of Appeal sentenced Khawaja to life in prison, in part due to his refusal to relinquish his extreme beliefs. He remains at the Special Handling Unit, a federal super-max prison in Sainte-Anne-des-Plaines, Quebec.

Key Points

According to available information, Khawaja (1) gave evidence of a sudden change in behavior, appearance, and ideology, (2) held a conviction that something had to be done to help oppressed Muslims, (3) traveled to a terrorist camp under false pretenses (visiting family), (4) believed in the narrative, and (5) has shown no signs of remorse or contrition.

Sayfildin Tahir Sharif

In January 2011, the RCMP arrested Tahir Sharif (also known as Faruq Khalil Muhammad 'Isa) in Edmonton following a joint RCMP-FBI investigation into a Tunisian foreign fighter–facilitation network. Tahir Sharif is accused of conspiracy to commit terrorism and of participation in several suicide attacks in Iraq in 2009 in which US soldiers were killed. The US government sought his extradition for trial in the United States. In October 2012 an Edmonton judge ruled that there was enough evidence to send Tahir Sharif to the United States, and he was extradited on January 23, 2015.[47]

Tahir Sharif, an ethnic Kurd, was born in Iraq and immigrated to Canada as a refugee in 1993, attaining citizenship in 1996. He worked in the construction industry and had a common-law relationship with a convert to

Islam. Although his partner originally told the Canadian media that Tahir Sharif was a kind and loving husband and father to her and her four children, she later told US authorities that the relationship was dysfunctional and that Tahir Sharif was controlling, dictating where she could go and with whom.

US officials allege that Tahir Sharif provided support to an extremist group and encouraged a woman in Morocco to travel to Iraq to partake in a suicide mission. He also expressed an interest in going to Iraq for similar purposes, and there are allegations he may have contemplated an attack in North America. Tahir Sharif confided to his mother that his greatest wish was to die a martyr and be greeted by "seventy virgins in paradise." He sent funds to mujahideen in Iraq, encouraging them to attack Americans.

Tahir Sharif reportedly was angry about the US invasion of Iraq and wanted to take revenge on the United States. He believed that he could support his brothers in Iraq from Canada if his efforts to travel were thwarted.

Key Points

Tahir Sharif (1) was obsessed with martyrdom, (2) was linked to an online extremist community, (3) acted as a radicalizer, encouraging others to engage in terrorism, (4) provided financial support to mujahideen in Iraq, (5) was angry about the US invasion of a Muslim county and desired to punish the United States, and (6) may have had a misogynous streak.

Said Namouh

Said Namouh, a resident of the small Quebecois community of Maskinongé, northeast of Montreal, was arrested in September 2007 in connection with a threat to bomb targets outside of Canada. A Moroccan-born permanent resident who arrived in Canada in 2003, Namouh was believed to be a member of the Global Islamic Media Front (GIMF), an international network of Al Qaeda sympathizers who translate and distribute extremist propaganda. Namouh was linked to an extremist cell in Austria that wanted to punish Austria and Germany for the presence of their troops in Afghanistan.

Although allegedly not a practicing Muslim in his native Morocco, Namouh's landlady in Maskinongé noted that he prayed regularly, abstained from alcohol, and refused to eat meals that were not halal. He had an online alter ego known as Ashraf (or "Achrafe" in French) on the GIMF website where he posted extremist messages. He posted support for a war between Islam and the infidels (also phrased a *war for existence*, a *war between right and wrong*, and a *war against tyranny*), reflections on his belief that the West seeks to eliminate Islam, and admonitions to Muslims who do not support jihad or the mujahideen. Namouh was also virulently anti-Shia. He had in his possession hundreds of videos and images of bomb-making materials and suicide packs.

Namouh was originally charged with conspiracy to cause death, but later charges were added, including participating in the activities of a terrorist group, facilitating terrorist activity, and committing an offense on behalf of a terrorist group. The cell with which he was associated was planning to explode a car bomb in Vienna and may have been targeting the 2008 UEFA European Football Championship in Austria and Switzerland, as well as planning attacks on large crowds and political figures.

Namouh's lawyer stated that his client was penniless and homeless (he had worked at a wood-processing plant) and that the Crown's charges were circumstantial. Nevertheless, Namouh was convicted on four terrorism-related charges in October 2009 and later sentenced to life in prison. Once he serves his sentence (a minimum of ten years in Canada), the Canadian government intends to deport him to his native Morocco.

Key Points

In his plans for terrorism, Namouh (1) desired to punish the West for its actions against Muslims, (2) believed strongly in the narrative, (3) held a strong hatred for Shia, (4) was obsessed with Al Qaeda–linked extremist websites, and (5) admonished Muslims who do not see jihad as necessary.

The In Amenas Attack

In January 2013, international media reported that two Canadians played a major role in a terrorist attack that resulted in at least forty deaths at a gas plant in southeastern Algeria that was manned by many foreign workers.[48] Among the dead, the bodies of Xristos Katsiroubas and Ali Medlej of London, Ontario, were identified by the RCMP in April. They had traveled to Morocco in 2011 and on to Mauritania and Mali, where they were allegedly trained by Mokhtar Belmokhtar, a North African terrorist linked to Al Qaeda in the Islamic Maghreb. A third Londoner, Aaron Yoon, was arrested in Mauritania and spent two years in jail on terrorism charges before returning to Canada in 2013.

Katsiroubas and Yoon were converts to Islam—Katsiroubas born into a Greek Orthodox household while Yoon's family was Korean Christian. Medlej's family immigrated to Canada from Lebanon. All three attended London South Collegiate Institute, where former classmates described them as average teenagers. Medlej played football, was a described as a bit of a bully, and had issues with authority at school. By the end of high school, he had slowly disassociated himself from the larger school community, dropped out of football, and began to limit his contacts to their clique of three. Katsiroubas converted to Islam in grade ten, and his mother began to have concerns about his choice of friends. Yoon's conversion to Islam occurred later, apparently under Medlej's influence.

After high school the trio became more overtly devout and eschewed post-secondary education for a move to Edmonton to find work. They were evicted from their apartment for causing damage, and court records point to a shoplifting offense. The three then traveled to Morocco and on to Mauritania where Yoon claimed to be studying Arabic and Islam. It is not clear how Katsiroubas and Medlej ended up participating and dying in the attack in Algeria.

Key Points

The London trio (1) disassociated themselves from former friends and activities, (2) trained with a terrorist group, and (3) had raised flags with their families over their behaviors.

THE SYRIAN FOREIGN FIGHTERS

Canadian officials have stated that at least thirty Canadians have left for Syria to join an extremist group or fight in the conflict in that country. Travel for fighting is not new in Canada: individuals have traveled to any number of war zones. The number and increased interest in Syria appears to be new, however. Information on some of those who have gone is publicly available. The following sections summarize what we know on three of the cases.

Damian Clairmont

In early 2014 Canadian media reported that a young man from Calgary had died fighting jihad in Syria.[49] Clairmont had attended a *musallah* (Islamic prayer center) in downtown Calgary where he studied Islam. His conversion to Islam was accompanied by a more worrisome set of changes: He tried to convince his best friend from childhood, a fellow Nova Scotian, to convert to Islam as well and criticized him for his lifestyle choices. He told his friend that he was "going down the wrong path." When his friend expressed an interest in joining the Canadian Armed Forces, Clairmont disagreed with the decision, stating that the Canadian military was killing Muslims. He was particularly upset at events in Syria and said that he wanted to do something to help.

Clairmont's mother also noticed changes in her son. He became secretive and argumentative. He subscribed to conspiracy theories about 9/11 and criticized the media for not telling the truth about what was happening to Muslims around the world. He started working out, joined a prayer group, and began to talk about going to a Muslim country to study Arabic.

Canadian security and law-enforcement agencies apparently believe there was at least one facilitator in Calgary who helped Clairmont along his radicalization path. *The National Post* has reported that several individuals in Calgary have traveled to Syria for jihad.

Damian told his mother of his plans to go to Cairo in November 2012. In actual fact, he flew to Istanbul and made his way to the Syrian border. There are reports that he joined the al-Nusra Front, an Al Qaeda affiliate in Syria. In correspondence with this mother and a *National Post* reporter, Clairmont claimed to be doing what was necessary and rejected suggestions that he was being exploited by extremists. According to Clairmont, women and children were being tortured in Syria. He criticized his former life in Canada as one where people "indulge in fornication and infidelity and stagger around poisoned on intoxicants." He extolled the benefits of the afterlife and wrote of his desire to become a martyr. He claimed to be engaged in "life-changing" work and to be growing in his new faith.

It was reported that Clairmont was killed near Aleppo, Syria, sometime in late 2013 or early 2014.

Key Points

In his short life, Clairmont (1) converted to Islam after a difficult youth and possible exposure to individuals with extreme ideology, (2) ended up rejecting the Canadian and Western lifestyle, (3) was intolerant of other views, (4) had some belief in conspiracy theories, (5) was convinced that Islam was under attack and no one was doing anything to save Muslims, and (6) was obsessed with foreign jihad.

Textbox 4.1

TERRORISM IN TIMMINS?

Timmins is a city in northeastern Ontario known for mining, forestry . . . and Shania Twain. The multiple Grammy Award winner for country music was born in Windsor but moved to Timmins as a child. The town even built a center in her name.

But Shania may no longer be Timmins's most famous citizen. Andre Poulin was born in Timmins, where he converted to Islam after a few run-ins with the local constabulary. He—well, let's let him tell his own story.

Textbox 4.1   Cont.

The following is a transcript of excerpts from a video posted online by the Islamic State in July 2014. In the first half, Poulin (now known as Abu Muslim) talks to the camera about his life in Canada and his decision to fight in Syria. Pictured with a weapon, and wearing a white bandana and fatigues, the boyish Poulin, sporting John Lennon–type glasses and a wispy beard, says

> I was like any other Canadian. I watched hockey. I went to the cottage in the summertime. . . . I liked outdoors, I liked sports. . . . But Allah guided me from the darkness of *kufr* [the infidel] to the light of *iman* [faith]. . . . Before I came to Syria, I had money, I had family, I had good friends. . . . I always had family to support me. . . . It's not like I was some kind of social outcast. . . . Life in Canada was good. . . . But at the end of the day it's still *Dar al-Kufr* [the world of the infidel]. . . . They [Canadians] use these taxes in their war on Islam. . . . [Contributions to the Islamic State] are obligatory on us. . . . There is no better land than Sham [Syria/Levant], so come and join.

Poulin went on to encourage others to travel to Syria to help the violent jihad, boasting that life was very good in the midst of a war zone.

Then a narrator comes on and says that Poulin was from the few of the few of the few. He is shown in battle, his body displayed on the battlefield.

The video lionizes Poulin and his commitment to the cause, sacrificing his life.

Ali Dirie

Ali Dirie is unique in the annals of Canadian terrorist history. He is the only person to date to have been convicted of a terrorist offense, served prison time, and been released, only to leave Canada to join a terrorist group overseas.[50]

Dirie was a member of the Toronto 18. He was arrested in August 2005 at the Fort Erie border crossing along with Mohamed Yassin when their rental car, which had been secured on a credit card belonging to Fahim Ahmad, was searched. Weapons were found in the car, and the two went on to be tried and convicted. Dirie maintained contact with Ahmad while in prison and used coded language to advise him on aspects of the Toronto 18 plot. He was reconvicted while still in prison when the group was arrested in June 2006 and served a total of seven years, some of which was at the Special Handling Unit in Quebec, Canada's super-max prison for its most dangerous inmates. He was released in 2011 and returned to Toronto. Dirie left Canada in 2012, possibly using a stolen passport, and ended up in Syria, where his death was reported in September 2013. He was alleged to have fought with Jabhat al-Nusra, a Syrian extremist group.

While in prison, Dirie actively tried to convert fellow inmates to Islam and talked about "dirty white people." This is not to suggest that conversion in itself ought to be considered a security concern: on the contrary, religion often serves as a protective and beneficial influence for those in prison. It does become problematic, however, when the person leading the conversion process is a convicted Al Qaeda–inspired extremist. Dirie told a parole-board hearing in 2010 that upon release his actions would "speak louder than words."

Dirie's story raises significant questions about the longevity of the threat from Al Qaeda–inspired extremists once the ideology takes hold. That is, Dire clearly neither was rehabilitated nor abandoned his violent ideology while in prison. In fairness, he did not undergo a programmed deradicalization process with a qualified religious instructor. Had he received such instruction, things may have turned out differently. We will return to the topic of deradicalization in chapter 5.

Key Points

Ali Dirie (1) demonstrated a clear singleness of purpose (keeping the fire of violent jihad burning while in prison and seeking to reengage after his release), (2) held a strong desire to join a foreign jihad, (3) separated society into us-versus-them, and (4) used subterfuge to travel in order to avoid scrutiny.

John Maguire

John Maguire was born in Kemptville—thirty minutes south of the nation's capital. And in what has become something of a trend, he was featured in an Islamic State video released in early December 2014.[51] In the video, Maguire alludes to his "normal" upbringing (like Andre Poulin, he mentions playing hockey) and comes across as an average Canadian young man. His message is anything but normal, however. He claims that the October 2014 attacks in Canada that killed Nathan Cirillo and Patrice Vincent were directly tied to Canada's role in the "war against Muslim people." His thinking went something like this: Canada is part of the global war on Islam and will suffer proportionately, and Canadians have no right to live in security when Muslims cannot. He cited the notion that jihad is an individual obligation for all Muslims and that Canada must be punished; those that do not submit to Islam will suffer damnation.

Maguire urged Muslims living in Canada to travel to live under the caliphate declared by the Islamic State (i.e., to perform hijra). He left his listeners them with the choice of hijra or jihad and encouraged them to emulate the example of Martin Couture-Rouleau (the killer of Patrice Vincent) and carry out attacks in Canada.

Despite being mocked in a series of articles in Canadian Press, Maguire's video repeats classic exhortations to engage in jihad and would appeal to some in Canada.

In mid-January 2015, an Islamic State Twitter user claimed that Maguire had been killed near Kobanî, a town on the Syrian border with Turkey.[52] Despite this alleged death, the RCMP charged Maguire with terrorism offenses in February 2015.[53]

Key Points

Like many extremists, Maguire (1) believed that the West is at war with Islam, (2) saw jihad as an individual obligation, (3) believed that true Muslims should perform hijra, (4) saw signs that the end-times (judgment day) were coming, (5) wanted Canada to be punished for its perceived anti-Islamic actions, and (6) feared that Canadian Muslims are living in *Dar al-Harb* [the house of war].

Farah Shirdon

People in Canada and around the world were introduced to Calgary resident Farah Shirdon through two online videos in 2014. In the first, Shirdon, the nephew of a former prime minister of Somalia and a student at the Southern Alberta Institute of Technology,[54] is seen burning his Canadian passport and boasting, "We are coming for you!"[55] Shortly after, despite rumors of his death, Shirdon gave a lengthy online interview to VICE News.[56] A summary of what he said is provided in the following:

- He was not "recruited."
- He refers to Canada and America as *tawaghit* (plural of *taghout*).
- He claims he made hijra and left comfort for Allah.
- He believes Islam's biggest enemies are the world, the coalition, and those fighting Islam.
- He hopes for many martyrdom operations.
- He is fighting because Muslims are not being "left alone."
- Muslims want to be free and to be able to live under sharia law.
- The *kuffar* are always attacking Muslims.
- Allah is on his side.

- Regimes such as Saudi Arabia and the United Arab Emirates are apostate.
- He expresses a desire for martyrdom ("I want *shahada*").
- Extremists are on the attack because they have been attacked.
- He makes a reference to *janna* (heaven) and *firdaus* (paradise).
- He boasts of future beheadings and the enslavement of women and children.

DISCUSSION

Having looked at a number of Canadians who have radicalized to violence and gone on to put their ideologies into action, it would be interesting to examine what, if any, similarities there are among them. Table 4.1 represents an initial attempt to compare the seventeen cases just discussed (measured as cases rather than as individuals) to see whether the twelve indicators were present in the radicalization-to-violence process.

In the table we see that each of the indicators is present at least once in these cases. Given that this comparison is based solely on open-source data (and that the accounts are not exhaustive), and given that it is likely there are other indicators in particular cases that have not been made public, the data strongly supports the conclusion that the twelve indicators are a useful tool in identifying those on the path to violent radicalization.

"WANNABES"

As noted, CSIS has stated publicly that it is engaged in several hundred ter-rorism investigations at any given time.[57] Assuming that the majority of these

Table 4.1

Indicator	Number
Sudden increase in intolerant religiosity/change in behavior	7
Intolerance for certain Muslim beliefs	1
Intolerance for non-Muslims	3
Rejection of Western ways	5
Rejection of Western policies	7
Change in social circles	5
Obsessive Internet use of violent sites	3
Obsession with foreign conflicts	4
Belief in the common narrative	6
Obsession with violent jihad	5
Obsession with martyrdom	6
Obsession with end-times	1

are tied to Al Qaeda—in keeping with the annual CSIS report which states that Al Qaeda–linked extremism is the Service's priority—this implies that a large number of people have neither been arrested nor left the country to join a terrorist group. So, the question remains, what are these people doing?

Practitioners term them *couch jihadis*. These people are radicalized and do support the use of violence, but, for a variety of reasons—perhaps lack of opportunity or motive or resources—have yet to act. Given that CSIS and the RCMP do not want to spend resources on individuals who may be unlikely to do anything, what *should* be done in these cases? I emphasize that there are reasonable grounds to suspect that these individuals are engaged in activity that poses a threat to national security. This suspicion is what CSIS uses, under its legislation, to launch an investigation. There are compelling reasons to not prolong investigations, however, ranging from a practical need to manage workload to the more serious requirement that the state not unreasonably subjects its citizens to intrusive investigation.

This is a vexing and challenging question. I stress once again, as I often have throughout this book, that there is no single process of violent radicalization. There is also no model predictive of who will move from advocating violent extremism to engaging in violent action. It is thus impossible, given the current state of knowledge and understanding, to determine who should be monitored and for how long. Obviously, if a person demonstrates a clear abandonment of violent extremism, they are no longer of immediate concern to either security or law-enforcement agencies. Caution must be exercised here, however, in that saying one no longer entertains extremist views does not mean one has truly abandoned them.

Getting this wrong has severe consequences. Hence, a constant re-evaluation and triage is required to determine where to allot precious few resources. Agencies are subject to review to assure that they are operating within their legislative mandates.

One of the most famous examples of a triage that went badly is the case of Mohammad Sidique Khan, ringleader of the July 7, 2005, attacks in London. Khan was on the radar of MI5, the UK's security intelligence service,[58] but went on to be judged "not essential" because there was no intelligence to suggest that he was planning an act of terrorism. This assessment turned out to be wrong.

Before proceeding, it is important to emphasize that saying that MI5 failed to determine the level of threat posed by Khan is *not* a criticism of the abilities or capabilities of MI5. The agency has to allot its resources in accordance with the competing priorities it encounters. MI5 cannot and surely would not want to look at everyone. They make the best decision at the time based on the best information available. In this case, an individual not believed to be an imminent threat turned out, unfortunately, to be exactly the opposite.

No one should be so smug as to suggest that the monitoring of violent extremists is easy or that deciding who poses the greatest danger is an obvious choice. Decisions are often made when exhaustive information is not available. Agencies make the best choices possible under the circumstances. It is hoped that those choices are the correct ones. There is never a guarantee, however: actions taken or not taken may not prevent a given act of terrorism from taking place.

DO CANADIAN AL QAEDA–INSPIRED EXTREMISTS POSE A THREAT TO OTHER COUNTRIES?

We have seen that Canada has been the target of individuals radicalized to violence in this country (Toronto 18, Samossa, etc.). But do these people pose a threat to other nations?

The simple answer is, obviously, yes. Canadians were involved in the In Amenas gas plant attack in Algeria, the planned attack in Southeast Asia, attacks in Riyadh, attacks in Somalia, and on and on. In light of the numbers of Canadians (and other Westerners) fighting in the Syrian Civil War, it would be surprising if some did *not* move on to acts of terrorism elsewhere once they quit the conflict.

For Canadian decision makers, however, there may be no greater fear than a Canadian link to an attack in the United States. The US-Canada economic relationship is of crucial economic importance to this country, and a successful plot in the United States perpetrated by a Canadian could be catastrophic to bilateral relations.

So, is this threat credible? US officials will often raise the specter of Ahmed Ressam, a Montreal-based extremist who was arrested at the British Columbia-Washington state border in December 1999 while on his way to Los Angeles International Airport where he planned to carry out a New Year's Eve attack. Some still claim that a few of the 9/11 hijackers came from Canada: in 2009, both former Secretary of Homeland Security Janet Napolitano and Senator John McCain repeated this inaccuracy.[59]

To my mind, the issue has been overblown. It has been used by many in the United States to criticize Canadian policies, ranging from immigration to security to multiculturalism. Canada is the United States' "porous" northern border in this narrative (and apparently of more concern that the southern Mexican border, through which hundreds of thousands of illegal migrants have moved to the United States). The truth is that today's Al Qaeda–inspired extremist is multinational. Individuals travel on multiple occasions to join groups, seek training, or engage in violent jihad. They can strike anywhere by taking advantage of international travel opportunities. Anyone can go anywhere. While it is entirely possible that a Canadian will cross the border into the United States to carry out an act, and the United States will probably remain a priority target for extremists for the foreseeable future, it is just as easy for US extremists to travel north. It is probably not a coincidence that members of the Toronto 18 began their plotting after a visit by Ehsanul Islam Sadequee and Syed Haris Ahmed, two Georgian (US) terrorists later arrested in the United States in the wake of the FBI's Northern Exposure investigation.[60]

SUMMARY

This chapter has provided a general overview of the major Al Qaeda–inspired terrorism cases in Canada since 9/11. I encourage the reader to consult the wealth of public material available for most of these cases for more information.

These incidents provide strong support of everything that has been discussed so far in this book with respect to Al Qaeda–inspired radicalization to violence in Canada. The individuals presented show that anyone from any background is susceptible to this phenomenon: men and women, immigrants and native-born, converts and born Muslims, married and single, highly educated and high school dropouts, people on social assistance and those with high-paying jobs. In other words, there is nothing to suggest a particular profile or checklist that could be used to isolate those at risk of violent radicalization.

We also saw the same themes over and over again: the narrative, the perceived oppression of Muslims, a rejection of life in the West, the belief that Islam forbids democracy, a fascination with foreign conflict, and so on.

Are there implications for future incidents? While it is impossible to predict whether Canada will face another attack, it is nevertheless likely that more individuals will radicalize to violence. Some may choose to act here and others abroad. I address this subject at greater length in chapter 6.

Now that we have described and explained radicalization at some length, it is time to consider what can be done to confront it. That is the subject of the next chapter.

NOTES

1. Steven Chase and Tu Thanh Ha, "Suspect in Quebec Attack Was Arrested by RCMP This Summer," *The Globe and Mail* (Toronto), last updated October 21, 2014, http://www.theglobeandmail.com/news/national/quebec-hit-and-run/article21187200/.

Isobel Teotonio "The Toronto 18," *The Toronto Star*, June 13, 2011, http://www3.thestar.com/static/toronto18/.

2. Chris Cobb, "Final Arguments to Be Heard in Sher Trial," *Ottawa Citizen*, last updated March 20, 2014, http://ottawacitizen.com/news/local-news/final-arguments-to-be-heard-in-sher-trial; Chris Cobb "Trip to Park Wasn't 'Training Camp,'" *Ottawa Citizen*, April 5, 2014; Colin Freeze, "Domestic Terror Group Was Building Bombs, Police Say," *The Globe and Mail* (Toronto), last updated August 23, 2010, http://www.theglobeandmail.com/news/national/domestic-terror-group-was-building-bombs-police-say/article1378351/; "Three Terrorism Suspects Charged in Ontario Court; Docs Name More Suspects," Canadian Press, August 26, 2010; "Fourth Man Charged in Terror Case Remains in Custody on Unrelated Charge," Canadian Press, August 29, 2010; Canadian Press, "Terror suspect Ahmed granted bail after relatives post $625K in bonds," CP24, September 28, 2010, http://www.cp24.com/terror-suspect-ahmed-granted-bail-after-relatives-post-625k-in-bonds-1.557385; Canadian Press, "Doctor arrested in terror plot gets bail under strict conditions," *Toronto Star*, October 13, 2010, http://www.thespec.com/news-story/2173480-doctor-arrested-in-terror-plot-gets-bail-under-strict-conditions/; Tony Spears, "Accused Terror Doc 'Groomed' for Violence: Defence," *St. Thomas Times-Journal*, March 31, 2014, http://www.stthomastimesjournal.com/2014/03/31/defence-argues-dr-khurram-syed-sher-had-no-clue-his-friend-had-gone-to-the-dark-side; QMI Agency, "'Right-Hand Man' Sought Explosives: Crown," *The Calgary Sun*, May 15, 2014.

3. Andrew Seymour, "'It Feels Great,'" *Ottawa Citizen*, August 20, 2014, http://www2.canada.com/ottawacitizen/news/city/story.html?id=430b016e-48cb-4e7d-8c6d-34c826be8dff.

4. Chris Cobb, "Misbahuddin Ahmed Sentenced to 12 Years for Terrorism Crimes," *Ottawa Citizen*, last updated October 24, 2014, http://ottawacitizen.com/news/local-news/misbahuddin-ahmed-sentenced-to-12-years-for-terrorism-crimes.

5. Nazim Baksh and Adrienne Arsenault, "Terrorism-Related Charges Laid against Ottawa Men with Alleged ISIS Ties," CBC News, last updated February 3, 2015, http://www.cbc.ca/news/canada/3-ottawa-men-with-alleged-isis-ties-face-terrorism-related-charges-1.2943313.

6. Reuters, April 22, 2013; *The Toronto Star*, April 23, 2013; *The Toronto Star*, May 1, 2014; *The Globe and Mail* (Toronto), April 23, 2013; CTV, April 26, 2013; CBC News, May11, 2013; CBC News, April 26, 2013; *National Post* (Toronto), March 21, 2014; *National Post* (Toronto), March 12, 2014; *Canadian Press*, April 24, 2013; *Canadian Press*, June 4, 2013; *L'Acadie Nouvelle*, March 15, 2014.

7. *National Post* (Toronto), February 7, 2015.

8. *The Toronto Star*, February 6, 2015.

9. *Montreal Gazette*, February 3, 2015.

10. *National Post* (Toronto), February 7, 2015.

11. "John Nuttall, Amanda Korody Found Guilty in BC Legislature Bomb Plot," CBC News, last updated June 4, 2015, http://www.cbc.ca/news/canada/british-columbia/john-nuttall-amanda-korody-found-guilty-in-b-c-legislature-bomb-plot-1.3094670.

12. Peritz, Ingrid, Tu Thanh, Ha and Perreaux, "Les Martin Couture-Rouleau's shift into extremism played out on social media." *The Globe and Mail*. Tuesday, October 21, 2014. Last updated Wednesday, October 22, 2014. http://www.theglobeandmail.com/news/national/extremism-in-canadas-borders/article21217185/.

13. Mark Gollom and Tracey Lindeman, "Who Is Martin Couture-Rouleau?" CBC News, last updated October 22, 2014, http://www.cbc.ca/news/canada/who-is-martin-couture-rouleau-1.2807285.

14. Rhiannon Coppin, "Michael Zehaf-Bibeau, Ottawa Gunman, Asked B.C. Judge to Send Him to Jail," CBC News, last updated October 24, 2014, http://www.cbc.ca/news/canada/british-columbia/michael-zehaf-bibeau-ottawa-gunman-asked-b-c-judge-to-send-him-to-jail-1.2810683.

15. "Michael Zehaf-Bibeau, Slain Ottawa Shooter, Had Criminal Record in Quebec, B.C.," CBC News, last updated October 23, 2014, http://www.cbc.ca/news/canada/montreal/michael-zehaf-bibeau-slain-ottawa-shooter-had-criminal-record-in-quebec-b-c-1.2809562.

16. "Ottawa Shootings: Canada Not Intimidated Says PM Harper," BBC News, October 23, 2014, http://www.bbc.com/news/world-us-canada-29735163.

17. "Ottawa Shooting: The Victim and the Sergeant-at-Arms," BBC News, October 23, 2014, http://www.bbc.com/news/world-us-canada-29736853; Andrew Seymour and Glen McGregor, "Shooter Zehaf-Bibeau Was Staying at Ottawa Mission Before Rampage: Witnesses," *Ottawa Citizen*, last updated October 23, 2014, http://ottawacitizen.com/news/national/shooter-zehaf-bibeau-was-staying-at-ottawa-mission-before-rampage-witnesses.

18. Dean Beeby, "Ottawa Shooting: Michael Zehaf-Bibeau Not among 90 Being Probed, RCMP Say," CBC News, last updated October 24, 2014, http://www.cbc.ca/news/politics/ottawa-shooting-rcmp-update-probe-into-gunman-s-attack-1.2810113.

19. See indicator #12 in chapter 4.

20. Mark Hume, "Previous Assessment Described Ottawa Shooter as Deeply Troubled but Not Mentally Ill," *The Globe and Mail* (Toronto), last updated October 23, 2014, http://www.theglobeandmail.com/news/national/previous-assessment-described-ottawa-shooter-as-deeply-troubled-but-not-mentally-ill/article21277933/.

21. Rhiannon Coppin, "Michael Zehaf-Bibeau, Ottawa Gunman, Asked B.C. Judge to Send Him to Jail," CBC News, last updated October 24, 2014, http://www.cbc.ca/news/canada/british-columbia/michael-zehaf-bibeau-ottawa-gunman-asked-b-c-judge-to-send-him-to-jail-1.2810683.

22. Andrea Woo, "Burnaby Mosque in Spotlight after Ottawa Attack," *The Globe and Mail* (Toronto), last updated October 24, 2014, http://www.theglobeandmail.com/news/british-columbia/burnaby-mosque-in-spotlight-after-ottawa-attack/article21306810/.

23. "Michael Zehaf-Bibeau Was Asked to Leave Burnaby, B.C., Mosque," CBC News, last updated October 25, 2014, http://www.cbc.ca/news/canada/british-columbia/michael-zehaf-bibeau-was-asked-to-leave-burnaby-b-c-mosque-1.2812206.

24. Ottawa Citizen, October 29, 2014.

25. "Ottawa Shooting: Michael Zehaf-Bibeau Made Video, Police Say," CBC News, last updated October 27, 2014, http://www.cbc.ca/news/politics/ottawa-shooting-michael-zehaf-bibeau-made-video-police-say-1.2813798.

26. See chapter 6 for a few thoughts on the lone-wolf concept.

27. Jason Hanna and Dana Ford, "Sources: Ottawa Gunman Had Ties to Jihadists," CNN, October 23, 2014, http://www.cnn.com/2014/10/23/world/ottawa-shooting/index.html.

28. Stewart Bell, "Gunman Heard Extremist's Call," *National Post* (Toronto), October 25, 2014, available online at http://www.pressreader.com/canada/national-post-latest-edition/20141024/281492159579746/TextView.

29. "Commissioner Paulson's Appearance at SECU on the Zehaf-Bibeau Video," Royal Canadian Mounted Police (website), March 3, 2015, http://www.rcmp-grc.gc.ca/news-nouvelles/speeches-stat-discours-decl/2015/03-05-eng.htm.

30. "Canadian, Foreign Jihadists Comment on Attacks in Canada, Call for Further Attacks," SITEIntelGroup.com, n.d., http://ent.siteintelgroup.com/Jihadist-News/canadian-foreign-jihadists-comment-on-attacks-in-canada-call-for-further-attacks.html (registration required).

31. Stewart Bell, "ISIS Takes Credit for Inspiring Terrorist Attacks That Killed Two Canadian Soldiers," *National Post* (Toronto), last updated January 24, 2015, http://news.nationalpost.com/2014/11/21/isis-takes-credit-for-inspiring-terrorist-attacks-that-killed-two-canadian-soldiers/.

32. The details provided here are derived from *The Martyr's Oath*, *National Post* writer Stewart Bell's book on a case of homegrown Al Qaeda terrorism in Canada (Mississauga, Ont.: J. Wiley and Sons Canada, 2005).

33. See chapter 3 for a discussion on the notion of *bayat*.

34. *National Post* (Toronto), August 12, 2012.

35. Greg McArthur, Patrick White, Joe Friesen, Christie Blatchford, Martin Youssef, and Colin Freeze, "Folio: The Lost Boys of Winnipeg," *Globe and Mail* (Toronto), October 1, 2010, http://beta.images.theglobeandmail.com/static/folio/drone/LostBoys2010.PDF; Patrick White, Colin Freeze, and Joe Friesen, "Terrorism Probe of Trio Shocks Muslims," *Globe and Mail* (Toronto), October 2, 2010; Steven Chase and Patrick White, "Be on Lookout for Radicalized Youth, Toews Says," *Globe and Mail* (Toronto), October 4, 2010; Chris Kitching/*Winnipeg Sun*, "Vanished in Pakistan," *Toronto Sun*, last updated October 1, 2010, http://www.torontosun.com/news/winnipeg/2010/10/01/15555471.html; Steve Lambert, "Three Muslim Students Have Gone Missing, CSIS Searching, Says Muslim Group," *Canadian Press* (Toronto), October 2, 2010; Douglas Quan, "Westerners Training as 'Foreign Fighters' a Growing Threat, Says Study," *Postmedia News*, October 2, 2010; Nick Martin and Bruce Owen, "Missing Students Joined Jihad According to CSIS," *Winnipeg Free Press*, October 2, 2010, http://www.winnipegfreepress.com/local/missing-students-joined-jihad-according-to-csis-104200139.html; Mary Agnes Welch, "Wake-Up Call for Muslim Community," *Winnipeg Free Press*, October 2, 2010, http://www.winnipegfreepress.com/local/wake-up-call-for-muslim-community-104200164.html; "Manitoba RCMP Lay Terrorism-Related Charges," *Winnipeg Free Press*, March 15, 2011, http://www.winnipegfreepress.com/breakingnews/RCMP-investigating-terrorism-117995989.html; Mike McIntyre, "NYC Bomb-Plot Trial Begins," *Winnipeg Free Press*, April 4, 2012, http://www.winnipegfreepress.com/local/nyc-bomb-plot-trial-begins-146059995.html; "Maiwand Yar," Royal Canadian Mounted Police (website), last modified March 29, 2011, http://www.rcmp-grc.gc.ca/en/wanted/maiwand-yar.

36. In 2005 the Danish newspaper *Jyllands-Posten* published twelve cartoons of the Prophet Muhammad, a perceived insult to Islam that led to riots worldwide and several foiled terrorist plots in Denmark.

37. Patrick White, Colin Freeze, and Joe Friesen, "Winnipeg Muslims Shocked Local Trio Target of Global Terrorism Probe," *Globe and Mail* (Toronto), last updated August 23, 2012, http://www.theglobeandmail.com/news/national/winnipeg-muslims-shocked-local-trio-target-of-global-terrorism-probe/article4190408/.

38. Stewart Bell, "Muhamad Mahmoud Al Farekh, Former University of Manitoba Student, Charged with Supporting Terrorism," *National Post* (Toronto), last updated April 2, 2015, http://news.nationalpost.com/news/canada/muhanad-mahmoud-al-farekh-former-university-of-manitoba-student-charged-with-supporting-terrorism.

39. Adam Goldman and Tim Craig, "American Citizen Linked to al-Qaeda Is Captured, Flown Secretly to U.S.," *Washington Post*, April 2, 2015, http://www.washingtonpost.com/world/national-security/american-citizen-suspected-of-being-al-qaeda-member-captured-brought-to-us/2015/04/02/48e8cc4c-d89c-11e4-8103-fa84725dbf9d_story.html.

40. Stewart Bell, "Canadian Linked to Terrorist Group Was Killed in Suicide Attack in Somalia: Community Source," *National Post* (Toronto), April 15, 2013, http://news.nationalpost.com/2013/04/15/canadian-linked-to-terrorist-group-was-killed-in-suicide-attack-in-somalia-community-source/.

41. Alex Ross, "Missing Student 'Killed in Battle' for Somali Militia," *The Varsity* (Toronto), March 22, 2010, http://thevarsity.ca/2010/03/22/missing-student-%E2%80%98killed-in-battle%E2%80%99-for-somali-militia/.

42. Raveena Aulakh and Isabel Teotonio, "Somali Terrorists Lure Toronto Women," *The Toronto Star*, April 1, 2011, http://www.thestar.com/news/gta/2011/04/01/somali_terrorists_lure_toronto_women.html.

43. *The Toronto Star*, March 30, 2011; *The Globe and Mail* (Toronto), March 30, 2011; *National Post* (Toronto), April 2, 5, 11, 29, and 30, 2014, May 7, 2014.

44. "Toronto Man Convicted of Terrorism Charges, Setting Canadian Precedent," CBC News, last updated May 30, 2014, http://www.cbc.ca/news/canada/toronto/toronto-man-convicted-of-terrorism-charges-setting-canadian-precedent-1.2659864.

45. CBC News, July 24, 2014.

46. *The Globe and Mail* (Toronto), March 31, 2004; *The Globe and Mail* (Toronto), May 23, 2006; *The Globe and Mail* (Toronto), May 1, 2007; *The Globe and Mail* (Toronto), October 29, 2008; *The Globe and Mail* (Toronto), December 18, 2010; Postmedia News, January 35, 2012, Postmedia News, May 4, 2013; *The Canadian Press* (Toronto), April 2, 2004; *The Canadian Press* (Toronto), March 12; *The Canadian Press* (Toronto), April 14, 2009; *National Post* (Toronto), April 15, 2004, December 21, 2005; *Fifth Estate* (television program), January 12, 2005; *Ottawa Citizen*, June 23, 2008; *Ottawa Citizen*, April 10, 2009; *Ottawa Sun*, February 6, 2009.

47. Thomson Reuters, "Canadian Sayfildin Tahir Sharif Extradited to U.S. to Face Terror Charges," CBC News, last updated January 23, 2015, http://www.cbc.ca/news/canada/edmonton/canadian-sayfildin-tahir-sharif-extradited-to-u-s-to-face-terror-charges-1.2930365.

48. *The Globe and Mail* (Toronto), April 6, 2013; *National Post* (Toronto), April 6, 2013; *The Toronto Star*, April 2, 2013.

49. *National Post* (Toronto), January 15, 2014; *National Post* (Toronto), April 26, 2014.

50. Michelle Shephard, "Toronto 18: Ali Mohamed Dirie, Convicted in Plot, Dies in Syria," *The Toronto Star*, June 13, 2011, http://www.thestar.com/news/gta/2013/09/25/toronto_18_ali_mohamed_dirie_convicted_in_plot_dies_in_syria.html.

51. "Canadian IS Fighter Calls Countrymen to Execute Lone-Wolf Attacks or Travel to Join Group," SITEIntelGroup.com, December 7, 2014, http://ent.siteintelgroup.com/Multimedia/canadian-is-fighter-calls-countrymen-to-execute-lone-wolf-attacks-or-travel-to-join-group.html (registration required).

52. Stewart Bell and Adrian Humphries, "Canadian Extremists Paying the Price, with Six Reported Dead over the Past Two Months," *National Post* (Toronto), last updated January 14, 2015, http://news.nationalpost.com/2015/01/14/pro-isis-twitter-account-claims-canadian-who-started-in-video-threatening-attacks-back-home-is-dead/.

53. Bruce Campion-Smith and Michelle Shephard, "RCMP Charge John Maguire and Two Others in Terror Investigation," *The Toronto Star*, February 3, 2015, http://www.thestar.com/news/canada/2015/02/03/rcmp-to-announce-terrorism-arrest-and-charges-at-3-pm.html.

54. "Farah Mohamed Shirdon of Calgary Fighting for Islamic State of Iraq and Syria," CBC News, last updated June 19, 2014, http://www.cbc.ca/news/canada/farah-mohamed-shirdon-of-calgary-fighting-for-islamic-state-of-iraq-and-syria-1.2680206.

55. Stewart Bell, "New Details about Canadian Jihadist Farah Shirdon Reveal Militant Ideology behind ISIS," *National Post* (Toronto), last updated January 24, 2015, http://news.nationalpost.com/2014/10/07/new-details-about-canadian-jihadist-farah-shirdon-reveal-militant-ideology-behind-isis/.

56. Jesse Tahiralli, "'Dead' Canadian Jihadist Reappears to Warn of 'Attacks in New York,'" CTV News, September 25, 2014, http://www.ctvnews.ca/canada/dead-canadian-jihadist-reappears-to-warn-of-attacks-in-new-york-1.2025277.

57. This according to 2012 testimony by then-CSIS director Richard Fadden to a Senate special committee on anti-terrorism. "Proceedings of the Special Senate Committee on Anti-terrorism, Issue 2, Evidence, Meeting of April 23, 2012," Parliament of Canada (website), April 23, 2012, http://www.parl.gc.ca/content/sen/committee/411/ANTR/02EV-49469-e.HTM.

58. Duncan Gardham, "7/7 Inquest: Mohammed Sidique Khan on MI5's Radar Before 9/11," *The Telegraph* (London), May 6, 2011, http://www.telegraph.co.uk/news/uknews/terrorism-in-the-uk/8497204/77-inquest-Mohammed-Sidique-Khan-on-MI5s-radar-before-911.html.

59. Lee-Anne Goodman, "9/11 Terrorists Came from Canada, McCain Insists," *The Toronto Star*, April 24, 2009, http://www.thestar.com/news/world/2009/04/24/911_terrorists_came_from_canada_mccain_insists.html.

60. "The Path to Terror: The Jihadists of Georgia, Part 1," Federal Bureau of Investigation (website), December 15, 2009, http://www.fbi.gov/news/stories/2009/december/jihadists_121509.

Chapter 5

Where Do We Go from Here?

FROM RECKLESSNESS TO REMORSE? SAAD KHALID

Serving a twenty-year sentence for his part in the Toronto 18 plot, Saad Khalid engaged in an exchange of letters with the CBC over a six-month period in 2013 and 2014 from his prison cell in Millhaven, a maximum-security prison in Ontario. In these letters, Khalid noted he immigrated to Canada from Pakistan at the age of eight and lived a typical middle-class life in Mississauga. Following his mother's sudden death, he began to hang around other Muslims at his high school and eventually became more religious, leading Friday prayers. He went on to university, where he discovered the lectures of Anwar al-Awlaki and became "hooked." He felt he had an obligation to do something, to engage in jihad. The rest is history: he became involved with others in the Toronto 18 cell and was arrested on June 2, 2006, while unloading three tons of fertilizer into a storage shed.

Having had almost a decade to think about his actions, Khalid wrote to the CBC that he didn't hate Canada or Canadians but Canadian foreign policy—specifically, our military presence in Afghanistan. He became convinced that he could make a difference in Canada and that violence was the answer.

Khalid stated that he now sees how wrong and "abhorrent" his actions were. He wants to work at his rehabilitation and eventual reintegration into the world, postprison. He hopes to be a productive member of Canadian society one day.[1]

CHAPTER ABSTRACT

In this chapter we examine some possible responses to violent radicalization. We will examine "soft" and "hard" measures, ranging from early intervention in what has been called the *precriminal* space to counter-radicalization, investigation, arrest and incarceration, and deradicalization. We will critique a number of programs ongoing in Canada and around the world.

Assuming that the threat from Al Qaeda–inspired terrorism is active, it is important that we ask what Canada can do and what is already being done to deal with violent radicalization and individuals engaged in extremist activity. There are several possible answers that depend on the stage individuals and groups are at in the radicalization-to-violence process.

I have already noted that the phenomenon of radicalization to violence in Canada is a problem, albeit one that appears, to the best of our available knowledge, to affect a very small number of Canadians. If we conclude that this problem is serious enough to warrant a response at multiple levels of Canadian society (both governmental and nongovernmental)—and that conclusion is debated by some—we need to decide what that response should be. Does the response necessitate huge influxes of cash? How does this problem compare with other problems requiring equal or greater amounts of money?

Other countries have considered this issue and have developed strategies and programs to deal with it. The strategies vary from country to country and range from early intervention to the deradicalization of convicted terrorists in prison. There is much literature on these efforts available to the public. Even if lessons can be drawn from the experiences and best practices of other nations, it is best to create a "made in Canada" plan that addresses Canada's particular circumstances.

From a Canadian perspective, the approaches to the radicalization problem can be divided into three broad categories: (1) security and law-enforcement action, (2) counter-radicalization, and (3) deradicalization. All three seek to either prevent acts of violence from occurring or to deal with radicalized individuals once they have been stopped or incarcerated for planned or successful attacks. In addition, all three have advantages and disadvantages and important implications for greater society.

In this chapter, we examine each approach, including their policy and operational perspectives. I must stress that, as radicalization is an individual process, so is the attempt to prevent or undo it. It is very unlikely that there is a one-size-fits-all model, although, just as in radicalization, there are probably general underlying principles that apply in the majority of cases.

APPROACH 1: SECURITY AND LAW-ENFORCEMENT ACTION

Seeing radicalization to violence as primarily a security and law-enforcement issue is the easiest approach. It is also the one that Canada has relied upon most frequently to date. Both the Canadian Security Intelligence Service and the Royal Canadian Mounted Police cite Al Qaeda–inspired violent extremism (recall that radicalization is the precursor and feeder to violent extremism) as the single greatest national security threat, and they devote a large number of resources to thwarting it. It is also beyond doubt that the agencies are doing so successfully in Canada. Most of the plots directed inside the country have been detected and neutralized. On the foreign-fighter front, the success rate has not been as high, for a variety of reasons (lack of exit controls, lack of intelligence, greater acceptance in communities that the fight is valid, etc.). The recent conviction in the Mohamed Hersi case may make it easier to prosecute those intent on joining groups abroad.[2]

Both agencies are clearly doing a lot that works. The Toronto 18 case and the Via Rail plot both demonstrated that getting a human source or agent right up against a terrorist cell is within the capability of Canada's security and law-enforcement partners. Cells and individuals have been investigated, monitored, followed, and neutralized to the point where they no longer pose a threat to Canada. The right combination of human intelligence, communications intercept obtained under federal court warrant, and surveillance has clearly led to success.

But what of the "failures"? Are the responsible agencies not doing everything possible to stop people from carrying out terrorist acts? The available information paints a less-clear picture.

If we start with the so-called "foreign fighter" issue, it is evident that many of the individuals who left Canada to join terrorist groups or engage in terrorist acts were known to either CSIS or the RCMP. So, why were they allowed to leave? The reasons are complex. CSIS of course does not have the power to stop anyone from doing anything (it has no law-enforcement powers and was harshly criticized by the Security Intelligence Review Committee in 2010 for engaging in "disruptions,"[3] although this power was granted to the service in 2015 in the proposed bill C-51[4]). The agency collects intelligence and can disclose or advise the RCMP when intelligence points to criminal activity. The RCMP, on the other hand, can arrest individuals and disrupt criminal activity. So, again, why are known radicals allowed to leave Canada to engage with terrorist organizations abroad?

In many cases, it is not clear that the individual in question is engaged in criminal activity (not surprisingly, not everybody writes on Facebook about their intentions to join Al Qaeda). Perhaps the investigation has not have progressed to a point where there is a critical mass of evidence that can be used in court. In addition, as good as our agencies are, they are not everywhere and do not have the resources to devote to every investigation. Sometimes there is simply not enough information to go on—there are always gaps that cannot be easily filled (not every investigation lends itself to the use of a human source, for example). The measures contained in the Canadian government's

Bill C-51 seek to provide the CSIS and the RCMP with additional tools to help close these gaps and stop extremists from leaving the country.

Even when everything possible is done, it is on occasion still inadequate. Let's turn to the two attacks in Canada in October 2014. Martin Couture-Rouleau had had his passport seized, had been counseled by religious leaders and the RCMP, and had led officials to believe that he was aware of the mistakes and poor decisions he had made. And yet he still was able to kill Warrant Officer Patrice Vincent. Had a surveillance team been following him on October 20, it is still not certain that law enforcement would have been able to stop his terrorist attack. The CBC reported in January 2015 that the RCMP had tried to restrict his movements weeks before he killed Vincent, but prosecutors said they hadn't had enough evidence to obtain a peace bond (which would have restricted his movements).[5]

As for Michael Zehaf-Bibeau, who killed Corporal Nathan Cirillo in an attack on Parliament Hill, it is still unclear what could have been done to stop him. How much was already known at the time of his attack and what was already being done in his particular case may never be made public.

While the foiling of plots has generally been a success at one level (only two people have died of terrorist-related attacks on Canadian soil), on another level it constitutes a failure. Individuals who otherwise may have been contributing members of society are in prison, dead, or saddled for life with the reputation of being a terrorist. Families of extremists are left to deal with the loss of a son or daughter who has been killed or is in jail. Communities are faced with accusations that their members are terrorists. Unhelpful factions label all Muslims potential terrorists, leading to intercommunity tension and the undermining of Canadian multiculturalism.

Security and law-enforcement agencies are in the business of stopping terrorism, not specifically stopping radicalization. Nor should they be expected to lead someone off the path to violence, since they may not be qualified to address the issues that may have led to the radicalization itself. Do we as a society want the CSIS or the RCMP—or the government of Canada, for that matter—to engage the young on religious or political issues? There are undoubtedly among us people better qualified to perform these tasks.

At the same time, however, it should be recognized that both agencies know a great deal about radicalization. Over the course of an investigation, they learn about an individual's particular pathway, some of which may be disclosed in the event of a court case, but much of which will remain hidden. Some of this knowledge has been made available to the larger Canadian public through access to information requests and through newspaper articles. Much more undoubtedly exists, gained through intelligence operations that may include human sources or agents and intercepted communications.[6]

One of the difficulties or challenges for the CSIS mainly and the RCMP to a certain extent in raising radicalization awareness is the lack of trust and understanding of these agencies' mandates—particularly challenging in the case of the CSIS. As government agencies entrusted with national security files, they investigate, advise, and—in the case of the RCMP—arrest people engaged in threatening activities. Some in Canada would prefer that these bodies pass on their suspicions to community leaders to deal with these matters rather than proceed with actions that could lead to arrests and prison. While this is, in theory, a viable approach, which will be developed in more detail in the next section, there are nevertheless cases where an individual or group has advanced along the radicalization trajectory so far that some kind of state corrective action is required. Believing that in all events a person needs only a talking-to to convince them of the error of their ways is naive at best. Sometimes a criminal threshold has been crossed and legal action must be taken. As the RCMP noted in Alberta in March 2015 after the arrest of an alleged foreign fighter in Edmonton, "While early intervention is our primary approach, after assessment, arrests and charges may be the only option in the interest of public safety. This also ensures that the individual has access to necessary support and assessment services."[7]

In addition, the best efforts and intentions of well-meaning community members and leaders are not guaranteed to succeed. Some extremists will ignore or reject interventions by others in the community. In May 2014, a Canadian fighting in Syria posted to a blog that Irshad Manji, Robert Heft, Syed Soharwardy, Tarek Fatah, Toronto 18 source Mubin Shaikh, and other Canadian Muslims opposed to extremist violence are "deviant" and "sell-outs."[8] In such, community intervention would have little to no effect.

It must be noted that communities may not always cooperate in identifying potential extremists to law enforcement and security officials or other government agencies (public health, community resources, etc.). The reasons for this reluctance range from denial (i.e., "There is no problem") to fear ("I don't want my son to get arrested") to distrust of authority. If the only solution is some type of state sanction, rather than counselling, the hesitation to inform is understandable. However, the October 2014 attacks demonstrated that inaction can lead to needless deaths in Canada. Communities aware of individuals who appear to be heading down a path of radicalization to violence need to take some type of action, if only to speak with fellow Muslims or local leaders. Mosque officials have to stop kicking problematic people out of their places of worship: this merely displaces the problem.

It has been my experience that the veil of denial is not as large as it once was. Ten years ago, few in the Muslim communities wanted to talk about radicalization to violence. Today, and especially in the wake of the October 2014 attacks, there is a realization that we have a problem in Canada and that we all, governments and communities, have to work together to tackle it. Communities are now asking for help and guidance, and they are more willing to work with security and law-enforcement agencies. Muslim leaders are taking the initiative to create programs—as we will discuss in the next section—and work with law-enforcement agencies.

Regardless of the successes of counter-radicalization or deradicalization strategies in the months and years to come, both the CSIS and the RCMP will likely have no shortage of work to do in detecting and neutralizing threats from people who have radicalized to violence.

COUNTER-RADICALIZATION

The field of counter-radicalization encompasses, among other things, awareness raising (i.e., what radicalization is and what it looks like) and community outreach, countering the extremist narrative, and early intervention programs (to get people off the path to violence). Let's examine some of these efforts.

It is first important to distinguish between counter-radicalization and deradicalization. The former is appropriate before radicalization occurs or when the process is in its earliest stages. It aims at preventing radicalization from taking place or creating the groundwork in which it cannot—or at least is difficult to—grow. Deradicalization occurs after someone has already been radicalized. It seeks to undo the process and reacquaint the individual with their preradicalization way of thinking. Most people intuitively agree that countering radicalization is preferable and probably more effective than attempts to deradicalize.

Awareness Raising and Community Outreach

If we want to be in a position to stop violent radicalization from taking place, we must have the best information available. Qualified and experienced people have to provide that information, and in order to do so they need to know what is of relevance and have the opportunity and means to get that information to those in the best position to act upon it.

In this regard, there are a number of existing programs that are beginning to bear fruit in Canada. One, managed by the RCMP, is called the Counter Terrorism Information Officer program—CTIO.[9] This three-day course is offered across Canada to frontline officials at the municipal, provincial, and federal levels with the goal of providing participants the requisite knowledge to understand potential threats and when to call the appropriate authorities (in cases of national security, that would be the RCMP's Integrated National Security Enforcement Teams). The course consists of a series of lectures and exercises that discuss a wide range of threats from across the ideological spectrum. It also contains a detailed section on Al Qaeda–inspired violent radicalization that closely reflects the principles and indicators discussed in this book. The CTIO course, which began in British Columbia, has been delivered in a large number of Canadian cities since its inception, and the feedback from participants has been encouraging. The RCMP also announced its Terrorism Prevention Program in early 2015.[10]

Several Canadian federal government agencies engage in regular community outreach sessions that aim to demystify the mandates of these agencies, build trust with communities, and share information. With regard to violent radicalization, the agencies usually involved include Public Safety Canada, the CSIS, the RCMP, the Canadian Border Services Agency, and, occasionally, Citizenship and Immigration Canada.[11] A number of sessions have been held with communities, including, but not exclusively, immigrant communities. The meetings can be raucous at times as Canadians voice their opinions, and concerns, over the roles and actions of our security agencies.

The RCMP has an initiative called the Junior Police Academy, which provides Canadian youth with a chance to see what the federal police force is all about. This effort may be particularly useful in creating allies among communities where Canadians were born in or at one point lived in countries where security and law-enforcement agencies are not seen as helpful or are seen as heavy handed or were even deadly. Junior Police Academy events may also include a section on radicalization. In conjunction with community leaders, youth have been exposed to the government's concerns about violent radicalization in the hopes that Canadians can work together to identified and combat it.[12]

The Citizenship Engagement section of Public Safety Canada, in collaboration with PSC's National Security Policy branch, has undertaken a series outreach events to dialogue with youth and communities on preventing and countering violent extremism. As of March 2015, eleven sessions have already taken place in Hamilton, London, Windsor, and St. Catharines in Ontario, in Calgary and Edmonton in Alberta, and in Montreal, Quebec. Through the use of composite case studies based in part on real cases in Canada, the sessions aim to provide information on the precursors, warnings, and other threads common among individuals who radicalize to violence, identify and discuss key intervention points for an individual who may be on the path to violent extremism, discuss tools needed by individuals and communities to prevent and counter violent extremism, and build trust with the participants. The sessions held to date have been well received. In March 2015, PSC was invited to share its approach with the Canadian Council of Imams in Toronto, a two-day event that brought government and communities together to discuss violent radicalization.[13]

The Canadian government created the Cross-Cultural Roundtable on Security (CCRS) in 2005 to engage Canadians and the government of Canada in a long-term dialogue on matters related to national security. The round-table brings together citizens who are leaders in their respective communities and who have extensive experience in social and cultural issues. The group focuses on emerging developments in national security matters and their impact on Canada's diverse and pluralistic society.

Within the CCRS is a subcommittee on countering violent extremism. The subcommittee has held a series of meetings in which experts and government officials from across Canada have discussed violent radicalization and suggested strategies to confront it. CCRS members have been instrumental in building bridges with Canadian communities and establishing contacts between average Canadians the security and law-enforcement world.

COUNTER-NARRATIVES

A great deal of study has been, and is continuing to be, devoted to countering the Al Qaeda single narrative. Most people in Western governments recognize that we have done little to challenge Al Qaeda's view of the world and have left the field wide open for extremist groups to exploit conflict, interpret it to their advantage, and use a panoply of media to manipulate and recruit new members. In the war of ideas, we are being beaten badly.

If the single narrative is wrong and misinterprets history, current events, and Islam, it would thus seem a straightforward matter to deconstruct its elements one by one and replace it with a more accurate story that will appeal to a large audience. As the single narrative begins to lose appeal, there should be a drop in effectiveness, visible in a decrease of those inspired by it.

Muslims around the world have been criticized for "not doing enough" about terrorism and not speaking out to condemn Al Qaeda and other groups. This criticism is unfair and unfounded. Community leaders have frequently and continuously raised their objections to and otherwise outright rejected terrorism. These communities can rightly point to a lack of media coverage of their condemnations. After all, finding a cleric who supports Al Qaeda is more newsworthy that reporting the thousands who reject the terrorist group.

There are several aspects of counter-narratives that should be considered. First, it is important that the right representative be chosen for developing a competing story. Governments are probably not the best-placed agents: they lack the required religious backgrounds, and there are also credibility and trust issues between governments and communities. As a result, community members need to take the lead for any counter-narrative to succeed.

Another issue that needs to be acknowledged is that the single narrative does have its strengths. It has been successful, and there must be reasons to account for its longevity and appeal. These include

- *Ease of understanding.* One does not have to be a religious scholar or historian to understand what the narrative is saying. The creators use real events and present them in a way that readers easily understand what is happening.
- *Changeability.* One of the greatest strengths of the narrative is its constant adaptation to events. As newer conflicts arise or another perceived attack on Islam appears, extremists go into overdrive to exploit the new situation. The early 2014 conflict in the Central African Republic, where proponents of the narrative have described the intervention of the French military as yet another example of the West's interference with the interests of Muslims, is illustrative in this regard.[14]
- *Emotional appeal.* The narrative is effective in part because it registers at the emotional level. Images of dead bodies and accounts of atrocities are used to anger readers and viewers. Academic treatises of the war in Syria cannot compete with the graphic detail of how Muslims are suffering and how the West is once again deaf to the plight of Islam.
- *Real solutions to real problems.* The narrative does not concern itself solely with a theoretical explanation of what is happening in the Muslim world and why it is happening. It is also a call to action. The action proposed by extremists is jihad, which is presented as a solution to a clear and present danger. Abdullah Azzam once said, "No negotiations, no dialogues and no conferences: jihad and the rifle alone."
- *Religious appeal.* The religious aspect of the narrative has often been underestimated or dismissed as unimportant. Whether or not the use of faith is an accurate representation of Islam, the central position of faith in the narrative cannot be ignored. While it is true that much of the narrative speaks of politics and history, its use of religion likely contributes to its success. People will support a given cause for a variety of reasons— political, ideological, social, etc. It might be speculative, but is it possible that, for some, divine sanction is paramount? If an individual chooses to fight and die because they believe that God has asked them to do so, what human authority or agency can convince them otherwise?

The narrative should not be seen as unassailable, but at the same time its strengths should not be underestimated.

An interesting counter-narrative effort in Canada is the Kanishka Project, which was announced by the government of Canada on June 23, 2011. The project—named for the 1985 bombing of an Air India flight off the coast of Ireland that killed 329 people, mostly Canadians—is a five-year,

$10 million initiative that will invest in researching pressing questions for Canada on terrorism and counterterrorism, such as preventing and countering violent extremism.

One of the recipients of Kanishka funding is the UK-based Institute for Strategic Dialogue, which is developing a series of film and educational resources to challenge extremist propaganda. According to the ISD website, this project will

- produce original counter-narrative films to tell the stories of former violent extremists and the survivors of violent extremism
- design an education resource pack for teachers, youth, and community workers with tool kits, lesson plans, and study guides to help them use the films in school and community settings
- leverage new analytical tools to devise a targeted dissemination strategy to guarantee the films reach the target audience, followed by analysis to understand their reach and impact online
- and build capacity among teachers, youth, and community workers through training workshops to ensure they have the skills and confidence to use the films and education resources effectively.

The initiative was launched in Canada in early 2015 to great fanfare.[15]

A number of ongoing initiatives address the issue of countering the Al Qaeda narrative. Clearly, the task is not an easy one, and success is not assured. Al Qaeda and other extremist groups have a head start, and there is a need to make up for a lot of lost time.

A slightly different approach would be to provide alternative narratives, which would consist of developing a series of stories without trying to deconstruct what the extremists are saying. Canada and the West remain a destination of choice for millions around the world, and many aspects of life in the West have a great appeal. Inclusiveness and openness and the freedom to worship, among other advantages, are desirable. By focusing on the plus side, the negative narrative propounded by Al Qaeda can be undermined.

EARLY INTERVENTION

One approach that is beginning to take shape in Canada is the development of an early intervention strategy for individuals and groups at risk of violent radicalization. Several other countries already have programs in place: the UK's Channel initiative[16] and Denmark's SSP (schools, social services, and Police)[17] are the best known.

An early intervention program aims at what is known as the *precriminal space*—that is, tackling an issue before it enters a law enforcement sphere. The idea is to identify individuals exhibiting early signs of violent radicalization and provide the necessary intervention (from parents, teachers, religious leaders, healthcare professionals, etc.) to stop the process from advancing. The RCMP has stated that it is looking into developing such an initiative in Canada. Successful intervention is not only cheaper (full-blown investigations are very expensive), but encouraging someone to turn back from the path of violence could also save lives and prevent family tragedy.

What would a successful early intervention program look like? Several elements need to come together to improve the chances of effectiveness: Accurate information on the nature of the activity of the individual(s) believed to be radicalizing must be procured (and protected—only those involved in the intervention effort should have access to personal data). The right people from a variety of backgrounds (social workers, health professionals, community resources, law enforcement) need to come together to decide who is best placed to intervene. Importantly, these people have to receive the necessary training to understand what radicalization to violence is and how to recognize it. A detailed program has to be devised, on an individual-case basis, outlining the services offered. These efforts need to be monitored, evaluated, and adapted as the circumstances dictate.

It is also necessary to point out that even the best intervention strategies will fail on occasion. Communities, families, and friends must recognize that at times individual cases will have to be referred to security or law enforcement, for it is these agencies that determine whether a serious threat to national security exists. It is also possible that some cases will vacillate between softer intervention and harder investigation. In addition, it will be a challenge to determine just exactly when an intervention should take place.[18]

There are several early intervention pilot programs in place across Canada as of early 2015. The mayor of Montreal, Denis Coderre, has also thrown his support behind a similar initiative in Quebec.[19]

OTHER PREVENTION PROGRAMS

Seizure or Revocation of Passport

One of the more controversial suggestions made to deal with violent extremists suspected of seeking to travel outside Canada to engage in terrorism, or perhaps seeking to return after their sojourn abroad with fellow extremists, covers measures to prevent travel in the first place. There are conditions under which the Canadian government can seize (for investigative purposes) or cancel valid passports where there is evidence that the bearer intends to leave Canada to commit an offense. Passport seizure or revocation does achieve the goal of not allowing a Canadian extremist to become someone else's problem and besmirch Canada's reputation abroad. People intent on leaving can always attempt to obtain fraudulent passports or use another valid passport (for instance, where the individual holds dual citizenship). Furthermore, a dedicated extremist may see the Canadian government's passport seizure or cancellation as interference with their plans to engage in violence, since the extremists are strongly committed to act. It is not a stretch to suggest that a canceled passport may convince an extremist to turn their attention inward—as in, "If I can't leave Canada to fulfill my desire, I'll just do something here." The possibility of such a decision may be rare (for some, the inability to travel may lead them to abandon their plans altogether), but it cannot be discounted. The October 2014 attacks in Saint-Jean-sur-Richelieu and Ottawa appear to be have been carried out by those whose plans to travel had been thwarted.

Cancellation of Citizenship

The revocation of citizenship opens a different set of issues. Is it legal to revoke citizenship in the first place? If a person has dual citizenship, revoking Canadian status allows them to retain their original citizenship. Can a government render someone stateless (it appears not)? There is also the issue of whether acts committed after citizenship is granted can be used to subsequently cancel status in Canada. Furthermore, someone born in Canada with unique Canadian citizenship cannot, it would seem, become stateless. Nor can the government deport these individuals (they are ours, after all). Should the government not take ownership of the problems its own citizens create? Why would they pass these extremists on to others and force them to deal with the situation?

There has also been some debate on whether cancelling citizenship or passports for those currently abroad (hence preventing their return and the opportunity to carry out an act in Canada or radicalize others) is the best solution. Some have argued that returnees, especially those who are disenchanted, could be used to convince others to not make the same mistakes they did.

No doubt the debate on the merits and drawbacks of these administrative measures will continue for some time.

DERADICALIZATION

What should be done if all the above-noted efforts fail? In other words, what action is required for those who radicalize to the point of violence?

One or more of the discussed initiatives may have been tried and have failed (there is certainly no guarantee that a counter-radicalization strategy will succeed), or the person or group may have escaped detection and scrutiny by family, friends, community, or security or law-enforcement agencies. As a result, an individual develops into an extremist.

One approach that has been adopted in a number of countries *deradicalization*. As stated earlier, deradicalization aims to undo the radicalization process and return the extremist to the mainstream. Countries that have implemented such program include Saudi Arabia,[20] Singapore,[21] and Yemen.[22] There is also a program in Germany called Exit Deutschland,[23] which was conceived to treat far-right and neo-Nazi extremists and has recently been adapted to deal with that country's growing Al Qaeda–inspired population.

Within these programs, governments bring in family members, religious leaders, and social workers to address a variety of issues that may have led to radicalization. All these efforts can play a crucial role in dealing with violent radicalization, but they suffer from three significant shortcomings:

- Many people who enter the program may not actually be extremist. Mass arrests of suspected terrorist often bring together people at various stages of radicalization, and some are arrested undoubtedly for being at the wrong place at the wrong time. If someone is not truly radicalized, can they be deradicalized?
- The programs are recently incepted, and we do not have good data on their success rates. It is not enough to point to a decrease in terrorist activity, because such a drop may be temporary. It remains unclear how to measure true deradicalization and what constitutes permanent abandonment of the ideology. It is also very hard to measure a negative: Did the program prevent someone from becoming a terrorist? How do we know what that person may eventually do?
- Some programs (the Yemeni effort is particularly egregious in this regard) may claim to have convinced extremists to eschew violence in their native countries, but program administrators were not as concerned about the use of violence by participants in other countries. There are many cases of "graduates" who were released, only to fight and die in a foreign jihad.[24]

An important distinction is also often lost in the debate surrounding deradicalization—that is, the difference between deradicalization proper and *disengagement*. Deradicalization is the proven rejection of violent ideology. It is very difficult to measure, as it is unclear how to reliably determine whether an individual's claims to have changed truly reflect their inner beliefs.

Disengagement is quite different. A person disengages when they abandon certain behaviors and associations. Unlike deradicalization, disengagement is plainly observable. If an extremist stops posting on certain websites or stops hanging out with their extremist friends, the changes in behavior can be monitored and verified.

Critically, disengagement without deradicalization is of concern. Someone who disengages but does not abandon adherence to the ideological underpinnings of violent extremism can re-engage. Disengagement is a good result—disengaged people do not join terrorist groups—but does not guarantee that someone will not revisit extremist activity in the future.

Perhaps disengagement is all we can really hope for and it is to this end that we should work. If someone disengages, they are no longer active: in other words, they are not acting on extremist thoughts or ideology and engaging in terrorism. Extremist thoughts are not necessarily criminal—we do not want to act as thought police, after all. Since we cannot look into people's heads, disengagement strikes me as a feasible and measurable goal. It is not perfect and does not preclude future acts of ideologically-motivated violence, but it can at least be tracked and evaluated.

What about Canada? Are there any deradicalization programs here? Officially, no. Canada is not in a position to deliver a state-driven program that at some point would have to deal with religious beliefs. Other states may be able to do so—for example, Saudi Arabia, where the state is seen as the protector of Islam.

To date, there appear to have been so few people in Canada who have radicalized to violence (and not been killed) that perhaps there is no strong need to warrant a national, government-sponsored or -administered approach. There are convicted terrorists in Canadian prisons, and there are reports that some prison imams have counseled these individuals (with some initial promising results).[25] In addition, there is anecdotal reporting of efforts by leaders in the community to talk to youths and convince them that the path they are traveling along will not end well.

One such program is the twelve-step radicalization-prevention program developed by Sayyid Ahmed Amiruddin of the Ahlus Sunnah Foundation of Canada Spiritual Wellness Centre in Mississauga.[26] According to the ASFC website, through this program "individuals are made aware of the theological, ethical, and legal aspects pertaining to clarifying the beliefs, states, and actions that give rise to criminal extremism and are empowered with knowledge of psychospiritual perfecting paradigms within their culture so the light of true self-knowledge reigns." The AFSC website also contains praise and testimonials of its success in bringing people back from the brink of violence. Amiruddin began his efforts in the wake of the arrests of the Toronto 18. Programs such as the ASFC's constitute one strategy in dealing with violent radicalization, and it is of note that the program is entirely community-driven and -managed.

Robert Heft, a Canadian convert to Islam, also claims to be involved in deradicalization efforts.[27] Other programs will undoubtedly be developed in the years to come.

A CAUTIONARY NOTE

Over the last several years I have read or heard of a number of ideas and proposals purporting to be the "solution" to radicalization and terrorism. These remedies appear in government meetings and op-ed pieces and come from all levels (state, academia, civil society, etc.). Their proponents suggest that, if we work at achieving these goals, we will significantly reduce the incidence of those radicalizing to violence.

Among the antidotes are:

- employment (something akin to "The devil finds work for idle hands")
- education (the thinking being that more someone is educated, the less likely they will be to follow a radically violent path)
- better integration
- putting more money into mental health
- a true understanding of Islam
- and addressing grievances (current or historical).

While all of these are noble efforts—and should be pursued—they are not in and of themselves solutions to radicalization. We saw in the first chapter that higher levels of employment, education, and integration do not correlate with lower levels of radicalization. It is true that our societies do not spend nearly enough dealing with mental health issues, but it is far from true that mental illness leads to violent radicalization. The oft-pronounced view that extremists have a poor grasp of Islam and only need to be nudged (or coerced) back to the true path is overly optimistic. Extremists believe they are the only true believers and see others—including religious leaders—as apostates and enemies. Furthermore, what is "true" religion, anyway? Does any one person or body have a monopoly on religious interpretation? As for righting wrongs (grievances), we have seen that the "resolution" of a particular conflict simply creates a vacuum for another (real or perceived) to enter.

The fact remains that radicalization to violence is a personal, complicated journey to which anyone in theory is susceptible (and that anyone in theory can deliberately choose). In addition, we need to move away from the notion that radicalized people are "victims," identified, recruited, and brainwashed by evildoers. There are undoubtedly some whose personalities open them

Textbox 5.1

ALL HAIL SOHAIL

Sohail Qureshi's father was very concerned about his son's descent into extreme ideologies in late 2006. Frantic and not knowing what to do, the Calgary doctor reached out to a local imam.

The imam tried to talk Sohail out of his plans to engage in violent jihad and, when the young man said his mind was made up, threatened to call the authorities. This led Sohail to say he had changed his mind.

Six months later, Sohail Qureshi traveled to Afghanistan, where he was arrested and jailed on suspicion of planning a suicide attack. Released six months later, he made to return to Canada, where he next sought to join the insurgency in Iraq but was detained, en route, in Jordan. He was returned to Canada.

He now claims that he has changed his life.

Source: Dawn Walton, "I Wanted to Join the Insurgency but Nothing Ever Happened," *Globe and Mail* (Toronto), last updated February 9, 2013, http://www.theglobeandmail.com/news/national/i-wanted-to-join-the-insurgency-but-nothing-ever-happened/article8421438/?page=3.

up to exploitation. But it is my experience that many individuals opt for this pathway willingly for reasons often known solely to themselves.

So, let us continue to identify those at risk of radicalization and provide the counselling and advice germane to their particular cases. But let us at the same time not gloss over the tremendous challenge this phenomenon presents by offering general, simplistic cures.

SUMMARY

In this chapter a number of approaches have been discussed that seek to address individuals and groups radicalizing in part through the Al Qaeda narrative. Each approach has its strengths and weaknesses, and each focuses on a particular part of the radicalization spectrum.

It is unlikely that other programs will be devised and implemented in the years to come. As a society, it will be necessary for us to decide whether the violent-radicalization problem is large enough to warrant taxpayer funding and support. Canada has many other issues to tackle, and each of these requires money and people. It is uncertain where radicalization to violence lies on the list of our nation's priorities. In the lead-up to the October 2015 federal election, opinion polls show that the vast majority of Canadians worry much more about the economy than they do terrorism.[28] In any event, the best response to the problem will include all the stakeholders: government (at all three levels—federal, provincial/territorial, and municipal), communities, and families.

It is also certain that all the agencies and actors discussed—security and law enforcement, families, friends, religious leaders, those working in the health and education sectors, etc.—have roles to play. The right agency or person for the job will depend crucially on the particulars of each case of violent radicalization. In a perfect world, we would detect behavioral and ideological changes early and effect intervention. We all know, however, that the world is not perfect and that it will be necessary to allow our intelligence and law-enforcement organizations to do what they were created to do—detect and thwart terrorism.

NOTES

1. Janet Thompson and Manmeet Ahluwalia, "Toronto 18 Bomb Plotter Saad Khalid Tells His Story," CBC News, last updated April 16, 2014, http://www.cbc.ca/news2/interactives/homegrown-terrorist/.

2. Hersi is the first Canadian convicted of trying to join a terrorist group. See chapter 4 for more details on his case.

3. Colin Freeze, "Spy-Watchers Urge a Shorter Leash for CSIS," *Globe and Mail* (Toronto), last updated August 23, 2012, http://www.theglobeandmail.com/news/politics/spy-watchers-urge-a-shorter-leash-for-csis/article1381179/.

4. "Bill C-51: CSIS Oversight Body Lacks Resources, Former Member Bob Rae Says," CBC News, last updated February 7, 2015, http://www.cbc.ca/news/politics/bill-c-51-csis-oversight-body-lacks-resources-former-member-bob-rae-says-1.2948639.

5. Chris Hall, "Martin Couture-Rouleau Peace Bond Denied Weeks before Fatal Attack," CBC News, last updated January 18, 2015, http://www.cbc.ca/news/politics/martin-couture-rouleau-peace-bond-denied-police-weeks-before-fatal-attack-1.2911867.

6. Canadian government agencies can apply to federal court to obtain permission to collect and analyze telecommunications. These powers are outlined in Section 21 of the CSIS Act for CSIS and are known as Criminal Code Part VI warrants used by the RCMP under the Canadian Criminal Code.

7. Tony Blais, "Edmonton Area Teen Facing Charges for Allegedly Trying to Join ISIS," *Edmonton Sun*, last updated March 20, 2015, http://www.edmontonsun.com/2015/03/20/edmonton-area-teen-facing-charges-for-allegedly-trying-to-join-isis.

8. ICA, "Calgary Man Turned Islamic Terrorist: Jihad Is Becoming as Canadian 'As Maple Syrup,'" Midnight Watcher's Blogspot (blog), May 8, 2014, https://midnightwatcher.wordpress.com/2014/05/08/calgary-man-turned-islamic-terrorist-jihad-is-becoming-as-canadian-as-maple-syrup/.

9. "The RCMP and Canada's National Security," Royal Canadian Mounted Police (website), last updated May 8, 2012, http://www.rcmp-grc.gc.ca/nsci-ecsn/nsci-ecsn-eng.htm.

10. "RCMP Supports Revolution to Prevent Tragedies," Royal Canadian Mounted Police (website), last updated March 6, 2015, http://www.rcmp-grc.gc.ca/features-vedette/2015/03-06-womens-day-jour-femmes-eng.htm.

11. "Community Outreach and Engagement to Counter Violent Extremism," Public Safety Canada, last updated March 4, 2014, http://www.publicsafety.gc.ca/cnt/ntnl-scrt/cntr-trrrsm/cntrng-vlnt-xtrmsm/cmmnt-trch-eng.aspx.

12. An excellent summary of one such event in Hamilton in 2013 can be found at Julia Chapman, "Hamilton Muslims Reach Out to the RCMP," CBC News, last updated April 30, 2013, http://www.cbc.ca/news/canada/hamilton/news/hamilton-muslims-reach-out-to-the-rcmp-1.1397863.

13. "Ontario Muslim Leaders Hold Conference on 'Countering Violent Extremism,'" *IQRA*, March 24, 2015, http://iqra.ca/2015/ontario-muslim-leaders-hold-conference-on-countering-violent-extremism/.

14. Associated Press, "French President 'Vigilant' after Jihadist Threat," *USA Today*, March 11, 2014, http://www.usatoday.com/story/news/world/2014/03/11/france-qaeda-hollande-terror/6286081/.

15. Reid Fiest, "New School Program 'Extreme Dialogue' to Fight Radicalization of Canadian Youth," *Global News* (Burnaby, BC), February 17, 2015, http://globalnews.ca/news/1834907/new-school-program-extreme-dialogue-to-fight-radicalization-of-canadian-youth/.

16. Her Majesty's Government, *Channel Duty Guidance: Protecting Vulnerable People from Being Drawn into Terrorism; Statutory Guidance for Channel Panel Members and Partners of Local Panels* (London: Crown, 2015), https://www.gov.uk/government/uploads/system/uploads/attachment_data/file/118194/channel-guidance.pdf.

17. Bologna Institute for Policy Research, "Managing the Risk from Violent Political Extremism: Swimming Upstream" (department memo), Johns Hopkins University, February 25, 2013, http://www.bipr.eu/PROFILESUMMARIES/20130225.pdf.

18. For an interesting analogy, see how the gun debate in the United States is giving rise to intervention questions: Joe Nocera, "Guns and Public Health" (op-ed), *New York Times*, November 3, 2014, http://www.nytimes.com/2014/11/04/opinion/joe-nocera-guns-and-public-health.html.

19. Katherine George, "Montreal Announces New Deradicalization Centre," *Humber News* (Toronto), n.d., http://humbernews.ca/montreal-announces-new-deradicalization-centre/.

20. Marisa L. Porges, "The Saudi Deradicalization Experiment," Council on Foreign Relations (website), January 22, 2010, http://www.cfr.org/radicalization-and-extremism/saudi-deradicalization-experiment/p21292.

21. Mohamed Bin Ali, "CO08100: De-radicalisation Programmes; Changing Minds?" S. Rajaratnam School of International Studies (website), last updated August 10, 2014, http://www.rsis.edu.sg/rsis-publication/rsis/1120-de-radicalisation-programmes/#.VZNEdvlViko.

22. Reins82, "De-Radicalization Programs Used to Combat Islamist Extremists," StudyMode (website), December 18, 2012, http://www.studymode.com/essays/De-Radicalization-Programs-Used-To-Combat-Islamist-1322801.html (registration required).

23. "EXIT-Germany: We Provide Ways Out of Extremism," EXIT-Deutschland (website), n.d., http://www.exit-deutschland.de/english/.

24. One account can be found at Peter Beaumont, "'Living Suicide Bomb' Returns to Wage Jihad," *Guardian* (London), January 18, 2014, http://www.theguardian.com/world/2014/jan/18/suicide-bomb-al-qaida-saudi-ahmed-al-shayea.

25. Wendy Gillis, "Is Canada Doing Enough to 'De-radicalize' Convicted Terrorists?" *Toronto Star*, August 11, 2013, http://www.thestar.com/news/crime/2013/08/11/is_canada_doing_enough_to_deradicalize_convicted_terrorists.html.

26. "ASFC Spiritual Wellness Center: Psycho-spiritual Rehabilitation Therapy," ASFC (website), copyright 2010–2012, http://www.alsunnahfoundation.org/12Steps.html.

27. http://www.mheft.com/ (website).

28. Bill Curry, "Economy a Higher Priority than Terrorism for Canadian Voters: Poll," *Globe and Mail* (Toronto), last updated April 10, 2015, http://www.theglobeandmail.com/news/politics/economy-a-higher-priority-than-terrorism-for-canadian-voters-poll/article23728296/.

Chapter 6

Conclusion

A LONELY WOLF?

In the immediate aftermath of the attack by Michael Zehaf-Bibeau at the National War Memorial and on Parliament, Canadian and international media went into a frenzy of speculation. As information on the attacker trickled in, the "instant analysis" went into overdrive. Experts from a variety of backgrounds chimed in with such "certainties" as:

- The attacker was mentally ill, and it was this illness that led to his actions.
- He was a drifter with little focus in life.
- His drug addiction was clearly a factor in the shootings.
- He was a true lone wolf, and it was unreasonable to expect anyone to have fingered him as a potential terrorist.
- This was a spontaneous act and may have been a copycat action modeled on the running down of Warrant Officer Patrice Vincent two days prior.

We have already noted that it is unlikely that the whole story will ever come out, in part because Zehaf-Bibeau was killed by parliamentary security. Nevertheless, it's helpful to ask how the instant analysis fared in light of subsequent information: not well, unfortunately.

- He may have had mental "issues," but he was judged not mentally ill by a psychiatrist. Furthermore, Royal Canadian Mounted Police Commissioner Paulson told a Senate committee on March 6, 2015, that the RCMP was not pursuing the "mental-health" angle in its ongoing investigation. As well, in his video testament Zehaf-Bibeau came across as lucid and logical.
- Zehaf-Bibeau did move around but had several jobs across Canada.

- He did have drug addiction issues, but there is no evidence to suggest these problems led to his decision to attack: Commissioner Paulson noted that there were no drugs or alcohol found in Zehaf-Bibeau's body during the autopsy.
- Zehaf-Bibeau left clues as to his ideology wherever he lived, including several of the twelve behavioral indicators presented in chapter 3.
- He toured Centre Block three weeks before his attack, stood in line at a Service Ontario kiosk to get a license for a car he had just bought, and fashioned a reasonable facsimile for a license when he failed to get a real one.

The intent here is not to cast aspersion on the instant analysts but, rather, to call for caution and considered analysis before offering trite and flippant conclusions. Violent radicalization may be complicated, but it is usually detectable—if you know what to look for.

In a 2002 article in *Foreign Affairs*, Paris-based researcher Grenville Byford said, "Wars have typically been fought against proper nouns (Germany, say) for the good reason that proper nouns can surrender and promise not to do it again. Wars against common nouns (poverty, crime, drugs) have been less successful. Such opponents never give up. The war on terrorism, unfortunately, falls into the second category."[1] This is profound. It speaks to the improbability, if not impossibility, of waging a war against a concept. While progress may have been made in fighting certain societal ills—smoking, teenage pregnancy, drunk driving, etc.—these have not been eliminated completely and arguably never will. This point of view is reflected in the 2014 report by five Nobel Prize–winning economists titled "Ending the Drug Wars" (a report of the London School of Economics expert group on the economics of drug policy), which calls for an end to the war on drugs and a battle to change international drug policies.[2]

A better-named campaign may have been to declare a War on Al Qaeda (one can substitute any other group's name here). Al Qaeda is a tangible organization with borders and finite members, even if these have shifted and changed over the decades. As a group or organization, its members can be killed, arrested, or neutralized, and its attraction can wane. Furthermore, Al Qaeda is a proper noun. And, as we have seen in the years since 9/11, the group has suffered significant losses, arguably culminating with the death of Bin Laden in May 2011. Many have claimed that Al Qaeda is all but finished and that we no longer need to spend as much blood and treasure pursuing it.

But, to paraphrase Mark Twain, it can be argued that rumors of Al Qaeda's death have been largely exaggerated. The group has proven remarkably resilient over time. In my view, some version of it will be around for some time.

Recall the brief discussion of the different levels of Al Qaeda in the introductory remarks. I repeat it here for ease of reference.

- *Al Qaeda core.* The original group created in large part by the late Osama Bin Laden and now headed by his lieutenant, Ayman al-Zawahiri
- *Al Qaeda affiliates.* Groups that either carry the Al Qaeda brand name (Al Qaeda in the Arabian Peninsula, Al Qaeda in Iraq, Al Qaeda in the Islamic Maghreb, etc.) or enjoy a relationship (financial, ideological, personnel, etc.) with the original Al Qaeda core (Al-Shabaab in Somalia and Jemaah Islamiyah in Southeast Asia are two examples)
- *Al Qaeda–inspired.* Individuals or groups that subscribe to the ideology propagated by Al Qaeda but that have no tangible links to the group or to its affiliates

Even if Al Qaeda core is completely crushed, two levels remain. In contrast to Al Qaeda core, the affiliates seem in the aggregate to be thriving. Some, such as the Somali group Al-Shabaab, have, like Al Qaeda itself, been declared dead or at least moribund many times.[3] The April attacks in Kenya were an all too gruesome a reminder that the group is anything but dead.[4] Others, such as Al Qaeda in the Islamic Maghreb or Al Qaeda in the Arabian Peninsula have had their ups and downs over the past decade. The Islamic State is clearly on the ascendant as of early 2015. Yet others may form in the years to come. In summary, it is most likely that some affiliates will present a threat for some time.

Those inspired by Al Qaeda, the focus of this book, are the largest and most difficult category to eradicate for a variety of reasons. First, they probably represent the single largest number of extremists. Second, they are spread in countries around the world. Third, they are not subject to the organizational pressures of large groups and, hence, may not be subject to the normal rivalries and infighting that all such groups inevitably go through.[5] And, last but not least, they are the equivalent of Byford's "common noun."

Where are those inspired by Al Qaeda headed? It is very difficult to say at this time. In all likelihood they will continue to morph and adapt in the same way that the narrative to which they subscribe morphs and adapts. Thus far they have at times managed to stay at least one step ahead of security and law-enforcement agencies in their abilities to plan and carry out attacks.

Most interestingly, they do not appear to have suffered from the setbacks that the more formal groups have suffered and do not appear to have been discouraged by the arrests and failed plots across the Western and non-Western worlds since 9/11.

More chillingly, the reasons and motivations that lead some to radicalize to violence show no signs of ebbing. To illustrate, consider foreign conflict as interpreted through the narrative.

Immediately after 9/11, the deployment of US and allied forces into Afghanistan in an effort to eradicate Al Qaeda core led to the radicalization of individuals, some of whom fought to oppose this perceived new invasion of a Muslim country by non-Muslim countries. Canada was seen as part of this invasion when it decided to send troops as well. The identification of the enemy shifted somewhat when the United States invaded Iraq, and extremist ideologues issued a new call to arms. In the intervening years, African (largely but not exclusively Kenyan and Ethiopian) forces in Somalia were targeted by Al-Shabaab and foreign fighters (including Canadians). In addition, extremists have portrayed the following actors as the enemies of Islam and called for jihad against them:

- France (in Mali, Niger, and, most recently, the Central African Republic)
- Myanmar (formerly Burma) (for its actions against the Rohingya minority in the northwestern state of Rakhine)
- Sri Lankan Buddhists (for their attacks on Muslims in that country)

Add to these all the long-standing conflicts that remain unresolved (Palestine, the Caucasus, Western China, Kashmir, etc.), and there exists a whole host of enemies against whom the extremists call for jihad. In other words, any conflict where Muslims are attacked can be construed and molded into a casus belli. In view of the human propensity to create armed conflict, there will likely be many opportunities, where Muslims are concerned, for the extremists to exploit. In view of Russia's 2014 annexation of Crimea, for example, it will be interesting to monitor what happens if Russian nationalists are seen to be abusing Tatars (a Muslim people) on the peninsula.[6] The US and allied air strikes against the Islamic State in Syria and Iraq are also feeding the narrative. The October 2014 attacks in Saint-Jean-sur-Richelieu and Ottawa were a shocking illustration that Canadians too can react to our actions abroad.

And finally, the waves of Islamophobia and right-wing fearmongering over immigration levels and the increasingly mosaic nature of societies in many Western countries will undoubtedly feed the narrative (recall that the first part of the narrative states that the West hates Islam).[7] There have been many incidents in recent years, ranging from the Swiss referendum against immigration[8] to the despoiling of mosques with pig's blood in several European countries (there have also been incidents in Canada[9]), all of which allegedly "confirm" what the extremists have been shouting about for years. There was a spike in anti-Islamic incidents following the October 2014 attacks in Canada.[10]

In view of this rather depressing outlook, is there hope for a resolution that does not involve another war or the use of force?

Thankfully, Al Qaeda–inspired terrorism and violent radicalization will most probably remain a rare phenomenon embraced by a very small number of people. It is true that a small group can do a great deal of damage, but none of the Al Qaeda forms—core, affiliated, or inspired—has ever posed an existential threat to any Western country (the same cannot be said for nations such as Iraq, Syria, Somalia, Libya, Yemen, or Afghanistan). Neither is any one of them likely to do so in the near to mid-future. They do represent a menace, yes, but not something that requires a war to end all wars.

Furthermore, the West has some advantages. Knowledge on violent radicalization is better now than ever, thanks to the work done by law-enforcement and security agencies and academics. There are more programs in place to identify those at risk or those in the initial stages of radicalization. Even if learning what works and what does not moves slowly and mistakes continue to be made, great progress has been registered since the early 2000s. If necessary, in the end, security and law-enforcement agencies will act to thwart plots.

And yet the most crucial factor is the reality that the vast majority of the world's Muslims, including a very high percentage in Canada, reject the Al Qaeda way of doing things.[11] Even if there is some sympathy for the plight of Muslims as interpreted by the narrative, there is little desire to resort to the levels of violence and mayhem that have plagued many countries over the last few decades. As some have pointed out, including the Counter Terrorism Center at West Point in the United States, all the Al Qaeda groups combined have killed many more Muslims than they have *kuffar*.[12] This is not good publicity for groups that claim to be defending Muslims from their sworn enemies.

So, in the end, it is probable that some group or individual aligned with or inspired by the Al Qaeda brand will carry out an occasional attack somewhere in the West, including Canada. Terrorism will likely remain a low-frequency, high-impact event. Western intelligence and law-enforcement agencies are well positioned to catch most of them before they act, but some may get through the security dragnet.

Recent attacks in the West—from mid-2013 to early 2015—have led to wide concern and speculation that things might be getting worse. A few of these attacks are listed in table 6.1.

Are these signs of a "new wave," as I have heard it called? I do not believe so. To my mind, they are a wrinkle on an existing phenomenon. We appear to be in the phase of "all of the above." By this I mean that we are experiencing attacks that may have been assisted (if not entirely directed) by Al Qaeda core or affiliates (that is to say the competing claims of responsibility for the *Charlie Hebdo* murders), those carried out by local "cells," and some the acts of lone individuals. Scholars and governments are busily studying this rash of events to determine whether something truly unprecedented is at play. Are "lone wolves" really new? Not at all: anarchist terrorists of the nineteenth century usually carried out their attacks without assistance or guidance.

Table 6.1

Country	Date	Attack	Perpetrators	Fatalities
UK	May 2013	Car, knife against UK soldier	2 Nigerian converts	1
Belgium	May 2014	Gun against Jewish museum	French returnee from Syria	4
Canada	October 2014	Car, shotgun (2 separate attacks) against 2 soldiers	2 converts thwarted from leaving	4 (including perpetrators)
Australia	October 2014	Knife against 2 police officers	Australian whose passport had been seized	1 (perpetrator only)
Australia	December 2014	Gun, hostage taking	Self-styled cleric	3 (2 hostages and perpetrator)
France	January 2015	Gun at offices of *Charlie Hebdo*	2 French Algerians	12; perpetrators later killed
France	January 2015	Hostage taking	Algerian with ties to Yemen	5 (including perpetrator)
Denmark	February 2015	shootings	Palestinian convict	3 (including perpetrator)

What is important to remember is that all these atrocities are consistent with the larger narrative we have discussed at length here. Regardless of the nature of the attack or whether the perpetrators were truly ordered by a higher body to act, they all are tied to a widespread notion that Islam is under attack (through invasion or satire in the case of the *Charlie Hebdo* attack) and that Islam mandates a response to which a chosen few have responded. The variety of terrorist actions would support the notions that the appeal of the narrative remains strong and that it is perversely (for us) flexible enough to apply to a broad spectrum of perceived slights or attacks against the Islamic faith.

While security and law-enforcement agencies have had great success in detecting and thwarting plots in Canada and the West over the past decade (Belgian security forces killed two alleged Syrian returnees planning an attack, and the United States foiled an alleged Capitol Hill plot in January 2015), past success is no guarantee of future success. The attacks in Canada October 20 and 22, 2014, demonstrated that. More people could conceivably succeed in carrying out an attack at some point in Canada. Hopefully, such an attack will be small in scope and will not result in many casualties. Learning more about violent radicalization and putting measures in place to stop it at an earlier stage is a preferred option. That is the challenge facing all of us in Canada as well as facing our friends and allies in the West.

FINAL THOUGHTS

I have been thinking about terrorism and working in the counterterrorism field for many years. During that time I have tried to better understand what motivates people to violence and to come up with ways to identify these people, not only to help my colleagues do their jobs but also because the field is vast and challenging. I have been fortunate to be surrounded by dedicated people as we collectively faced this threat.

I hope that this book has been of use to those who read it. It is my wish that perhaps it can provide some insight into the radicalization-to-violence process and lead others to engage in their own analysis, sharing the views developed through their own experiences. The terrorism field is a large one, and there is a great deal still to be studied. Terrorism will remain a threat for a long time, granting us all more than enough opportunity to make contributions to our collective understanding. I very much look forward to reading those contributions.

NOTES

1. Grenville Byford, "The Wrong War," *Foreign Affairs* 81, no. 4 (July/August 2002), https://www.foreignaffairs.com/articles/2002-07-01/wrong-war.

2. Jacob Kastrenakes, "Nobel Prize Winning Economists Call for End to War on Drugs," The Verge, May 7, 2014, http://www.theverge.com/2014/5/7/5690428/nobel-prize-winning-economists-call-for-end-to-war-on-drugs.

3. Joshua Kato, "Al-Shabaab Defeated, Says Somali President," *New Vision* (Kampala), March 16, 2013, http://www.newvision.co.ug/news/640693-al-shabaab-defeated-says-somali-president.html.

4. On April 2, 2015, gunmen opened fire in Garissa University College in Garissa, Kenya, killing 147 people.

5. Although it is worth repeating that the Toronto 18 did split into two groups after the two leaders had a falling out.

6. Taras Kuzio, "Tatars Fear a Future under Russia," Al Jazeera America, April 2, 2014, http://america.aljazeera.com/opinions/2014/4/ukraine-crimean-tatarsinputin-srussia.html; Robert Coalson, "Crimean Tatars Complain of Campaign of Harassment, Intimidation," Radio Free Europe/Radio Liberty, October 3, 2014, http://www.rferl.org/content/crimean-tatars-ukraine-harassment-intimidation-russia/26618766.html.

7. Kourash Ziabari, "Islamophobia: The West's Crusade against Muslims," Global Research (website), July 8, 2012, http://www.globalresearch.ca/islamophobia-the-west-s-crusade-against-muslims/31821.

8. Catherine Bosley, "Swiss Vote to Curb Immigration in Referendum," Bloomberg Business, last updated February 9, 2014, http://www.bloomberg.com/news/2014-02-09/swiss-voters-support-immigration-limits-with-50-3-srf.html.

9. CBC News, "Quebec Mosque Vandalized with Possible Pig Blood," last updated September 2, 2013, http://www.cbc.ca/news/canada/montreal/quebec-mosque-vandalized-with-possible-pig-blood-1.1395867.

10. Joan Bryden, "Prime Minister's Silence on Anti-Muslim Backlash Disheartens Muslim Groups," November 1, 2014, available online at http://o.canada.com/news/harper-silence-anti-muslim-backlack-538391.

11. "Osama bin Laden Largely Discredited among Muslim Publics in Recent Years," Pew Research Center (website), May 2, 2011, http://www.pewglobal.org/2011/05/02/osama-bin-laden-largely-discredited-among-muslim-publics-in-recent-years/.

12. Yassin Musharbash, "Surprising Study on Terrorism: Al-Qaida Kills Eight Times More Muslims than Non-Muslims," *Der Spiegel*, December 3, 2009, http://www.spiegel.de/international/world/surprising-study-on-terrorism-al-qaida-kills-eight-times-more-muslims-than-non-muslims-a-660619.html.

Appendix 1

Books on Al Qaeda–Inspired Extremism

Thousands of books and articles have been written on terrorism since 9/11. I have had the opportunity to read or at least browse through many of them. For what it is worth, here are my top recommendations.

Bell, Stewart. *Cold Terror: How Canada Nurtures and Exports Terrorism around the World*. Mississauga, Ont.: J. Wiley & Sons Canada, 2007.
   The first comprehensive look at terrorism in Canada

Bell, Stewart. *The Martyr's Oath: The Apprenticeship of a Homegrown Terrorist*. Mississauga, Ont.: J. Wiley & Sons Canada, 2005.
   A history of the Jabarah brothers

Bin Laden, Osama. *Messages to the World: The Statements of Osama Bin Laden*. Edited and introduced by Bruce Lawrence. London and New York: Verso, 2005.
   All of Bin Laden's statements up to 2005

Bonney, Richard. *Jihād: From Qur'ān to Bin Laden*. New York: Palgrave Macmillan, 2004.
   A comprehensive look at jihad across history

Habeck, Mary R. *Knowing the Enemy: Jihadist Ideology and the War on Terror*. New Haven: Yale University Press, 2006.
   The best little book on Al Qaeda terrorist thought

McGrory, Daniel, and Sean O'Neill. *The Suicide Factory: Abu Hamza and the Finsbury Park Mosque*. London: Harper Perennial, 2006.
   An excellent book on the life and influence of recently convicted UK firebrand Abu Hamza

[Scheuer, Michael]. *Imperial Hubris: Why the West Is Losing the War on Terror*. Washington, DC: Brassey's, 2004.
   An excellent look at Al Qaeda ideology, written anonymously by then-CIA analyst Michael Scheuer

Appendix 2

The Twelve Indicators

For ease of reference, I repeat the twelve indicators of Al Qaeda–inspired radicalization and violence, presented at length in chapter 3.

1. Sudden increase in intolerant religiosity
2. Rejection of different interpretations of Islam
3. Rejection of non-Muslims
4. Rejection of Western ways
5. Rejection of Western policies (domestic, military, foreign, social, etc.)
6. Association with like-minded people
7. Obsession with jihadi sites
8. Obsession with the narrative
9. Desire to travel to conflict zones
10. Obsession with jihad
11. Obsession with martyrdom
12. Obsession with end-times

Appendix 3

Radicalization-to-Violence Matrix

In determining the extent to which an individual has embraced violent radicalization, the following matrix can be applied. Information on the variables listed is plotted, and, if necessary, the degree to which a given variable is present (where degrees of presence are logical) can also be noted. These variables follow very closely the twelve indicators presented in chapter 3.

As emphasized several times, any one observation should not be magnified or taken out of context. This tool needs to be used in conjunction with other observations.

Variable	Not observed	Seldom observed	Frequently observed	Very frequently observed
Religious beliefs				
Intolerance of other Muslims				
Sense of superiority				
Regular criticism of others				
Rejection of Shia				
Rejection of Sufis				
Rejection of other sects (Ahmadis, Ismailis, etc.)				
Hatred of Jews				
Hatred of Christians				
Hatred of other faiths (Hinduism, Buddhism, Bahaism, etc.)				
Rejection of religious authority				
Overt challenge of religious authority				
Belief in *Al Wala' wal Bara'*				
Use of *takfiri* terminology				
Search for fatwas to justify violence				

Variable	Not observed	Seldom observed	Frequently observed	Very frequently observed
Change in associates and lifestyle				
Sudden change in friends				
Limits exposure to only those with similar exclusionary views				
Sudden change in long-standing activities (sports, clubs, etc.)				
Participation in physical activity (paintball, martial arts) associated with preparation for violent jihad				
Sudden departure from work or school without explanation				
Sudden change in physical appearance				
Vehement rejection of former associates or lifestyle				
Sudden criticism or rejection of family				
Refusal to engage in debate or compromise				
Family and friends notice sudden changes in individual				
Influence				
Attempts to influence others to adopt violent views				
Efforts by others to influence/radicalize individual				
Views on West				
Rejection of democracy				
Rejection of Western law				
Demand for imposition of sharia in Canada				
Violent criticism of Western foreign or military policy				
Identification of Westerners as *kuffar*				
Identification of Westerners as *taghout*				
Refusal to recognize rights and validity of non-Muslims				
Desire to punish West for its policies				
Severe misogyny or homophobia				
Obsession with foreign conflict				
Identification of particular zone of conflict or grievance				
Efforts to travel to fight				
Efforts to conceal true travel patterns				
Efforts to obtain false travel documentation				
Correspondence with violent extremists in conflict zones				

Variable	Not observed	Seldom observed	Frequently observed	Very frequently observed
Belief in need for hijra				
Desire to return to conflict zone				
Belief in the narrative				
Conviction that West is at war with Islam				
Belief that West must be punished for its actions				
Belief that true Muslims must act				
Internet use				
Browsing of violent Web sites				
Participation in chat rooms of violent Web sites				
Sharing of violent material				
Exhortation to violence on Web sites				
Use of social media to promote violent jihad				
Efforts to hide Internet browsing of violent sites (encryption, file erasing)				
Use of alias to hide identity				
Views on violent jihad				
Jihad as *fard `ayn*				
Violent jihad as obligation				
Praise for mujahideen				
Rejection of need for authority to justify jihad				
Views on martyrdom				
Overt desire for martyrdom				
Sudden repayment of outstanding debt				
Sudden asking for pardon and forgiveness				
Promotion of martyrdom				
End-times				
Belief in imminent end of world				
Desire to travel to attend battle at end-time				

Appendix 4

At Tibyan Publications

At Tibyan Publications (or ATP—also known as Al Tibyan Publications) is a collection of essays and short books that provides would-be extremists with religious justification for violence. Fahim Ahmed of the Toronto 18 was a prolific contributor to the ATP Web site.[1] The site (or rather *sites*, as many other Web pages have copied the ATP material) has dozens of papers, all of which deal with some aspect of jihad.

ATP material is somewhat dated and is but a drop in the ocean of violent material available online today. It is worth examining some of the documents, nevertheless, as they give a flavor of the mentality and meticulous argumentation made to support violent jihad.

The ATP material is usually presented in the following manner: The author raises an issue and shows how some Muslims have been misled or have misunderstood what Islam demands of them on the issue. Through the use of Quranic verses, hadiths (sayings of the Prophet Muhammad), and quotations from Muslim scholars over the centuries, the author seeks to teach and correct the reader. The research presented appears legitimate and is written in an appealing manner. Certainly to some less informed of Islamic history or jurisprudence, the texts can be convincing. It is not difficult to see why some would be swayed by them.

The authors of the writings are generally dismissive of "apologists, defeatists, modernists, and moderate Muslims" who have been misguided by the "Orientalists" (Western scholars who have studied Islam). The extremist authors believe that they have a monopoly on the true interpretation of Islam and of history and want others to recognize their superiority in these matters.

In the following sections, I summarize some of the ATP papers and show how they provide guidance on why jihad is necessary.

THE PAPERS

"Thirty-Nine Ways to Serve and Participate in Jihad"

Written by one Muhammad bin Ahmad As-Salim, this paper states that Islam is under attack from all corners and that jihad is an obligation to all Muslims. The author provides useful suggestions that anyone can follow to embrace and/or support jihad. These steps include:

Making a clear intention to fight
Asking Allah for martyrdom
Leaving for jihad
Using one's wealth and/or sending money to the mujahideen
Supporting the families of those who have left for jihad
Training physically in preparation for jihad (including swimming, riding
    horses, and shooting—three classic sports associated with jihad)
Hating the disbelievers
Raising one's children to love jihad

These suggestions are presented along with verses of the Quran and hadiths and are written to convince readers that they have the ability to engage in jihad.

"The Slicing Sword"

Written by Abd Allah ibn Abd Al-Bari Al Ahdal, this treatise discusses a Muslim's obligation to retake lands conquered by non-Muslims and, if living in those lands, to not accept the beliefs and practices of non-Muslim rulers. Several Quranic verses refer to the admonition that Muslims not take Christians and Jews as friends for fear of becoming "one of them." Furthermore, Muslims are never to make allegiances with non-Muslims and are to reject non-Muslim justice systems. Muslims living in lands controlled by non-Muslims are to leave (i.e., perform hijra—flight) as it is preferable to live where Islam is dominant. Should a Muslim embrace another religion, he is to be labeled a hypocrite for abandoning Islam and should be punished accordingly.

"Essay regarding the Basic Rule of the Blood, Wealth and Honour of the Disbelievers"

This paper is based on classic Muslim dictates on warfare and what is considered legitimate war booty. The author criticizes those who try to reform Islam in concordance with "modernism" or those who seek to "please" the disbelievers. For those nonbelievers who embrace Islam, their blood and wealth are "protected"; those who refuse conversion may be killed and their wealth taken. The paper notes that the wealth of the *kuffar* can be taken in the course of warfare or as tribute or tax paid to Muslim conquerors. This concept has been used to justify theft or fraud, since the wealth of the *kuffar* is considered there for the taking.

"Jihad and the Effects of Intention Upon It"

Penned by jailed extremist scholar Shaykh Abdul Qadir Ibn Abdil Aziz, this paper provides advice on those who are interested in jihad. Potential jihadists should not prepare themselves in order to be seen as courageous or to gain glory and adulation from others. Nor are concerns of financial gain or status to be considered. Muslims must not use other distractions or commitments as an excuse to not train for jihad. This paper emphasizes that jihad remains an obligation for all Muslims, as ordained by Allah.

"The Doubts regarding the Ruling of Democracy in Islam"

Written allegedly as a clarification in response to an online debate as to whether Muslims could vote in elections in the West, this paper notes that the root of the word *democracy* (the Greek words for "people" and "governance") implies that authority is placed in the hands of human beings, in whom mastery is thus also placed. This is at "odds with the very essence of Allah's exclusive right of legislation." Furthermore, it is equivalent to *shirk*— elevating mankind to the level of Allah. Those elected are then set up as false deities to be worshipped alongside Allah. The paper notes that without elections, democracy would be impossible: since it is not compulsory (at least in some nations), participation by Muslims is discouraged. Interestingly, the author approves involvement in certain political activities (demonstrations, rallies, and campaigns), as these do not lead to *shirk*.

Other Papers

The above small sample should provide an adequate overview of the kinds of material published under the At Tibyan banner. A few more titles are listed below.

"The Exposition regarding the Disbelief of the One Who Assists the Americans"
"Can Makkah [Mecca] Become *Dar Al-Harb*?"
"Fundamental Concepts regarding al-Jihad"
"Verdict regarding the Permissibility of Martyrdom"

"When Jihad Is for the Sake of America"
"Debate: The Sword vs. the Pen"
"The Ruling on the One Who Insults the Prophet of Allah"
"Strangle the Last Arab Tyrant . . . with the Entrails of the Last Palace
Scholar(!)"

SUMMARY

Despite their often densely written style, the essays in the ATP collection
are, in my view, effective and influential for a number of reasons: First, they
cite recognized Islamic sources (the Quran, hadiths, and reputable scholars),
even if there remains debate in the Muslim world over the issues discussed.
Second, they seek to answer questions that are apparently on the minds of
people—for example, jihad, participating in Western society, the suffering
of Muslims—and provide definitive answers. Third, they raise Muslims and
Islam to a higher level of respect and status, treating followers as a chosen
people in a sense.

More sophisticated readers may be able to deconstruct the arguments
presented in the ATP articles. There is a long tradition in Islam of debating
the meanings of scripture and scholarship, and there are undoubtedly many
individuals capable of undermining the message of violence promoted in ATP.
It is probable, however, that the majority of those downloading ATP papers
are not Islamic scholars or even well versed in history or politics. The emotive
nature of the works would likely appeal to these readers and, crucially, provide
the theological justification for violence that many of them seek.

Similar messages can be found in online magazines such as *Inspire* (the
product of Al Qaeda in the Arabian Peninsula), *Azan* (issued by the Taliban
in Afghanistan), and *Dabiq* (put out by ISIS). All have high production values
and feature short articles calling on Muslims to fight.

While there are other sources on the Internet that have proven effective
in relaying the extremist message and issuing a call to action, it is not clear
how Twitter or texting can "radicalize" someone. These tools do not allow
for detailed argumentation and a full explanation of why violence is both
needed and obligatory. I am not claiming that these media are not important
but, rather, that it takes more than a 140-character tweet to radicalize an
individual.

NOTE

1. Michelle Shephard, *Decade of Fear: Reporting from Terrorism's Grey Zone*
(Vancouver: Douglas & McIntyre, 2011), 11,593.

Bibliography

Baran, Zeyno. "Fighting the War of Ideas." *Foreign Affairs* 84, no. 6 (November/ December, 2005). https://www.foreignaffairs.com/articles/europe/2005-10-01/ fighting-war-ideas.

Beinart, Peter. "Bill Maher's Dangerous Critique of Islam." Global. *Atlantic Monthly*, October 9, 2014. http://www.theatlantic.com/international/archive/2014/10/ bill-maher-dangerous-critique-of-islam-ben-affleck/381266/.

Beirich, Heidi. "White Homicide Worldwide." *Intelligence Report* no. 154 (Summer 2014). http://www.splcenter.org/get-informed/intelligence-report/browse-all-issues/2014/summer/White-Homicide-Worldwide.

Bell, Stewart. *The Martyr's Oath: The Apprenticeship of a Homegrown Terrorist.* Mississauga, Ont.: J. Wiley and Sons Canada, 2005.

Berntzen, Lars Erik. "The Collective Nature of Lone-Wolf Terrorism." *Terrorism and Political Violence* 26, no. 5 (2014): 759–79.

Bhui, Kamaldeep, Nasir Warfa, and Edgar Jones. "Is Violent Radicalisation Associated with Poverty, Migration, Poor Self-Reported Health and Common Mental Disorders?" *PLoS One* 9, no. 3 (March 5, 2014). doi:10.1371/journal.pone.0090718. http://journals.plos.org/plosone/article?id=10.1371/journal.pone.0090718.

Bin Ali, Mohamed. "CO08100: De-radicalisation Programmes; Changing Minds?" S. Rajaratnam School of International Studies (website). Last updated August 10, 2014. http://www.rsis.edu.sg/rsis-publication/rsis/1120-de-radicalisation-pro-grammes/#.VZNEdvlViko.

Bologna Institute for Policy Research. "Managing the Risk from Violent Political Extremism: Swimming Upstream" (department memo). Johns Hopkins University, February 25, 2013. http://www.bipr.eu/PROFILESUMMARIES/20130225.pdf.

Byford, Grenville. "The Wrong War." *Foreign Affairs* 81, no. 4 (July/August 2002). https://www.foreignaffairs.com/articles/2002-07-01/wrong-war.

Citizens for Public Justice. *Poverty Trends Highlights: Canada 2013.* Ottawa: CPJ, 2013. http://www.cpj.ca/sites/default/files/docs/Poverty-Trends-Highlights-2013. pdf.

Corda, Tiziana. "The Caliphate and Its Followers." Geostrategic Forecasting (website), n.d. http://www.geostrategicforecasting.com/the-caliphate-and-its-followers/.

Corner, Emily, and Paul Gill. "A False Dichotomy? Mental Illness and Lone-Actor Terrorism." *Law and Human Behavior* 39, no. 1 (2015): 23–34.

Dag. "Imam Aly Hindy's Previous Job." No Dhimmitude (blog), June 4, 2006. http://nodhimmitude.blogspot.ca/2006/06/imam-aly-hindys-previous-job.html.

El Akkad, Omar, and Greg McArthur. "Hateful Chatter Behind the Evil." *Globe and Mail* (Toronto), last updated August 22, 2012. http://www.theglobeandmail.com/news/national/hateful-chatter-behind-the-veil/article1203257/?page=all.

Environics. *Focus Canada: The Pulse of Canadian Public Opinion; Report 2006-4.* Ottawa and Ontario: Environics Research Group Ltd., 2007.

EXIT-Deutschland (website). "EXIT-Germany: We Provide Ways Out of Extremism," n.d. http://www.exit-deutschland.de/english/.

Federal Bureau of Investigation (website). "The Path to Terror: The Jihadists of Georgia, Part 1," December 15, 2009. http://www.fbi.gov/news/stories/2009/december/jihadists_121509.

Filiu, Jean-Pierre. *Apocalypse in Islam.* Berkeley: University of California Press, 2011.

Friscolanti, Michael. "It Comes Down to These Four: The 'Toronto 18' Terrorism Case Rests on a Core Group of Suspects." *Macleans*, June 9, 2008. Available online at http://www.thecanadianencyclopedia.ca/en/article/the-toronto-18-terrorism-case/.

Furnish, Timothy R. *Holiest Wars: Islamic Mahdis, Their Jihads, and Osama bin Laden.* Westport, CN : Praeger Publishers, 2005.

Gambetta, Diego, and Steffan Hertog. *Engineers of Jihad.* Sociology Working Papers, paper no. 2007-10. Department of Sociology, University of Oxford. http://www.sociology.ox.ac.uk/materials/papers/2007-10.pdf.

Gurr, Ted Robert. *Why Men Rebel.* Princeton: Princeton University Press, 1970.

Harris, David B. "Guest Column: Terror's Virus on the Northern Border." *The Investigative Project on Terrorism* (blog), October 7, 2014. http://www.investigative-project.org/4602/guest-column-terror-virus-on-the-northern-border.

Her Majesty's Government. *Channel Duty Guidance: Protecting Vulnerable People from Being Drawn into Terrorism; Statutory Guidance for Channel Panel Members and Partners of Local Panels.* London: Crown, 2015. https://www.gov.uk/government/uploads/system/uploads/attachment_data/file/118194/channel-guidance.pdf.

Horgan, John. "Don't Ask Why People Join the Islamic State—Ask How." *Vice News*, September 10, 2014. https://news.vice.com/article/dont-ask-why-people-join-the-islamic-state-ask-how.

ICA. "Calgary Man Turned Islamic Terrorist: Jihad Is Becoming as Canadian 'As Maple Syrup.'" Midnight Watcher's Blogspot blog), May 8, 2014. https://midnightwatcher.wordpress.com/2014/05/08/calgary-man-turned-islamic-terrorist-jihad-is-becoming-as-canadian-as-maple-syrup/.

IQRA (website). "Ontario Muslim Leaders Hold Conference on 'Countering Violent Extremism,'" March 24, 2015. http://iqra.ca/2015/ontario-muslim-leaders-hold-conference-on-countering-violent-extremism/.

Islamic Social Services Association, National Council of Canadian Muslims, and Royal Canadian Mounted Police. *United against Terrorism: A Collaborative*

Effort towards a Secure, Inclusive and Just Canada. Winnipeg: ISSA, NCCM, and RCMP, 2014. http://www.nccm.ca/wp-content/uploads/2014/09/UAT-HAND-BOOK-WEB-VERSION-SEPT-27-2014.pdf.

Kirchner, Lauren. "Marriage May Calm a Criminal Impulse in Men." *Pacific Standard Magazine*, July 15, 2013. http://www.psmag.com/navigation/health-and-behavior/marriage-may-calm-a-criminal-impulse-in-men-62504/.

Lewis, Bernard. "I'm Right, You're Wrong, Go to Hell." *The Atlantic* (May 2003). http://www.theatlantic.com/magazine/archive/2003/05/-im-right-youre-wrong-go-to-hell/302723/.

Life on the Left (blog). "Quebec's Debate on 'Reasonable Accommodation'—A Socialist View," December 16, 2007. http://lifeonleft.blogspot.ca/2007/12/quebecs-debate-on-reasonable.html.

Meleagrou-Hitchens, Alexander. *As American as Apple Pie: How Anwar al-Awlaki Became the Face of Western Jihad*. London: International Centre for the Study of Radicalisation and Political Violence, 2011. http://icsr.info/wp-content/uploads/2012/10/1315827595ICSRPaperAsAmericanAsApplePieHowAnwaralAwlakiBecametheFaceofWesternJihad.pdf.

Moulana Muhmmad A. "Will a Shahid (Martyr) Be Liable for His Debts?" Hadith Answers.com (website), March 22, 2014. http://www.hadithanswers.com/will-a-shahid-martyr-be-liable-for-his-debts/.

Mowatt-Larssen, Rolf. "Al Qaeda's Religious Justification of Nuclear Terrorism." Excerpt of forthcoming research report. Available online at belfercenter.hks.harvard.edu/files/aq-religious-justification.pdf.

Mulcaire, Camille. "Assessing al-Qaeda from the Teachings of Ibn Taymiyya." Student essay. E-International Relations: Students (website), written April 2013, published October 15, 2013. http://www.e-ir.info/2013/10/15/assessing-al-qaeda-from-the-teachings-of-ibn-taymiyya/.

Musharbash, Yassin. "Surprising Study on Terrorism: Al-Qaida Kills Eight Times More Muslims than Non-Muslims." *Der Spiegel*, December 3, 2009. http://www.spiegel.de/international/world/surprising-study-on-terrorism-al-qaida-kills-eight-times-more-muslims-than-non-muslims-a-660619.html.

O'Neill, Sean, and Daniel McGrory. *The Suicide Factory: Abu Hamza and the Finsbury Park Mosque*. London: Harper Perennial, 2006.

Pape, Robert A. *Dying to Win: The Strategic Logic of Suicide Terrorism*. New York: Random House, 2005.

PBS. "Trial of a Terrorist: A Terrorist's Testimony." *Frontline*, n.d. http://www.pbs.org/wgbh/pages/frontline/shows/trail/inside/testimony.html.

Peace with Realism (website). "*Jihad* in the *Hadith*," n.d. http://www.peacewithrealism.org/jihad/jihad03.htm.

Pew Research Center (website). "Muslim-Western Tensions Persist: Common Concerns about Islamic Extremism," July 21, 2011. http://www.pewglobal.org/2011/07/21/muslim-western-tensions-persist/.

———. "Osama bin Laden Largely Discredited among Muslim Publics in Recent Years." May 2, 2011. http://www.pewglobal.org/2011/05/02/osama-bin-laden-largely-discredited-among-muslim-publics-in-recent-years/.

Porges, Marisa L. "The Saudi Deradicalization Experiment." Council on Foreign Relations (website), January 22, 2010. http://www.cfr.org/radicalization-and-extremism/saudi-deradicalization-experiment/p21292.

Public Safety Canada. "Community Outreach and Engagement to Counter Violent Extremism." Last updated March 4, 2014, http://www.publicsafety.gc.ca/cnt/ntnl-scrt/cntr-trrrsm/cntrng-vlnt-xtrmsm/cmmnt-trch-eng.aspx.

———. "2013 Public Report on the Terrorist Threat to Canada." Last updated March 4, 2014. http://www.publicsafety.gc.ca/cnt/rsrcs/pblctns/trrrst-thrt-cnd/index-eng.aspx.

Reins82. "De-Radicalization Programs Used to Combat Islamist Extremists." StudyMode (website), December 18, 2012. http://www.studymode.com/essays/De-Radicalization-Programs-Used-To-Combat-Islamist-1322801.html (registration required).

Royal Canadian Mounted Police (website). "Commissioner Paulson's Appearance at SECU on the Zehaf-Bibeau Video." March 3, 2015. http://www.rcmp-grc.gc.ca/news-nouvelles/speeches-stat-discours-decl/2015/03-05-eng.htm.

———. "Maiwand Yar." Last modified March 29, 2011. http://www.rcmp-grc.gc.ca/en/wanted/maiwand-yar.

———. National Security Criminal Investigations. *Radicalization: A Guide for the Perplexed, June 2009* (Canada: Royal Canadian Mounted Police, 2009). http://publications.gc.ca/collections/collection_2012/grc-rcmp/PS64-102-2009-eng.pdf (archived).

———. "RCMP Response: *United Against Terrorism* Handbook." Last updated September 30, 2014. http://www.rcmp-grc.gc.ca/news-nouvelles/2014/09-30-uni-eng.htm.

———. "RCMP Supports Revolution to Prevent Tragedies." Last updated March 6, 2015. http://www.rcmp-grc.gc.ca/features-vedette/2015/03-06-womens-day-jour-femmes-eng.htm.

———. "The RCMP and Canada's National Security," last updated May 8, 2012. http://www.rcmp-grc.gc.ca/nsci-ecsn/nsci-ecsn-eng.htm.

Sampson, Robert J., John H. Laub, Christopher Wimer. "Does Marriage Reduce Crime? A Counterfactual Approach to Within-Individual Causal Effects." *Criminology* 44, no. 3 (2006): 465–508. Available online at http://scholar.harvard.edu/files/sampson/files/2006_criminology_laubwimer_1.pdf.

Shephard, Michelle. *Decade of Fear: Reporting from Terrorism's Grey Zone.* Vancouver: Douglas & McIntyre, 2011.

Silverman, Adam L. "Just War, Jihad and Terrorism: A Comparison of Western and Islamic Norms for the Use of Political Violence." *Journal of Church and State* 44, no. 1 (2002): 73–92. doi:10.1093/jcs/44.1.73.

Smith, Angus. "Words Make Worlds: Terrorism and Language." Royal Canadian Mounted Police (website). Last modified November 9, 2009. http://www.rcmp-grc.gc.ca/pubs/nsci-ecrsn/words-mots-eng.htm (original posting), http://pointdebascu-lecanada.ca/wp-content/uploads/2012/07/0%20org%20grc%20jihad%20english.pdf (screen capture).

Taylor, Max. Podcast featuring Marc Sageman. *Terrorism and Political Violence* (journal), May 2014. http://www.tandfonline.com/sda/4890/audioclip-transcript-ftpv.

pdf (transcript), http://www.tandfonline.com/sda/4890/audioclip-ftpv.mp3 (original podcast).

Wiktorowicz, Quintan. *Radical Islam Rising: Muslim Extremism in the West.* Lanham, MD: Rowman and Littlefield, 2005.

Ziabari, Kourash. "Islamophobia: The West's Crusade against Muslims." Global Research (website), July 8, 2012. http://www.globalresearch.ca/islamophobia-the-west-s-crusade-against-muslims/31821.

Index

About the Author

Phil Gurski served for more than thirty years as an analyst in the Canadian intelligence community. From 1983 to 2001 he worked as a multilingual analyst for Communications Security Establishment, Canada's signals-intelligence organization. In 2001 he joined the Canadian Security Intelligence Service, where he was a strategic analyst, specializing in homegrown Al Qaeda–inspired terrorism and radicalization to violence. In 2013 he moved to Public Safety Canada as senior strategic advisor on Canada's Countering Violent Extremism policy. He has presented on these issues across Canada and around the world. He is currently president and CEO of Borealis Threat and Risk Consulting Ltd. You can follow him at his blog, Terrorism in Canada and the West (pkgursk.wordpress.com), and on Twitter (@borealissaves).